IN THE NAME OF THE CHURCH

In the Name of the Church

Vocation and Authorization of Lay Ecclesial Ministry

Edited by William J. Cahoy

Charles A. Bobertz
Zeni Fox
Francis Cardinal George, OMI
Edward P. Hahnenberg
Jeffrey Kaster
Graziano Marcheschi
H. Richard McCord
Hosffman Ospino
Lynda Robitaille
Susan K. Wood, SCL

LITURGICAL PRESS

Collegeville, Minnesota

www.litpress.org

Cover design by Stefan Killen Design. Cover photo © Jesuit School of Theology in Berkeley, a Graduate School of Santa Clara University.

Excerpts from documents of the Second Vatican Council are from *Vatican Council II: The Basic Sixteen Documents*, by Austin Flannery, OP © 1996 (Costello Publishing Company, Inc.). Used with permission.

"Call To Ecclesial Ministry" on pages 172–77 © Archdiocese of Chicago. Used by permission.

Portions of text from pages 172–77 adapted from the English translations of *The Roman Missal* © 1973 and *Rite of Religious Profession* © 1974, International Commission on English in the Liturgy Corporation. All rights reserved.

1   2   3   4   5   6   7   8   9

Library of Congress Cataloging-in-Publication Data

In the name of the church : vocation and authorization of lay ecclesial ministry / edited by William J. Cahoy ... [et al.].
   p.   cm.
  ISBN 978-0-8146-3423-3 — ISBN 978-0-8146-3452-3 (e-book)
   1. Lay ministry—Catholic Church.   2. Laity—Catholic Church—Congresses.   3. Church—Authority.   4. Authority—Religious aspects—Catholic Church.   5. Vocation—Catholic Church.   6. Catholic Church—Government.   I. Cahoy, William John.

BX1920.I5   2012
262'.152—dc23   2012003268

Contents

Introduction

Collegeville Ministry Seminar II

William J. Cahoy

Leadership scholar Ron Heifetz makes a helpful distinction between technical and adaptive challenges. Technical challenges are those for which we have the necessary know-how and that can be fixed by an expert. For instance, I go to the doctor not feeling well. She diagnoses strep throat, prescribes an antibiotic, and in a few days I am back to normal. All goes on as before. Of course, it is not always as easy as that. The diagnosis may be something like a faulty heart valve that needs to be replaced in highly complex surgery. Simple or complex, what they have in common is that I as a patient can turn my problem over to an expert who fixes it for me. This is technical work.

Adaptive work is very different. Here there is no expert with the technical skill or knowledge to fix it for me. I need to be more actively involved in the solution and perhaps even in diagnosing the problem. This is more like heart disease, where the solution involves behavior and lifestyle changes that I need to make or I will not get better. The doctor cannot fix it for me and I will not be going back to "normal." I need to craft a new normal, a new way of life that allows me to be healthy and even thrive; a way of life in which I can do the things that are more important to me (like playing with my children, working, traveling) than the things I give up (bacon, donuts, not exercising). This is adaptive work. It is not easy. It typically involves changes we don't want to make, the loss of some things we enjoyed, and sorting out what is more and what is less important in our lives. Typically we try to avoid that work and do all we can to make our adaptive challenges technical ones that someone else can fix for us and that do not demand such changes (an antiobesity pill).[1]

Heifetz's contention is that this distinction applies also to the challenges faced by organizations or communities and their leaders. Some organizational problems are technical in that "they have known solutions that can be implemented by current know-how. They can be resolved . . . through the organization's current structures, procedures and ways of doing things."[2] It may take considerable skill and effort but the problem can be solved without significant changes to the way we do things. We can get back to normal and continue as before. For example, some economic and employment problems can be fixed through technical adjustments to the money supply; some energy problems by doubling the fuel efficiency of our engines. These are highly technical fixes by skilled experts that, like taking a pill, require little of the rest of us and enable us to maintain our normal ways of doing things.

Other organizational problems, the truly challenging ones, do not lend themselves to a technical fix and cannot be solved by a more expert application of our current structures and ways of doing things. More of the same will not fix it no matter how well we do it. These problems require more fundamental, pervasive adaptation on the part of the whole organization or community. Adaptive problems, says Heifetz, typically arise when there is a gap between the mission, vision, and values of an organization and the circumstances it faces that "cannot be closed by the application of current technical know-how or routine behavior."[3] The organization with its leaders must learn its way forward.[4] Like the heart patient, the organization needs to develop new ways of doing things, new capacities, if it is to be healthy enough to achieve its mission. This kind of adaptation involves innovation, even experimentation and improvisation, in an iterative process: "Try something, see how it goes, learn from what happened, and then try something else."[5] At the same time, says Heifetz, successful adaptation involves continuity. It builds on the past rather than jettisons it.[6]

Adaptive change thus requires a clear understanding of an organization's identity: of the difference between what truly defines the organization and what is more incidental. What defines us needs to continue. What does not define us can be changed without losing our identity, mission, or values. Significantly, this understanding of our identity is also part of the learning in adaptive situations. Indeed, it is typically the most significant, difficult, even painful learning as the reality of the situation we face often demands a rethinking of our identity. If we really can't go on as before with technical fixes; what can we change, what can we not, and why? Adaptive change requires wise discernment and courageous action. It also needs to involve the whole organization.

The most common leadership failure, Heifetz maintains, is treating an adaptive challenge as if it were a technical one. This failure is made all the more understandable when we remember that the members of the organization, from bottom to top, deeply want the problems to be technical. We all want to give our problem to the experts, our leaders, and have them fix it for us—and do so at very little cost to our normal way of doing things (see US politics). Hard as it may be, when we resist the temptation to avoid adaptive work, organizations often discover opportunities to do more than merely cope with a problem. It can present opportunities to reclaim or discover a deeper identity that may have been obscured or become crusted over. It may open up new ways of doing things that enable the organization to thrive by developing capacities to meet the problem successfully and advance its values and purposes.

What Heifetz and his colleagues write about the adaptive challenges and opportunities of organizations can be helpfully applied to the church.[7] To be sure, the church is the people of God, the body of Christ, the sacramental presence of the Spirit in the world. This is an article of faith, part of our identity that cannot change in any adaptation. However, it is also an article of faith à la the Council of Chalcedon—and empirically demonstrable—that the church is a fully human organization with all the blessings, temptations, triumphs, and failures that characterize other human organizations. As such it can be instructive to consider the history of the Roman Catholic Church since the Second Vatican Council as an extended period of adaptive change, with all the stresses that go with it. Without using the category per se, Susan Wood highlights the adaptive character of these changes: "The Second Vatican Council called for a theological and liturgical renewal emphasizing the Church as communion rather than as institution. The council called for a vision of the Church as sacramental rather than juridical. . . . This entails a fundamental change in the understanding of how sacred and secular realms relate to one another. It calls the laity out of passivity into active participation in the ministry of the Church, a call inherent in their baptism and in the example of Jesus of Nazareth."[8]

This has all the elements of an adaptive response to the challenge faced by the church in the (post)modern world, including a reclaiming or reaffirmation of its fundamental identity and mission with a different way of being church in the world. This is far from a technical matter that the experts or leaders can "fix" for us. It requires the involvement of the entire organization, of all the baptized, to address the challenge of being church. All of us are responsible for the work of the church, not just the ordained. From Heifetz's analysis of other organizations, it is hardly surprising that this would meet with resistance from some, excitement from others, and take time to sort out and learn our way into—a process that is still very much with us.

There is much we could learn from applying Heifetz's analysis to any number of issues in the church and its history since the council. Our focus here, however, is on one particular issue: the development of lay ecclesial ministry in the Roman Catholic Church in the United States. Ecclesiastically, there are two interrelated dynamics that have generated this adaptive challenge—and opportunity. The first is Vatican II's empowering call of the baptized to full participation in the work of the church, noted by Wood. This has both increased our sense of what the church should be and do, including our expectations of the ministry of the church, and, as she goes on to note, has led some to come forward to participate in that ministry in a more professional way but without ordination. The second factor, which Wood also notes, is the dramatic decline in the number of priests. In Heifetz's terms, these two factors create a gap between our mission and our circumstances. The ministry we need to carry out the mission of the church does not align with the number of priests available to do it. We need either to reduce our mission and ministry to fit the people available or to increase our communal capacity for ministry by finding new ways to bring in more people to do it. Our current structures and know-how are not sufficient to deal with the problem. A classic adaptive challenge.

Lay ecclesial ministry is an adaptive response to this challenge. Building on the theological and ecclesiological framework of Vatican II, it is an operational exploration of the idea that having all ministry done by priests is not as definitive of our identity as Catholics as we might have thought. When laypeople first began doing professional ministry in the church, it was not clear what all the implications might be of this move (which is not to suggest it is clear today) but we tried it. It was not a matter of implementing some program or theology of ministry. In most cases it was simply a matter of people seeing a need, feeling a call to meet it, and stepping forward. Why would we say no to that? So we found ourselves in the sort of innovative, experimental environment characteristic of adaptive change. To be sure, not all the experiments were successful (they rarely are), but the diversity of forms and approaches made for a very creative environment, even if a bit chaotic. We were learning our way forward in just the sort of iterative process Heifetz describes: try something, learn from it, try again. Significantly, the "we" doing this learning was the whole church, not just the experts or those in authority. All of us had to sort out how we relate to laypeople doing ministry. How do we understand them and their place in the church? What is their authority? What can we rightfully expect from them—and they from us? How do we empower them to do this work while maintaining the distinctive role of the ordained? From the other side, what is the distinctive identity of the nonordained ecclesial minister in the context of the call of all the baptized to the work of the church? If everything is ministry and all are ministers, what is the place of lay ecclesial ministry? These questions quickly take us into large-scale, fundamental theological issues such as ecclesiology, discipleship, baptism, orders, parish life, and the status of the nonparochial ministries of the church such as chaplaincy, education, social services, and health care. This is not the stuff of a merely technical fix. We are learning our way together into a new way to do the ministry of the church.

This book, with its particular focus on the vocation and authorization of lay ecclesial ministers, is meant to be a contribution to that learning and the adaptive work of the church. While we hope it stands on its own as a coherent volume, it is best understood in the context of a web of initiatives to which it is explicitly and intentionally related. The most ecclesially significant and authoritative context for this work is the series of documents on lay ecclesial ministry that have been produced by the US bishops.[9] Culminating in the publication of *Co-Workers in the Vineyard of the Lord* in 2005, these documents and their significance are reviewed here by H. Richard McCord in chapter 1. Significantly, the bishops resist the temptation to treat lay ecclesial ministry as a technical fix, a stopgap to keep things going until we get back to our "normal" ways of doing things, that is, with more priests. They are quite explicit in identifying lay ecclesial ministry as the work of the Holy Spirit to which we as a community must respond. Our work here on vocation and authorization is part of that response.

More specifically, this collection of essays is part of a series of initiatives organized by Saint John's School of Theology·Seminary in Collegeville, Minnesota. These initiatives are reviewed by Jeffrey Kaster with a particular focus on the connection between the symposium of 2011 and the theological essays in this volume. Here I will simply map out the major events to help locate the essays and points of convergence. Theologically, the most immediate progenitor for this book is *Ordering the Baptismal Priesthood: Theologies of Lay and Ordained Ministry*. That volume was the fruit of Collegeville Ministry Seminar I, a group of ten theologians led by Susan Wood who worked together from 2001 to 2003 on fundamental questions related to the theology of lay and ordained ministry. In addition to their essays, the seminar produced seven points of convergence agreed to by all the members. Central to this work and giving it its title is the argument that "both lay and ordained ministry represent an ordering of the baptismal priesthood of all the faithful."[10] The points of convergence in the present volume begin with an affirmation and restatement of these seven points.[11] The connection is also evident in their final point: "These principles call us to an ongoing ecclesial discernment and a fresh articulation of an ordering of ministries (e.g., installation, commissioning) in the Church in order to recognize emerging ministries and changes in church practice."[12]

The work of this volume is an intentional response to that call to ongoing ecclesial discernment. It also follows the method of *Ordering the Baptismal Priesthood* by bringing together, thanks to the support of an anonymous foundation, the nine authors in this book to work on the theology of vocation and authorization in what we called the Collegeville Ministry Seminar II. The work began in 2009 and culminated in the symposium held in August of 2011 in Collegeville, after which the essays were given a final revision for publication here.

As Kaster explains, there were two events between these two seminars that generated the topic and shaped the way the second seminar worked on that topic: the publication of *Co-Workers* and the 2007 symposium on lay ecclesial ministry in Collegeville. Originally conceived to consider the statewide certification process for lay ecclesial ministers adopted by the six dioceses of Minnesota, the 2007 symposium was reshaped in collaboration with the United States Conference of Catholic Bishops Secretariat of Laity, Marriage, Family Life, and Youth (USCCB-LMFLY) to address the initial reception and implementation of *Co-Workers*. To that end a network of sixteen cosponsors was built with practitioners, academics, and bishops participating in the work of the 2007 symposium.[13]

At the close of the 2007 symposium, Archbishop Gregory Aymond stated in his summative remarks that "there are two very important issues that need theological research and dialogue. First . . . is the theology of vocation in ministry. . . . The second . . . is authorizing people in ministry. . . . As we go forward with lay ecclesial ministry, we must continue to do conversation, prayer, and reflection around those issues." What does it mean to be called to this work? Can we speak of it as a vocation as we do the priesthood, religious life, or marriage? How can we not when so many lay ministers clearly articulate their work as a vocation and a calling? What does it mean to be authorized for this ministry? How does that authorization happen and by whom? It is not ordination but it seems it is also not the same as hiring a janitor, for example, even if that janitor sees his or her work as a form of ministerial service to the community. The bishops through the agency of the LMFLY secretariat asked Saint John's to continue its work on lay ecclesial ministry with a focus on such questions and the theology of vocation and authorization that would enable us to answer them responsibly.

The current volume is the fruit of that work. In consultation with staff of the secretariat (Sr. Amy Hoey, Sr. Eileen McCann, McCord) and individual bishops who worked with the seminar (Aymond, Michael Hoeppner, Blase Cupich), we convened a group of theologians in 2009, drafted a framework for our work, and determined the particular research topics to be addressed. It was clear the seminar needed to do foundational, conceptual work on the meaning of vocation (Edward Hahnenberg) and authorization (Wood) for lay ecclesial ministers and that we needed to explore the biblical roots of the call to lay ecclesial ministry (Charles Bobertz). We also determined that it would be educative to learn from our more recent history, hence Hosffman Ospino's essay on the early conversations about the identity of the director of religious education (DRE), arguably the first lay ecclesial ministers after Vatican II. It is not inconsequential that a consideration of the DRE as something of a case study in lay ecclesial ministry opens up connections with the ministry of catechist so important in many Hispanic/Latino communities. It was critical that the seminar also include a consideration of ritual in authorization (Zeni Fox and Graziano Marcheschi), as well as an exploration of the canonical issues and resources related to the authorization of lay ecclesial ministers (Lynda Robitaille). Ritual and canon law are essential ingredients in Roman Catholic life and thinking. This is how ideas acquire public standing and staying power. Any ideas, any theology, of the vocation and authorization of lay ecclesial ministers will become institutionally embodied in the life of community if they make their way into ritual and canon law. As framework for all this we included the essays by McCord on the documents of the US bishops on lay ecclesial ministry and Kaster on the activities surrounding these essays, as well as the keynote address by Francis Cardinal George on the meaning of "ecclesial" in lay ecclesial ministry, specifically the relation of the bishop to the lay ecclesial minister.

Like the first seminar, the authors here did independent research and came together on several occasions to critique and learn from each other's work. Our hope is that this gives the collection of essays coherence as part of an organic project, a real conversation. The authors also produced their own points of convergence on vocation and authorization that were agreed to by all the members of the seminar.

The second seminar went beyond the first, however, in its collaboration with practitioners, which brings us to the final formative element of this volume: the 2011 Collegeville National Symposium on Lay Ecclesial Ministry. Thanks to the support of the Lilly Endowment, we were able to organize a second symposium focusing on vocation and authorization. Building on our experience with the 2007 symposium, we put together a network of forty-four cosponsors, mostly national ministry organizations with some universities, schools of theology, and bishops committees.[14] The symposium was designed from the start to interact with the seminar, so at the 2010 planning meeting the authors presented drafts of their essays for review and critique by sixty-five representatives of the cosponsoring organizations and three bishops. The authors revised their essays and what all thought were final drafts were distributed to the 230 participants in advance of the symposium.

When we came together for the symposium, something remarkable happened. Instead of the typical unidirectional flow of information and ideas from academics to practitioners, theorists to implementers, there was genuine dialogue. As Kaster details, the authors learned from their engagement with the practitioners. Though they thought their research was done, they decided to revise their essays again in light of what they had learned. Thus the essays in this volume are shaped not only by scholarly engagement with theological literature and official documents, as one would expect, but also by discussion with the other members of the seminar and by sustained dialogue and *theological* engagement with practitioners.

Not to be overlooked in this dialogue is the engagement of the bishops throughout the process. As noted, the two symposia and the second seminar were undertaken in explicit collaboration with the USCCB Secretariat of Laity, Marriage, Family Life, and Youth. The Secretariat of Cultural Diversity in the Church and the Commission on Certification and Accreditation were also cosponsors of the 2011 symposium.

In addition, a number of individual bishops were participants in the conversation at various times, meeting with the seminar, participating fully in the symposia and planning meetings, serving on panels, offering summative reflections on what they heard at each symposium, and delivering keynote addresses.

This sustained, intentional listening and collaboration is perhaps the most distinctive aspect of the work of the seminar and the essays in this volume. It is also, if I may say so, the part of it we are most proud of. We at Saint John's think of it as a very Benedictine way of doing theology by listening and hospitable dialogue. It respects expertise, experience, and authority; yields good theology; and contributes to the critical adaptive work of the church. The development of lay ecclesial ministry and, even more, of a way of being church and carrying out our mission and ministry consistent with it is not a technical problem to be taken care of by the experts. It is an adaptive challenge and opportunity in which the whole community is learning its way forward in an iterative process. We try some things, learn from them, and move forward. It is critical to this learning, to our theological work, that we involve practitioners in the reflection as well as the experimentation. The involvement of practitioners is not just about more effective implementation of the experts' ideas. It is about making the learning more true and the ideas better. It is about deepening our theological understanding of how God is at work in the church and the world. Ultimately, we hope it makes the community more faithful disciples and better equipped to be and do what it is called to.

The points of convergence are an important example of this collaborative work. Originally drafted to reflect a consensus among the authors, they too were revised in light of the dialogue at the symposium. In the end, the eight points in this volume were endorsed by over three-fourths of the participants. As such they represent a consensus not only of a group of academic theologians but also of representatives of forty-four national ministry organizations and schools. While the process of adaptation to the changing circumstances of ministry needs to be innovative and experimental, it also learns. Some basic principles, definitions, and practices emerge. We need to solidify our learning by establishing them as a foundation if we are to continue to grow. Otherwise we keep going over the same issues again and again to everyone's frustration—a far too familiar experience in discussions of lay ecclesial ministry.

To avoid that, we need to establish a foundation, get the concrete poured, let it set, and then build on it. We cannot keep digging it up, remixing the concrete, adjusting the forms, and pouring it again. Could it be better? Undoubtedly. But if we waited for the perfect foundation, we would all be homeless. So it is with the theology of vocation and authorization for lay ecclesial ministry. We can actually answer some questions: What distinguishes lay ecclesial ministry from other work of the baptized? Leadership and authorization. Is lay ecclesial ministry a vocation? Yes. Who authorizes the lay ecclesial minister? The bishop. We have learned some things. We have built a good foundation. It is time to come to a shared, operative recognition of that foundation so we can stop repouring the foundation and get on with the work of building on it. After all, the foundation is only the beginning, not the building.

Co-Workers is a major contribution to establishing that foundation. It identifies some fixed points that make further conversation possible. The work of the theologians and practitioners reflected in this volume, particularly the points of convergence endorsed by such a wide cross-section of those working in and on lay ecclesial ministry, is meant to augment the theology of *Co-Workers*. Our hope is that the consensus that has emerged can help further solidify the foundation, establish some agreed upon fixed points that enable us to move forward together in the continuing adaptive work of building the church's capacity for ministry.

As I consider the multiple initiatives converging in the publication of these essays and, even more so, the development of lay ecclesial ministry in the years since the council and the work we have yet to do, I am reminded of the story of the conversion of Cornelius in Acts 10. The context is a dispute in the church (yes, even then) about whether Gentiles could be baptized. The answer seems so obvious to us baptized Gentiles that it may be hard to imagine the difficulties around what was arguably the most momentous decision in the history of the church. Indeed, if anything was obvious in the first century it was that Gentiles should *not* be baptized. After all, Jesus was a Jew. All the disciples were Jews. Jesus spoke to Gentiles and could have called them to be his followers had he wanted to, but he did not. Everyone who had ever been baptized was a Jew. What could be clearer than that baptizing Gentiles was against the will of Christ and tradition? This was a profound identity issue and it was clear their identity was Jewish.

Enter Cornelius the Gentile. One afternoon he had a vision in which an angel told him to send for Peter. Meanwhile, Peter was having his own vision that "what God has made clean, you must not call profane." Luke tells us that even after hearing this three times, Peter was still "greatly puzzled" (vv. 15, 17, NRSV). It was against everything he knew as the will of God. Nevertheless, he went to Cornelius, explaining that he was violating the law against visiting Gentiles because "God has shown me that I should not call anyone profane or unclean" (v. 28, NRSV).

Peter then proclaimed the Gospel to Cornelius and his household. "While [he] was still speaking, the Holy Spirit fell upon all who heard the word." Not surprisingly, "the circumcised believers who had come with Peter were astounded that the gift of the Holy Spirit had been poured out even on the Gentiles. . . . Then Peter said, 'Can anyone withhold the water for baptizing these people who have received the Holy Spirit just as we have?' So he ordered them to be baptized" (vv. 44-48, NRSV). A decision endorsed, after a good bit of controversy, at the Council of Jerusalem (Acts 15).

What does this have to do with our work here on the vocation and authorization of lay ecclesial ministers and the broader adaptive challenges around ministry in the Catholic Church? In both cases, the Spirit is acting, moving ahead of us in ways we did not, and perhaps could not, foresee. We struggle to keep up—to understand, respond, and adapt our practices and structures to what the Spirit is already doing. This is true of our individual lives as disciples. It is also true of our life as an institution. Like the Spirit's coming to Cornelius, the phenomenon of lay ministry stretches our categories and raises significant theological, as well as structural, questions. Our work here is meant to contribute to our collective efforts to think through those questions and adapt our structures and practices in response to the work of the Spirit.

How will ministry be done in the twenty-first century? Like Peter, we may be more than a little puzzled as we see ever fewer priests. Yet we go forward, confident that the Spirit is active in the church—even if in ways we did not expect. Thus it has always been. Figuring out the proper institutional response to the call of the Spirit is the great opportunity in the adaptive work we are about as church.

Notes

1. Heifetz introduces this idea and its implications for organizations and leadership in *Leadership Without Easy Answers* (Cambridge, MA: Belknap Press of Harvard University Press, 1994). He develops its implications for the life of the leader in *Leadership on the Line: Staying Alive through the Dangers of Leading*, with Marty Linsky (Boston: Harvard Business School Press, 2002); and offers

more concrete tips on implementing it in *The Practice of Adaptive Leadership*, with Alexander Grashow and Marty Linsky (Boston: Harvard Business Press, 2009). See specifically *Without Easy Answers*, 22–27, 35, 73–76, 87; *On the Line*, 13–20, 55–62; *Practice*, 2–3, 14–23, 69–87. Zeni Fox uses Heifetz's reflection on leadership explicitly in her consideration of lay ecclesial ministers as leaders in her chapter in this volume, pp. 193–94.

2. Heifetz, *Practice*, 19.

3. Heifetz, *Without Easy Answers*, 35.

4. Ibid., 87.

5. Heifetz, *Practice*, 10.

6. Ibid., *15*.

7. Though I am confident that most of the adaptive challenges faced by the Roman Catholic Church in the last fifty years have been or are being faced in their own way, *mutatis mutandis*, by other Christian churches, our focus here and throughout this volume is on the Roman Catholic Church with its particular organizational form and dynamics.

8. "Introduction: The Collegeville Ministry Seminar," in *Ordering the Baptismal Priesthood: Theologies of Lay and Ordained Ministry* (Collegeville, MN: Liturgical Press, 2003), vii.

9. These documents are *Called and Gifted: The American Catholic Laity* (1980), *Called and Gifted for the Third Millennium* (1995), and *Co-Workers in the Vineyard of the Lord: A Resource for Guiding the Development of Lay Ecclesial Ministry* (2005).

10. Wood, *Ordering*, x.

11. See conclusion below, pp. 209–10.

12. Wood, *Ordering*, 264.

13 For a list of cosponsors, see chap. 2, p. 31, n. 14.

14. For a listing of the cosponsors, see appendix, pp. 217–18.

Part I

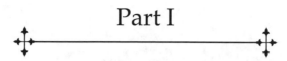

Context and Method

Chapter 1

Lay Ecclesial Ministry
Pastoral Leadership in a New Era

H. Richard McCord

Lay ecclesial ministry is a new form of pastoral leadership being carried out by laypersons who have discerned a vocation to this work and who have been properly authorized for it. The essays in this book provide a fuller discussion of what it means for a person to be called to lay ecclesial ministry and to receive authorization for it.

The present chapter serves as background for that discussion by providing a perspective on the origins and development of lay ecclesial ministry. It also seeks to advance the pursuit of excellence in lay ecclesial ministry by identifying and reflecting on a few challenges that exist in the landscape surrounding lay ecclesial ministry in the Catholic Church in the United States.

With these purposes in mind, I have organized this chapter around the following topics:

the meaning of lay ecclesial ministry
the origin and development of lay ecclesial ministry
ministerial leadership and lay ecclesial ministry

The Meaning of Lay Ecclesial Ministry

Lay ecclesial ministry is the term chosen by the US Catholic bishops to describe a new reality that has taken shape in the decades following the

Second Vatican Council. In their groundbreaking document *Co-Workers in the Vineyard of the Lord: A Resource for Guiding the Development of Lay Ecclesial Ministry* (2005), the bishops use this term as a generic, categorical name for many different ministerial leadership roles that are commonly found in US parishes and other church settings. A few of these roles are pastoral associate, parish catechetical leader, youth minister, school principal, director of music and liturgy, RCIA director, campus minister, and health care minister. The bishops offer four distinct characteristics of a person who could be considered a lay ecclesial minister:

1. *Leadership* in a particular area of ministry
2. *Authorization* of the hierarchy to serve publicly in the local church as leaders
3. *Close collaboration* with the pastoral ministry of bishops, priests, and deacons
4. *Preparation and formation* appropriate to the level of responsibility assigned to them.[1]

It should be noted that these characteristics apply to the person who does a ministry, not to any particular ministry itself. For example, catechesis is not a lay ecclesial ministry as such. Rather, the layperson responsible for directing a catechetical program would be considered a lay ecclesial minister. At the same time, the bishops are quick to point out,

> "Lay ecclesial minister" is not itself a specific position title. We do not use the term in order to establish a new rank or order among the laity. Rather, we use the terminology as an adjective to identify a developing and growing reality, to describe it more fully, and to seek a deeper understanding of it under the guidance of the Holy Spirit. (*Co-Workers*, 11)

The four characteristics listed above are meant to delineate a relatively small but growing number of laywomen and laymen who serve—mostly as employees—at parish, diocesan, and other levels of institutional church life. The characteristics attempt to distinguish the lay ecclesial minister from other laypersons who are carrying out ministerial duties.

The number of lay ecclesial ministers is small in comparison to the many thousands of laypersons who serve in church ministries on a volunteer and occasional basis, for example, reading or serving at Mass, helping to distribute Holy Communion, teaching in catechetical programs, visiting the sick and elderly, working with youth groups, assisting in charitable works, and so on.

Because *Co-Workers* does not propose or, much less, prescribe a definition of lay ecclesial ministry, there inevitably will be some blurring of boundaries and lack of consistency regarding who is considered a lay ecclesial minister. The bishops' document, by its own admission, claims no juridical force. It is an instructional, pastoral resource. Therefore, it leaves it to each diocesan bishop, guided by the four characteristics named in the document, to identify those roles that most clearly exemplify lay ecclesial ministry in his local situation. Thus, application of the term may vary from diocese to diocese.

In the years since *Co-Workers* was published there has been a common misunderstanding that someone needs to be on a church payroll in order to be considered a lay ecclesial minister. This is not true. Although lay ecclesial ministers are employed by the church on a full- or part-time basis, the bishops do not make this a necessary condition for lay ecclesial ministry. In some instances—perhaps in small parishes or in special cultural settings—it may not be possible to pay a lay ecclesial minister or it might not even be expected. Lay ecclesial ministry can still be present and viable in these situations.

The truth of this claim can best be demonstrated by focusing especially on the first characteristic used to describe lay ecclesial ministry, namely, leadership in a particular area of ministry. The role and responsibility of leadership are what must be emphasized, not whether the leader is paid. If a person is truly called to a role in pastoral leadership, is properly prepared for it, and is duly authorized to act in the name of the church in a particular faith community, then that woman or man can be considered a lay ecclesial minister.

The criterion of leadership was especially important to the bishops as they developed *Co-Workers*. In a very real sense it could be considered the primary characteristic of lay ecclesial ministry.

Leadership is a term that has no particular theological or scriptural meaning. Nonetheless, it does have a practical, existential meaning inasmuch as the church at all levels is a community of persons whose relationships and responsibilities must be organized and regulated in orderly, effective ways. Simply put, any group of people is normally able to distinguish the ones who are in leadership roles from those who are not.

In an ecclesial setting the responsibility of leading can, in certain situations, be regarded as pastoring. After all, the pastor or shepherd is the one charged with leading the flock. It is perhaps with this connection in mind that Cardinal Francis George has tended to use the phrase "sharing in the pastoring of people" as a distinguishing characteristic of the lay ecclesial minister. In so doing, he clearly states that a lay ecclesial minister is a leader, but a specifically pastoral one. Not all leaders, he seems to imply, are engaging in the pastoring of people, but only those whose ministry has a specifically pastoral character. This is an intriguing point that seems to invite more discussion.

The Origin and Development of Lay Ecclesial Ministry

The term lay ecclesial ministry can be traced through several decades of documents from the US Conference of Catholic Bishops. But prior to any mention in official statements, there was the experience of new forms of pastoral leadership especially in parishes.

The essay by Hosffman Ospino in this volume provides a valuable historical perspective on the emergence of the role of parish director of religious education (DRE) and the situational factors that promoted its growth, beginning in the late 1960s. It is generally agreed that the role of DRE was the first example of laywomen (and a few men) being entrusted with a responsibility of ministerial leadership and pastoral care. In a parish context they were lay ecclesial ministers even before the term was invented. The DRE role served as a forerunner and template for others that followed in the next decade or so, for example, youth minister, pastoral associate, liturgical coordinator.

In 1980 the bishops published a brief but influential statement titled Called and Gifted: The American Catholic Laity, in which they reflected on the many ways that laypersons had been responding to the summons of the Second Vatican Council for greater participation in the life and mission of the church. The bishops drew attention to the growing number of laypersons who "have prepared for professional ministry in the Church." They referred to these men and women as "ecclesial ministers" and welcomed them as a gift to the church (7). Among the people whom the bishops surely had in mind were those who had already begun to assume newly created leadership roles in parish ministry, such as director of religious education (DRE) and youth minister. In Called and Gifted the bishops chose to highlight the professional level of preparation and formation that this group of laypersons had undertaken. This would indicate, at least implicitly, that the bishops saw these "ecclesial ministers" acting in a leadership capacity.

In 1995 the bishops issued a second statement titled Called and Gifted for the Third Millennium. With the advantage of fifteen years of ad-

ditional experience, the bishops observed that lay ministry had continued to expand both within and beyond parishes. Laypersons had taken
on leadership roles in parish liturgical and social ministries as well as
schools, social service agencies, and health care institutions. The bishops
called this group "ecclesial lay ministers" whose roles were expressions
of ministry carried out "under the aegis of the Church" (16). The bishops also acknowledged that these ecclesial lay ministers would "speak
of their work, their service, as a calling, not merely a job. They believe
God has called them to their ministry, and often the parish priest is the
means of discerning the call" (17).

In this instance the bishops were reinforcing the leadership role of
these ministers by introducing the possibility that people could be called
to such a ministry and that they could be designated to carry it out with
the necessary degree of authority.

An expansion and refinement of thinking is certainly evident in the
progression from one document to another. This is so because in both
their statements the bishops were responding to pastoral realities as
they had been developing in the life of the church. This methodology
of response and reflection or leading by listening has been the bishops'
primary approach to lay ecclesial ministry up to the present moment.

In the period between their two official statements the US bishops
took an important step toward further understanding and responding to
the reality that would come to be known as lay ecclesial ministry. They
commissioned a national research project that was begun in 1990 and published in 1992 as *New Parish Ministers: Laity and Religious on Parish Staffs*.
This study produced the important baseline figure of 21,569 laypersons
and women and men religious employed at least twenty hours a week
as parish ministers in half of the 19,000 parishes in the United States.[2]

This study has been replicated two more times at seven-year intervals.
The third and latest study published in 2005 by the National Pastoral
Life Center found that the number of lay parish ministers employed
at least twenty hours a week had increased 42 percent to 30,632. The
percentage of parishes employing these ministers had increased from
one-half to two-thirds.[3]

The three studies told a story not only of numerical growth but also
of a developing identity in the ranks of these lay ecclesial ministers. In
various ways the research revealed the nature and extent of the leadership being provided by laypeople as well as their consciousness of being
called by God to this service and of being entrusted by the church with
responsibility for it.

Monsignor Philip J. Murnion, author of the 1997 research study, identified a significant characteristic of the "new parish ministers" when he wrote that "nowhere has the emergence of lay leadership been more dramatic than in parishes."[4] He observed that for a long time, even predating Vatican II, laity had undertaken leadership roles in church organizations, for example, the St. Vincent de Paul Society. So it was not the fact of their leadership that was new but rather the new place (parish) and the specific character (pastoral) of it.

The lay ministers whom he studied had "become part of the formal leadership as members of the parish pastoral and finance councils *and as pastoral ministers*."[5] Some of them, such as pastoral associates, were serving in roles once carried out by the ordained.

The bishops' conference paid attention not only to the research they had authorized but also to the "signs of the times" that were emerging in their dioceses and parishes. By the 1990s it was becoming abundantly clear that a new and different kind of lay participation had taken shape in the US Catholic community's experience. This type of participation could be seen as qualitatively different from—but not in opposition to—the service and witness offered by laypersons in the family, the marketplace, and the civic spheres of life. It was also distinct from but complementary to the many intraecclesial services that laity might offer—from the care of parish facilities to fundraising to reading at Mass. And, most important, it was essentially distinct from but complementary to the ordained ministries of bishop, priest, and deacon.

At the same time, theologian Edward P. Hahnenberg could justifiably make an observation about the newness of lay ecclesial ministry consisting of "not just new positions in ministry, but new ways of ministering, new ways of being a minister, new configurations of the church's ministerial structures, and new arrangements of its pastoral life."[6]

To develop an appropriate response to a new reality that they believed had "emerged and taken shape in our country through the working of the Holy Spirit" (*Co-Workers*, 14), the bishops decided in 1995 to establish a special Subcommittee on Lay Ministry to probe more systematically and to understand more fully the group of laity whom they had first called ecclesial ministers fifteen years earlier and who were being studied in the successive national research projects. In discharging its mandate the subcommittee conducted numerous consultations with theologians, pastoral experts, educators, and ordained and lay ministers. It sponsored national symposia and regional meetings that included many bishops. It issued a series of reports and working papers.

From the beginning, the subcommittee saw its task as more than just collecting data, more than just reporting trends, and even more than just providing theological grounding. Its work included all these dimensions and the additional one of providing a theological and pastoral "resource" for guiding how the church in the United States would integrate lay ecclesial ministry into its life and mission. The result of the subcommittee's work over a period of ten years was the approval and publication in 2005 of *Co-Workers in the Vineyard of the Lord* by the full body of bishops.

This document has proved to be significant for many reasons at theological, pastoral, and strategic levels. Its theological and pastoral impact has been the subject of much excellent writing.[7] In addition, however, the strategic importance of what the publication of *Co-Workers* has done for lay ecclesial ministry needs to be lifted up for consideration. I can summarize it in the following points.

First, in the document the bishops clearly and unequivocally identify lay ecclesial ministry as a work of the Holy Spirit and place themselves in a position of discernment about what is occurring under the Spirit's power. This is a fundamental assertion about the legitimacy and value of lay ecclesial ministry. It also implies that attentiveness to its development and openness to its potential are basic attitudes to maintain as we move into the future.

Second, *Co-Workers* shines a spotlight on a specific and significant population of lay ministers, namely, those who can be encompassed within the four descriptive characteristics of lay ecclesial ministry listed earlier in this chapter. The bishops focus on this group in order to point out their distinct identity and role within the church. The intent, however, is not to isolate lay ecclesial ministers but rather to connect and relate them to the fuller community of ministers that includes all the ordained and other members of the laity. As a result, therefore, the bishops take an essential first step toward the recognition and integration of lay ecclesial ministers.

Third, the very existence of *Co-Workers* as an official document and the sustained fact of the ten years' work that produced is an acknowledgment of lay ecclesial ministry as an accepted and acceptable part of the church's pastoral leadership in the United States. It has emerged in the stream of renewal begun at Vatican II and has taken hold for a variety of reasons that are both theologically supportable and pragmatically explainable. Regardless, however, the very existence of *Co-Workers* is a strategic statement about the inclusion of lay ecclesial ministry in the church's ministry of pastoral leadership.

Fourth, *Co-Workers* advances the understanding and acceptance of lay ecclesial ministers by describing in concrete terms who they are as a group. The four characteristics set forth by the bishops, namely, leadership, authorization, collaboration, and formation, represent an important advance in the matter of ministerial identity. They were not invented by the bishops. Rather, these characteristics emerged from the experience of the church and were confirmed as significant by the bishops.

Finally, the text of *Co-Workers* was organized around certain key topics (discernment of call, formation, authorization, utilization) that were intended to set direction for subsequent thinking and action about lay ecclesial ministry. This has proven to be the case—as is demonstrated, for example, by the topics chosen for the two national symposia on lay ecclesial ministry organized by Saint John's University School of Theology. The way in which the topics were presented in *Co-Workers* and the way in which they have been treated subsequently reinforce the understanding that lay ecclesial ministry is a valid expression of pastoral leadership and, as such, deserves to be institutionally integrated into and supported by the Catholic community in the United States. Achieving a better understanding of how lay ecclesial ministers can act "in the name of the church" by reason of their being called and authorized—as reflected in the chapters of this book—is an important step toward their integration into the ecclesial structures of leadership.

Ministerial Leadership and Lay Ecclesial Ministry

If the primary distinguishing characteristic of lay ecclesial ministry is leadership in an area of ministry that grants to a person a share in the pastoring of people, then I suggest that more attention should be given to questions about how leadership is exercised in a pastoral context and also about the social and ecclesial landscape in which pastoral leadership must operate today. In the remainder of this chapter I simply want to highlight some points about each of these areas.

Leadership Understood within a Specific Context
This is a question of the distinctiveness and the nuancing of leadership particularly within cultural communities. There are universal aspects to the role of a pastoral leader, to be sure. But significant differences exist in the processes by which potential leaders are identified, the expectations about what kind of preparation they need for their role, the

ways in which they carry out their responsibilities, the relationships they have with community members, and so on.

Lay ecclesial ministry has taken root and flourished in US parishes whose cultural heritage stems from European immigration and whose structure relies heavily on a core of paid, professional staff members (including clergy) who work with volunteers, committees, budgets, and other corporate-like systems. In this regard, lay ecclesial ministers clearly help to maximize the institutional potential of the parish for accomplishing its community-building and missionary goals.

While the parish-based model of church life remains strong, there are important changes taking place within parishes and outside of parishes that result from the changing demographics of US Catholicism. Simply put, we are becoming a church that is shaped more and more by Hispanic/Latino cultures. Often these communities bring with them a tradition of leadership that does not entirely fit the already-established templates of lay ecclesial ministry. For example, there might be less emphasis placed on the leader's professional or academic credentials and more weight given to equivalent experiences and accomplishments. Leadership roles might not be paid staff positions but rather volunteer positions that involve substantial responsibility and extensive collaboration.

Potential leaders are just as likely to surface in and through ecclesial movements, such as the charismatic renewal, than to work their way up through parish structures. This experience brings a different leadership perspective to parish ministry. It also raises the question of the extent to which lay ecclesial ministers can be found in nonparish settings that are connected more loosely with the oversight of the bishop.

These are but a few, sketchy examples of how lay ecclesial ministry as a form of pastoral leadership is already diversifying and developing in response to new social and ecclesial realities. Future agenda must include study and dialogue about these changes and their implications.

Leadership Understood within a Broad Landscape

In addition to focusing on the changing faces of the leaders themselves we must also consider certain factors and trends that are influencing how the leadership of lay ecclesial ministers is offered and received. I will mention only a few of the elements I see on the landscape and propose them as examples of the changing environment within which pastoral leaders must function. Their experience will continue to shape the future of lay ecclesial ministry.

In discussing the current and future environment for pastoral leadership there are many factors to mention, for example, the cultural diversity of the church, an aging population of ministers and core parishioners, differences among generational cohorts of Catholics, the impact of communications technology and the globalization of information, the erosion of trust in authority resulting from the sexual abuse crisis, the ongoing effects of an economic recession and the widening gap between rich and poor, and the decline in religious participation and sacramental practice.

However, because the most common arena for lay ecclesial ministry is the parish, I would like to focus briefly on three trends that together describe the reality of parish life today. These were identified and discussed at length by Dr. David DeLambo, a religious sociologist and pastoral planner, at a recent conference on parish life.[8]

1. *Intentionality*: Parishes are becoming more intentional, organized, and participative in their consultation and ministries. Examples are the increasing use of mission statements, parish pastoral councils, and other ways of broadening consultation with the laity by pastoral leaders. Dr. DeLambo sees these as indicators of a movement toward more shared responsibility for the mission and ministry of the parish as well as the desire by pastoral leaders to become more proactive in setting ministry priorities.

2. *Complexity*: The dual trends of larger parish size and multiple parish staffing are the leading indicators of complexity in parish life and ministry. Driven largely by a 35 percent decline in diocesan priests over the past twenty-five years and a continuing pattern of the same, there has been a net decline of 1,200 parishes (7 percent) in the last decade. Closings and mergers account for this reduction. Since the Catholic population has not declined proportionately, the result is larger parish size. Today the average number of registered parishioners is 3,277. This represents a 45 percent increase in ten years.

   A net decline in the number of parishes has been accompanied by the clustering or merging of remaining parishes under a single pastor with staff serving multiple parishes. Currently more than 40 percent of US parishes are served by a priest with responsibility for more than one parish. Pastors, pastoral life coordinators, or pastoral teams responsible for two parishes account for 62 percent of those parishes. Multiple staffing responsibility for three parishes is present in an additional 30 percent. The mere logistics of managing several parishes, often with different histories and cultures, multiple facilities and worship schedules, diverse programs, and the like, is a daunting challenge for ordained and lay ecclesial ministers alike.

3. *Vitality*: As the dynamics and structures of parish life change, there is a sharper focus on parish vitality and on the processes and practices that might enhance it or, in some cases, restore it. According to DeLambo's research, there is a heightened awareness of best practices or marks of pastoral excellence that exist in parishes that not only have viability but also vitality. These characteristics have been documented through research and can be made the basis for pastoral planning and renewal.[9]

Research by DeLambo and others is making it clear that parish vitality is closely linked with intentionality in ministry. In the face of the third trend, that is, parish complexity, this linkage can only be established and sustained by competent, collaborative, and even courageous pastoral leadership. Lay ecclesial ministers have a unique and necessary share in such leadership.

Notes

1. See USCCB, *Co-Workers in the Vineyard of the Lord: A Resource for Guiding the Development of Lay Ecclesial Ministry* (Washington, DC: USCCB Publishing, 2005), 10.

2. Philip J. Murnion, *New Parish Ministers: Laity and Religious on Parish Staffs* (New York: National Pastoral Life Center, 1992).

3. David DeLambo, *Lay Parish Ministers: A Study of Emerging Leadership* (New York: National Pastoral Life Center, 2005), 19.

4. Philip J. Murnion, *Parishes and Parish Ministers: A Study of Parish Lay Ministry* (New York: National Pastoral Life Center, 1997), 21.

5. Ibid.

6. Edward P. Hahnenberg, "Theology of Lay Ecclesial Ministry: New Trajectories," in *Lay Ecclesial Ministry: Pathways Toward the Future*, ed. Zeni Fox (New York: Rowman and Littlefield, 2010), 70.

7. See, for example, Donna M. Eschenauer and Harold Daly Horell, eds., *Reflections on Renewal: Lay Ecclesial Ministry and the Church* (Collegeville, MN: Liturgical Press, 2011); Zeni Fox, ed., *Lay Ecclesial Ministry: Pathways Toward the*

Future (New York: Rowman and Littlefield, 2010); Matthew H. Clark, *Forward in Hope: Saying Yes to Lay Ecclesial Ministry* (Notre Dame, IN: Ave Maria Press, 2009).

8. David DeLambo, "Changes in the Nature and Practice of Leadership and Ministry in American Catholic Parishes," *Origins* 41:12 (August 18, 2011): 189–94.

9. See, for example, Carole Ganin, ed., *Shaping Catholic Parishes: Pastoral Leaders in the 21st Century* (Chicago: Loyola Press, 2008); and Paul Wilkes, *Excellent Catholic Parishes: A Guide to Best Places and Practices* (New York: Paulist Press, 2001).

Chapter 2

Doing Theology Together to Advance Excellence in Lay Ecclesial Ministry

Jeffrey Kaster

Advancing understanding of faith practices comes from a deep communal listening to both the tradition and the lived experience of the faithful. This communal listening diffuses some of the polarization that prevents the church from making progress on important theological and pastoral issues. Listening is the essential ingredient in authentic dialogue, and authentic dialogue is an essential catalyst for transformation. Paulo Freire explains that authentic dialogue demands both reflection and action: "There is no true word that is not at the same time a *praxis*. Thus to speak a true word is to transform the world."[1]

During the last twelve years, Saint John's School of Theology·Seminary has convened conversations seeking to advance and sustain excellence in ministry. This initiative is called *Conversatio*, funded through generous grants from the Lilly Endowment. Saint John's Abbot John Klassen, OSB, explains, "*conversatio* is one of the three vows that a Benedictine monastic makes at profession. This virtually untranslatable Latin word has a two-fold meaning: to live the monastic manner of life and to commit oneself to the continual conversion required by the Gospel."[2] This second meaning of *conversatio* has been the inspiration for convening conversations seeking to foster transformation in ministerial practice. Over the last dozen years, Saint John's has learned that convening conversations imbued with listening and hospitality can lead to the change needed to advance excellence in ministry.

In the Name of the Church: Vocation and Authorization of Lay Ecclesial Ministry represents the latest step in an extended theological conversation focused on lay ecclesial ministry. Highlights of this twelve-year initiative include the publication of *Ordering the Baptismal Priesthood: Theologies of Lay and Ordained Ministry*[3] in 2003 and the convening of two national symposia in 2007 and 2011. This chapter reflects on doing practical theology together. It will explore the meaning that the process held for theologians and practitioners, explain the process, and draw conclusions about the process for advancing excellence in ministry.

Practical Theology

The method used throughout this initiative has been an intentional exercise in practical theology. The Association of Practical Theology defines practical theology "as an integrative hermeneutical endeavor at the heart of theological education, characterizing not only the ministerial sub-disciplines but also a manner and method of engaged reflection."[4] Kathleen Cahalan explains the goal of this interpretive endeavor as "the dialogue between text and experience toward the purpose of renewed faith in action."[5] Cahalan further explains that the methodologies of practical theology "begin with observation and attention to faith practice, engage theological content, and draw this 'new' meaning and insight into renewed action."[6] Essentially the methodology is an interpretive dialogue between experience and the Christian tradition that leads to action.[7]

Practical theology also raises the question of who is invited to be part of the dialogue. Too often theologians do not have occasion or sometimes the disposition to listen to the experiences of those outside the academy, much less from underrepresented populations. Freire warns that dialogue that does not closely listen to those on the margins can become a form of domination:

> Because dialogue is an encounter among women and men who name the world, it must not be a situation where some name on behalf of others. It is an act of creation; it must not serve as a crafty instrument for the domination of one person by another.[8]

Central to this twelve-year initiative to advance lay ecclesial ministry has been the inclusion of significant numbers of participants from underrepresented populations.

Interpreting the Christian tradition is the mainstay of Christian theology when it analyzes biblical, ecclesial, historical, and liturgical sources
to more fully understand and advance understanding of the tradition.
The essays in this book show theologians interpreting vocation and
authorization in lay ecclesial ministry through the lenses of church documents, Scripture, rituals, and canon law. What moves the process into
practical theological methodology is that the theologians also spent significant time listening to feedback from each other and from ministry
practitioners. The main argument in this chapter is that this theological
process of listening to the texts of the tradition and the texts of the lived
experience of practitioners was very beneficial in providing new theological insights and new action to advance excellence in lay ecclesial
ministry.

Perspectives of the Contributing Theologians

For this chapter I interviewed the seven authors of the essays used for
the 2011 symposium: Charles Bobertz, Zeni Fox, Edward Hahnenberg,
Graziano Marcheschi, Hosffman Ospino, Lynda Robitaille, and Susan
Wood. My primary question was about their impressions of doing theology together as an exercise in practical theology.

They were unanimous in describing their experience as exciting and
pleasurable, using descriptors such as "I loved it," "enjoyable," "wonderful," "essential," "intense," and "worthwhile." Fox said, "It was one
of the highlights of my theological life."

Why was this experience of doing theology together so meaningful? All the theologians mentioned how much they valued conversation about their essays before they were published—from each other
and from symposium participants.[9] In every case, the conversations
led to changes in their essays. Marcheschi explained that the feedback
he received from practitioners and his six colleagues resulted in major
revisions in his essay. He said it was exciting to have people read and
respond to his work before it was published. All the theologians agreed
that the feedback helped them improve their theological work.

For Wood, the process used at the symposium could be summarized
in one word: essential. For instance, she had an intense conversation
with a Hispanic leader in her symposium small group that led to a major
revision in her essay. She said that this dialogue led her to rethink the
theological categories she was using for authorization. Hearing the experiences of how Hispanic communities authorize their leaders did not

fit with the theological categories of authorization that she had prepared. As a result, she rethought and reframed an aspect of her treatment of the theology of authorization, particularly the addition of the terms *reception* and *election* and of new questions related to the terms.

Ospino shared the impact that diverse perspectives have on doing theology well. He said the variety of voices and points of view fostered mutual learning in amazing ways. The process was an invitation to realize that theological reflection about issues as important as lay ecclesial ministry must be done *en conjunto*—collaboratively. Ospino also observed that the seven authors did not exhaust reflection on vocation, authorization, and ritual within the context of lay ecclesial ministry. In fact, new questions emerged and others were nuanced. He said, "We must listen to God's people and the larger Tradition on a regular basis."

Robitaille was surprised that others did not know about canonical perspectives she took for granted. She found it very enjoyable to be in a community dialogue where the assumptions within her field of canon law were not accepted by everyone else. For her, it was intellectually exciting to listen and learn from these multiple perspectives. She said that none of the authors stayed stagnant and that they continued to learn throughout the entire process.

Fox agreed—she said that the in-depth sharing of perspectives was very enriching and dialogic in its truest sense, where the theologizing was constantly informed by the living church. "It was not just individuals doing theology. It was a broad section of informed folks doing theology together." The fruit of such effort was not simply an improvement in the essays but the experience of communion.

Hahnenberg explained that he typically crafts theological arguments alone and then sends out his work for feedback from a few individuals. Theologians often find their work to be a solitary experience. This was his first experience of doing theology in this communal way. He found the feedback from his colleagues on the writing team to be very beneficial, but it was harder—in a good way. "It is easier to craft an argument on your own. It certainly is more efficient. It is challenging to move together."

Bobertz expanded on Hahnenberg's comment about the solitary experience of doing theology, noting that biblical scholars often do their work in silos. They talk primarily with other biblical scholars within the guild and rarely have conversations about their work with other theologians outside their guild, much less with those practicing ministry. Bobertz found the feedback he received at the symposium to be very productive because it revealed points within his work that were most engaging for ministry practitioners. He said, "What most interested them was fascinating to me. I was amazed at what they were drawn to and what they saw in my work." He said he felt uplifted and a great sense of joy, realizing his work was making a contribution.

Doing theology together can be intimidating. Professors of theology live in a stratified world based on prestige factors, such as where they completed doctoral studies and who is publishing their research. Such stratification can lead to privileging some opinions more than others. A number of the symposium authors stated that they experienced community or even communion within the group. Listening was mentioned as the practice that most fostered community. Robitaille said that the hospitality she received and the respect she experienced enriched her experience of community, affirming the power of listening and hospitality for doing theology together.

Fox, Hahnenberg, and Wood all pointed out that the dialogue was not simply between the theologians and the practitioners at the symposium. It also included dialogue with the bishops. While several bishops were present at both symposiums, the primary way the bishops were included in the dialogue was through their document *Co-Workers in the Vineyard of the Lord*.[10] All the essays in this volume directly or indirectly referenced *Co-Workers*. The grounding of the conversation in *Co-Workers* meant that the dialogue was essentially a three-way conversation between the bishops, theologians, and practitioners.

The authors also underscored the significance of the points of convergence. Wood said that it was a significant theological breakthrough in 2003 when the theologians started asking together, "What are we saying here?" The breakthrough was in part the effort to speak in a communal theological voice. Fox reflected that this was of the Holy Spirit and one of the highlights of her theological career.

Hahnenberg thought that the significance of the 2011 symposium was bringing the eight points of convergence to the symposium participants for their critical discussion and feedback. Revising the points of convergence based on that process and having these points endorsed by the symposium participants was unique. "I really liked the idea that these were points of convergence and not necessarily consensus points because this left plenty of space for further dialogue and further theological exploration."

All seven authors concurred that this was their first experience of doing theology together and of having multiple rounds of dialogue with other theologians and ministerial practitioners. They all said they would do this again and seemed a bit surprised that they hadn't done it before. The authors said that doing theology together provides multiple perspectives that enrich theological reflection that is different than when one does theology alone.

Perspectives of Multicultural Leaders

I interviewed six multicultural leaders to listen to their insights and reflections about the process used at the symposium: Cecile Motus, assistant director, USCCB Cultural Diversity; Carmen Cervantes, executive director, *Fe y Vida*; Hector Medina, Diocese of Oakland; Sergio Canjura, Archdiocese of San Francisco, *Pastoral Juvenil*; Ruth Bolarte, IHM, Archdiocese of Philadelphia, *Federacion de Institutos Pastorales*; and Roberto Navarro, *National Catholic Network de Pastoral Juvenil*.

Similar to the experiences of the theologians, these church leaders were very positive about the process used to do theology together. Cervantes said that having two persons representing minority cultures at each table of eight was very significant. She highlighted the listening that happened and the openness to really hear the experiences of the minority. She said the two national symposia were marking a new way of working together, heightening the importance of including all voices, and paving the way for the whole church.

Motus echoed these sentiments, noting that she was particularly impressed with the level of listening. This was most evident with her table facilitator, who paid particular attention to those from cultural groups. "The facilitator continually invited us into the conversation and asked us what we thought." Motus also highlighted an ongoing tension that she experienced at the symposium. "With so many culturally diverse groups within Catholicism, it is challenging to listen to the various voices that make up the diverse church."

Medina emphasized deep conversation as the source of his appreciation for the symposium. He said it was a participatory process that reminded him of a national *encuentro* in Brazil he had attended ten years earlier. He observed that the participants of the symposium were protagonists in the process. They were helping to create not only the theology of vocation and authorization within lay ecclesial ministry but also an experience of church.

Both Cervantes and Canjura suggested that the symposium process could be adapted to be even more effective. They commented that reacting to a first draft of a theological work is less inclusive than being part of a conversation that would proceed and help prepare a first draft. "Once a first draft is written," Canjura said, "so much has already been set in stone that it is often difficult to change." Wood had said virtually the same thing about having the theologians discuss their topics more thoroughly before writing the first drafts.

Canjura and Medina both commented that many in the Latino community did not feel recognized because of the lack of Latino keynote speakers and authors at the 2011 symposium. Canjura said that seeing Latino leaders speaking in front of the symposium impacts feelings of representation. For example, on the first night of the symposium, no Hispanic leader was part of a panel discussion of the keynote address. Having Beverly Carroll, assistant director of the USCCB Committee on Cultural Diversity, an African American woman, on the panel was not sufficient and did not foster a feeling of being represented as a Latino at the symposium.

Navarro said the symposium process impressed him especially when the theologians said they would change their essays based on the feedback they received from participants. He saw movement from "you have a place at the table" to "you are heard at the table." He explained that at many church conferences representatives from cultural groups are invited to attend but often in such low numbers that their voices are not really heard. At the symposium there were enough diverse voices that they were actually listened to. Navarro also pointed to the context of fear and skepticism that sometimes occurs within the Latino community because of immigration and documentation issues. His experience at the symposium helped him to feel part of this group. "I want you to know my story. You will then know my context. I cannot love you, if I don't know you."

Bolarte summarized the experiences of many of those from culturally diverse populations at the symposium: "It was overall a very positive step and we were really happy to be part of it. But it is still too easy for us to be on the margins within the church." She said that the essays prepared for the symposium did not adequately address cultural diversity. One Latino author cannot cover diversity. Diversity should be the umbrella for all the essays. Bolarte summed up what all six leaders concluded: the symposium was a very positive step and a good process that provided a model of inclusivity for other ministerial conversations. Nonetheless, there is still a distance to go before we create authentic dialogue that listens to the diversity that is the church.

Case Study: A Twelve-Year Process of Advancing Lay Ecclesial Ministry

The experiences of the authors and the leaders of multicultural ministry suggest that the process had significant merit. Before drawing conclusions based on this experience, it will be useful to explain more thoroughly the process that Saint John's School of Theology·Seminary utilized through this twelve-year endeavor.

The Collegeville Ministry Seminar

The first major step in advancing a theological understanding of lay ecclesial ministry began in 2001. Saint John's School of Theology·Seminary received a grant from the Lilly Endowment to host a research seminar that would articulate a contemporary theology of lay and ordained ministry. The Collegeville Ministry Seminar brought together ten theologians for eight days in August 2001.[11] Their charge was "to discuss position papers on various aspects of lay and ordained ministry."[12] The theologians then developed seven convergence points contributing to a theology of ordered ministry.[13] The results of the seminar were published in *Ordering the Baptismal Priesthood* and two conferences were also held to disseminate this work.

Certification of Lay Ecclesial Ministers in Minnesota

Since 1998, Saint John's School of Theology·Seminary has worked collaboratively with the six dioceses of Minnesota and the other Catholic colleges and universities in the state to develop and advance a statewide certification process for lay ecclesial ministers. In 2002, the six dioceses opened a file with the United States Conference of Catholic Bishops Commission on Certification and Accreditation (USCCB-CCA) to certify lay ecclesial ministers serving as catechetical and youth ministry leaders.

During this time, Saint John's received a new Lilly Endowment grant as part of its sustaining pastoral excellence initiative. As part of that grant, Saint John's committed to foster a collaborative approach among the six dioceses on certification, believing that pastoral excellence would be served by insuring that lay ministers were well prepared for ministry. Part of that commitment was to plan and host a national symposium on lay ecclesial ministry certification in 2007.

Planning a National Symposium on Lay Ecclesial Ministry

In 2005, the plans for a Saint John's national symposium on certification based on the Minnesota experience changed with the publication by the USCCB of *Co-Workers in the Vineyard of the Lord*. It became apparent that a symposium focusing exclusively on certification of lay ecclesial ministers would be too narrow. Certification was only one piece of the bigger challenge of advancing lay ecclesial ministry. Saint John's approached the United States Conference of Catholic Bishops Committee on Laity, Marriage, Family Life, and Youth (USCCB-LMFLY) about collaborating on a symposium on lay ecclesial ministry that would include a focus on certification. The committee chair, Bishop Kicanus, endorsed this idea. The first step in planning was inviting universities and ministry organizations to cosponsor this symposium. Sixteen organizations joined Saint John's and the USCCB-LMFLY in cosponsoring the symposium.[14]

In 2006 cosponsors met in Denver to design the symposium. The group established four goals: (1) to amplify the national will to advance lay ecclesial ministry in the United States; (2) to foster theological and pastoral insight into certifying, forming, authorizing, and sustaining lay ecclesial ministry; (3) to create national recommendations for formation, authorization, pathways, and workplace issues that seek to foster excellence in lay ecclesial ministry; and (4) to generate organizational and personal commitments for implementing symposium recommendations.

Consistent with its third goal, the planning group agreed that symposium participants should develop and prioritize a set of recommendations to advance excellence in lay ecclesial ministry in the four areas of pastoral application outlined in *Co-Workers* (27–65). H. Richard McCord, executive director of the USCCB Secretariat of Laity, Marriage, Family Life, and Youth, made a pivotal recommendation. Rather than simply developing recommendations, the symposium should invite the cosponsoring organizations to make concrete commitments to advance the recommendations endorsed by the symposium participants. This has played a significant role in Saint John's twelve-year process of advancing lay ecclesial ministry because it grounded the idea that this doing theology together must include action. More specifically, it includes actions the participants themselves will undertake, not merely actions they recommend others undertake.

The planning group for the 2007 symposium also decided that it was very important to have diverse representation at the symposium. Funds from the Lilly Endowment and another anonymous donor supported participation from minority communities. The goal was to recruit 25 percent of the symposium participants from minority groups.

2007 National Symposium on Lay Ecclesial Ministry

The 2007 National Symposium on Lay Ecclesial Ministry: Working in the Vineyard of the Lord, was a direct response to the USCCB's call in *Co-Workers* for expanded study of critical issues facing lay ecclesial ministry and for dialogue about effective ways to support and advance ministry in the church. Nearly two hundred Catholic leaders gathered at Saint John's University in Collegeville, Minnesota, from July 31 to August 3, 2007, for that purpose.

The process used at the symposium included presymposium online discussions of theological essays on lay ecclesial ministry, keynote talks, panel discussions, and extended time for dialogue to produce recommendations and commitments for advancing excellence in lay ecclesial ministry. The process also focused on the personal experiences of participants' call to ministry. Symposium participants constructed a pathway to ministry map that they shared in their table discussion groups. This critical experience of personal call was placed in dialogue with the theological essays and keynote talks throughout the symposium.

By intention, small groups reflected the diversity of participants. Twenty of the participants were ordained, and eighteen served as parish-based lay ecclesial ministers. Fifty of the representatives were from Latino ministry organizations, and ten were from the National Association of Black Catholic Administrators. Also attending were several representatives from Pacific Islander and other minority groups. Each table discussion group of eight people had one ordained minister, at least one lay ecclesial minister, a leader of a ministry organization, and at least two people from underrepresented populations.

Having more than one-fourth of the ministerial leaders from underrepresented populations had a significant impact on the dialogue, recommendations, and commitments made at the symposium. Both the recommendations and organizational commitments reflected the diversity of the symposium population as illustrated by the recommendations and commitments for advancing lay ecclesial ministry in the four areas of pastoral application from *Co-Workers*.[15]

Each cosponsor of the 2007 symposium made organizational commitments to advance the recommendations made at the symposium. This was an essential aspect of the theological methodology used at the symposium. It coupled theological reflection and dialogue with action. Once again diversity issues were central to many of the organizational commitments.[16]

The process utilized at the 2007 symposium advanced the communal practice of practical theology through its dialogic process of listening to the Christian tradition and to the lived experience of symposium participants. The result was the development of recommendations and commitments to action. As stated by Ana Maria Pineda at the conclusion of the symposium, the diversity of the participants broadened and enriched the understanding of lay ecclesial ministry. This process of doing theology together also generated positive conversation about advancing lay ecclesial ministry nationally. A few months after the symposium, Charlotte McCorquodale, a consultant on certification working with Saint John's, said,

> As I travel around the country, there has been a high level of interest in the work happening in Minnesota around LEM certification, as well as the outcomes of the "Collegeville Symposium." Never in the history of lay ecclesial ministry in the U.S. Church has such a broad group of national organizations, dioceses, and higher education institutions come together with the common purpose to discern not what others should do to advance lay ecclesial ministry, but what they will do to advance it through organizational commitments.

Finally, the 2007 symposium recommendations and commitments provided the direction for theological research on vocation and authorization that would become foundational for the next steps in Saint John's initiative to advance lay ecclesial ministry.

The Collegeville Ministry Seminar II
    At the conclusion of the 2007 symposium, Saint John's School of Theology·Seminary made the following two commitments: (1) to continue to serve as conveners of the conversation at the national level and pursue funding to make it possible, and (2) to contribute to the development of a theology of vocation and a theology of authorization for lay ecclesial ministers. These two commitments spurred Saint John's in 2008 to secure funding for a second seminar of theologians to study the theology of vocation and authorization. Once again this effort developed into a partnership between Saint John's and the USCCB-LMFLY.
    The three-year process utilized in the second Collegeville seminar advanced the notion of communal practical theology begun at the first Collegeville seminar in 2001. The theologians whose essays are included in this volume created their chapters through the process of doing theology together. It began in February 2009, when the authors met with Bishops Gregory Aymond (Archdiocese of New Orleans), Michael Hoeppner (Diocese of Crookston), and Blase Cupich (Diocese of Spokane) to discuss the question: What theological, canonical, and pastoral issues

associated with vocation and authorization in lay ecclesial ministry have the most potential to advance lay ecclesial ministry in the United States? The conversation clarified needed areas of theological and canonical research and identified who was best suited for which topics.

Between February 2009 and August 2010, the theologians developed the first drafts of their theological essays on vocation and authorization in lay ecclesial ministry. Leadership from Saint John's and the USCCB-LMFLY helped the authors to sharpen the focus of the essays and clarify how they fit together. As part of the planning process for the 2011 symposium, the authors met in August 2010 to review the first drafts of their essays with sixty-five representatives from the symposium's cosponsoring organizations. The process for this planning meeting was designed to ground the discussion of the essays in the lived experience of lay and ordained ecclesial ministers, so it began with participants sharing the stories of their vocations and drawing out the key elements and commonalities. Then each author listened to specific feedback from the participants concerning their essays in terms of what ideas were most helpful for advancing the discussion of lay ecclesial ministry in the church, where the authors' ideas differed from those of participants, and what seemed to be missing from the essays. The process ended with identification of questions that would benefit from further discussion at the symposium itself and reflection on what movement of the Holy Spirit participants discerned in the planning process.

In September 2010, the authors again met in Chicago with leaders from the USCCB-LMFLY to discuss the written feedback they received from the symposium planning meeting. At this meeting, the authors clarified changes or new directions they intended for their final drafts and began the discussion of the themes or theological convergence points that emerged from all the essays. During the next eight months, the theologians completed what we assumed would be the final drafts of the essays. These were sent to the 2011 Collegeville National Symposium participants prior to the symposium. The authors also worked during this time to complete their points of theological convergence prior to the 2011 symposium.

2011 Collegeville National Symposium on Lay Ecclesial Ministry

Two hundred and thirty participants engaged in extended dialogue on the theology of vocation and authorization in lay ecclesial ministry from August 2–5, 2011, at Saint John's University in Collegeville, Minnesota. More than a fourth of the participants were Latino, African

American, Asian, Pacific Islander, or American Indian. Forty-four organizations cosponsored this second symposium, including fourteen universities, twenty-five ministry organizations, two dioceses, and three USCCB committees or departments.

Key aspects of the process included the following:

1. Presymposium reading of the seven essays on vocation and authorization in lay ecclesial ministry
2. Keynote addresses by Dr. Nancy Ammerman and Francis Cardinal George
3. Feedback from the symposium participants on the essays
4. Presentation of the authors' theological convergence points
5. Participant response to the convergence points followed by their revision
6. Endorsement of the convergence points by symposium participants
7. Development and prioritization of recommendations to advance excellence in lay ecclesial ministry
8. Commitment to action by cosponsoring organizations to advance excellence in lay ecclesial ministry
9. Capstone talks by Bishop Blase Cupich, Diocese of Spokane, and Diana Macalintal, director of worship, Diocese of San Jose, on discerning the movement of the Holy Spirit through the dialogue of the symposium.

The 2011 symposium used a dialogic process of theological reflection and action. It included the essays by theologians and thoughtful presentations by keynote speakers. Significant and sustained conversation by participants explored the theological ideas framing the symposium and produced new theological insights leading to revisions in both the essays and theological convergence points. This dialogue also focused specific, concrete recommendations and commitments for action that would insure that the excitement generated during the four days in August would not fade as people left campus. One strategic way to reinforce the commitment to action was a $30,000 fund generated by cosponsor fees that would support collaborative initiatives to advance excellence in lay ecclesial ministry.

A review of the recommendations again highlights the significance of cultural diversity. It was the most frequently mentioned topic and included the recruitment of lay ecclesial ministers from underrepresented populations, investing financial resources, and the need for further dialogue with representatives from culturally diverse groups about the cultural implications impacting lay ecclesial ministry formation, certification, and authorization.

The second important category of recommendations focused on national certification of lay ecclesial ministers. These included approval and promotion of national certification standards by the USCCB as integral to determining competency for ministry, the need for colleges and universities to understand and utilize these standards in ministry formation, and a need for cultural sensitivity within the certification process.

Commitments by cosponsors also underscored cultural diversity. Saint Catherine University, for example, will renew efforts to reach out to, recruit, support, and educate/form persons from underrepresented populations for lay ecclesial ministry. Saint John's University School of Theology·Seminary will provide fifteen full tuition scholarships over the next three years for lay ecclesial ministers pursuing a master of divinity degree (with preference for those serving underrepresented communities). The National Conference for Catechetical Leadership will work with the Alliance for the Certification of Lay Ecclesial Ministers (organizations working together on national certification of lay ecclesial ministers) and its members to pursue the sponsorship of a "training the trainers" workshop on intercultural competencies in collaboration with the USCCB Secretariat of Cultural Diversity in the Church. The Association of Graduate Programs in Ministry will encourage member schools to meet the needs of minority and nontraditional students by increasing accessibility to its programs and offering alternative formation opportunities. The National Association of Pastoral Musicians commits to continue offering leadership and certification of lay ecclesial ministers in collaboration with other partner organizations of the alliance and in dialogue with organizations representing various cultural and ethnic groups, especially in exploring pathways and equivalencies.

Conclusions

Reviewing the twelve-year history of conversations on lay ecclesial ministry convened by Saint John's School of Theology·Seminary reveals an evolving process of practical theology, beginning with ten theologians dialoguing with each other about a theology of lay and ordained ministry and concluding with extensive dialogue among bishops, theologians, and diverse ministry practitioners. This dialogue led to an endorsement of the theological points of convergence by symposium participants and action to advance excellence in lay ecclesial ministry. What conclusions can be drawn from this process of doing practical theology?

Conclusion #1: The church is better served when theology emerges from intentional dialogue among theologians, ministerial practitioners, and bishops. The research into the meaning that this process held for the theologians suggests that better theology emerges through an intentional process of theological reflection and action with practitioners and bishops. It was surprising to hear how the theologians enjoyed doing theology together. Their conclusion was that this dialogue produced better theology. Their joy also resulted from their increased capability to fulfill their ultimate purpose to serve the church in advancing theological thinking about vocation and authorization in lay ecclesial ministry. This method of dialogue and action serves the church by producing better theology and fostering better faith practices.

In reviewing the data from the last twelve years, it was very interesting that the progress made on the main 2007 symposium organizational commitments are all having a positive impact on advancing excellence in lay ecclesial ministry. The USCCB Committee on Cultural Diversity, for example, has made great progress on developing competencies for multicultural ministry. The Alliance for the Certification of Lay Ecclesial Ministers has just received approval from the USCCB-CCA for their new national certification standards for lay ecclesial ministry. This approval will be the start of national certification for lay ecclesial ministers serving in a variety of ministerial roles. And this book makes its own important contribution to the theology of vocation and authorization in lay ecclesial ministry. These advancements have benefited from the method of theological dialogue that includes reflection and action in service of the church.

Conclusion #2: Theologians should utilize the methods of practical theology. All of the theologians mentioned that this was the first time they had participated in dialogue with other theologians and practitioners in such an extensive way. Theological work has been in silos for too long. The data discovered in this research suggests that theologians would greatly benefit from dialogue with other theologians in a systematic way and would also greatly benefit from dialogue with practitioners. If theology is in service of the church, then it needs to break out of its silos. Theologians may discover new vocational joy in this transformation. When a theologian states that "one of the highlights" of her theological career was extensive dialogue with nine other theologians, it suggests that something very important is happening.

Conclusion #3: Theologians must listen to the voices of underrepresented communities to adequately advance Christian practice. Two pivotal moments in the entire initiative were the decision in 2006 to have significant representation (25 percent) at the 2007 symposium from diverse communities and in 2011 when Sr. Susan Wood said publically that she would revise her essay because of conversation she had with Hispanic leaders. These moments challenge the church, in the words of Roberto Navarro, to move from providing minorities "a place at the table" to actually being "heard at the table." It is clear from listening to leaders from diverse communities that we still have a long way to go, but having significant numbers of minority voices in the conversation is essential for advancing excellence in ministry.

Conclusion #4: Doing theology together is a particularly effective method for advancing excellence in lay ecclesial ministry because it is an intentional process of listening to the movement of the Holy Spirit. The comment heard most often in researching this process of practical theology was "I really felt listened to." Something profound appears to happen in our polarized society when we provide space for authentic listening. Another comment that was prevalent throughout the twelve-year process was the phrase "movement of the Holy Spirit." It appears that listening is an essential practice in discerning the movement of the Holy Spirit. It was the intention of Saint John's School of Theology·Seminary that this initiative be an experience of *conversatio* where listening with the ear of one's heart becomes an essential part of the transformational process.

The fruits of this process of doing theology together suggest it is the work of the Holy Spirit. The symposium participants moved beyond particular positions to a larger communal conversation that produced insight for themselves and for theologians. They were able to critique and then endorse the theological convergence points, affirming as one of those points that lay ecclesial ministry is a work of the Holy Spirit. They were able to identify and name specific, concrete ways in which good ideas developed at the symposium would find embodiment in actions benefiting the work of the church to proclaim the Gospel. It is my contention that authentic listening is essential for theological dialogue precisely because it helps the church discern the movement of the Holy Spirit in matters of mission, ministry, and pastoral leadership.

Notes

1. Paulo Freire, *Pedagogy of the Oppressed*, New Revised 20th Anniversary Edition (New York: Continuum, 1996), 68.

2. *Conversatio*, Saint John's School of Theology·Seminary Newsletter (Winter 2003/2004): 4.

3. Susan K. Wood, ed., *Ordering the Baptismal Priesthood: Theologies of Lay and Ordained Ministry* (Collegeville, MN: Liturgical Press, 2003).

4. "About APT," The Association of Practical Theology web site, http:// practicaltheology.org/about-2/.

5. Kathleen A. Cahalan, "Locating Practical Theology in Catholic Theological Discourse and Practice," *International Journal of Practical Theology* 15, no. 1 (August 2011): 12.

6. Ibid.

7. Richard Osmer, *Practical Theology: An Introduction* (Grand Rapids, MI: Eerdmans, 2008), 23. Osmer explains how this methodology of interpretation brings about this new meaning by referring to Hans-Georg Gadamer's hermeneutical circle. Gadamer's five moments include (1) *preunderstanding*—the judgments with which we begin interpretation; (2) *being brought up short*—calling into question some aspect of our preunderstanding; (3) *dialogical interplay*—listening to the text, person, or object to reveal itself in a new way or to its new horizon; (4) *fusion of horizons*—"like a conversation, interpretation yields new insights when the horizons of the interpreter and the interpreted join together"; and (5) *application*—"new insights give rise to new ways of thinking and acting in the world."

8. Freire, *Pedagogy of the Oppressed*, 70.

9. There were three distinct times for feedback on the theological essays prior to the publication in this volume: (1) in August 2010 representatives from the forty-four cosponsors of the symposium provided feedback on the author's first drafts; (2) in September 2010 the theologians met to provide feedback to each other; and (3) in August 2011 participants provided feedback on the second drafts at the symposium.

10. USCCB, *Co-Workers in the Vineyard of the Lord: A Resource for Guiding the Development of Lay Ecclesial Ministry* (Washington, DC: USCCB Publishing, 2005).

11. The ten theologians were Michael Downey, Zeni Fox, Richard R. Gaillardetz, Aurelie Hagstrom, Kenan Osborne, OFM, David Power, OMI, Thomas P. Rausch, SJ, Elissa Rinere, CPR, Kevin Seasoltz, OSB, and Susan K. Wood, SCL.

12. Wood, *Ordering the Baptismal Priesthood*, x.

13. Ibid., 256–65. These seven convergence points are also listed in the conclusion of this volume.

14. Cosponsors of 2007 Working in the Vineyard of the Lord: A National Symposium on Lay Ecclesial Ministry included the following: Association of Graduate Programs in Ministry; Institute in Pastoral Ministries: Saint Mary's University of Minnesota; *Instituto Fe y Vida*; Federation of Diocesan Liturgical

Commissions; Minnesota Catholic Education Association; National Association of Black Catholic Administrators; National Association of Catholic Chaplains; National Association of Catholic Family Life Ministers; National Association for Lay Ministry; National Federation for Catholic Youth Ministry; Washington Theological Union; USCCB Commission on Certification and Accreditation; National Association for Pastoral Musicians; National Conference for Catechetical Leadership; National Leadership Roundtable on Church Management; USCCB Secretariat of Laity, Marriage, Family Life, and Youth; and USCCB Committee on Hispanic Affairs.

15. (1) Pathway recommendations emphasized ways for Catholic leaders to invite persons into lay ecclesial ministry; (2) formation recommendations focused on (a) formation for a culturally diverse church, (b) funding, (c) allowance for alternative modes of formation, and (d) availability and accessibility; (3) authorization recommendations called for further dialogue and study to clarify the meaning of authorization; and (4) workplace recommendations called for dioceses and parishes to establish personnel policies that are just.

16. A summary of organizational commitments: (1) commitments to discuss, study, promote, or integrate *Co-Workers* within their organizations; (2) commitments to address inclusion and cross-cultural ministry competence; (3) commitments to advance lay ecclesial ministry standards, competencies, or certification, including a significant commitment toward national certification; (4) commitments to publicize and engage the work of the symposium; and (5) commitments to advance the theology of vocation and authorization. A complete list of the recommendations and commitments have been archived on the 2007 symposium web site: http://www1.csbsju.edu/sot/symposium/2007symposium.htm.

Part II

The Vocation
to Lay Ecclesial Ministry

Chapter 3

Serving in the Name of the Church
The Call to Lay Ecclesial Ministry

Edward P. Hahnenberg

Can we speak about a "vocation" to lay ecclesial ministry? This question goes back almost to the beginning of the process that would produce the document *Co-Workers in the Vineyard of the Lord*. Early on in their deliberations, the US bishops' Subcommittee on Lay Ministry arranged a consultation with several lay ecclesial ministers serving on parish staffs in a variety of ministerial roles. As the conversation unfolded, several of the lay ministers began to share their experiences of being called to ministry. They spoke of the ways God had worked in their lives, and the many ways God was still at work in their lives. Their words resonated with the bishops who were present. Afterward, the committee members spent some time discussing what they had heard. Do these stories of call suggest a genuinely new vocation in the church? Is this a new diversification of God's call—a fourth vocation alongside the vocations to priesthood, religious life, and marriage? Is the call to lay ecclesial ministry comparable to the call to ordained ministry? Is it more like the consecrated life? How does the work of lay ecclesial ministers relate to the broader vocation of the laity in the world?

Here lived experience comes up against traditional categories. For centuries, Roman Catholics have practically identified the concept of vocation with priesthood and religious life. To "have a vocation" meant the call to be a priest or a nun—to enter, through vows or ordination, into a permanent, ecclesiastically approved state of life. The lived experience of lay ecclesial ministry, as a more or less full-time, long-term position of lay ministerial leadership, does not seem to fit neatly within such a definition. It is not a state of life. It does not entail the same kind of permanence or totality that has been historically associated with clerical or religious vocations. Still, these elements are not entirely absent—and this is one of the things that make the phenomenon so complex and so rich. Lay ecclesial ministers *do* make a significant commitment to ministry, and they enact that commitment in concrete ways (by pursuing education on their own and at their own expense, by moving a family to take a new position, by planning programs or projects that extend into the future, and so on). David DeLambo's 2005 study reports that nearly three-fourths (73.1 percent) of lay parish ministers believe that they are pursuing a lifetime of service in the church.[1] Clearly, their response to God's call is a life-orienting decision, one that profoundly impacts their faith, their families, and their future. Moreover, their own personal sense of call is consistent and strong. Those few lay ecclesial ministers who shared their experiences with the subcommittee are not the exception but the norm. DeLambo reports that more than half (54.2 percent) of lay ecclesial ministers say that the factor that most influenced them to pursue a lifetime of ministry in the church is a "call" from God. Seven in ten (69.3 percent) list "response to God's call" among the top three reasons for doing what they do. "So dominant was the response to God's call as a motivating factor that the next highest factor cited by laypersons totaled only 15.0 percent."[2]

To their credit, the bishops acknowledged the reality of this experience. In an initial report of the subcommittee, published in 1999, they wrote, "Lay ministers speak often and reverently of their call or vocation to ministry, a call that finds its origin in the call of God and its confirmation in the appointment to a specific ministry within the Church. . . . We conclude that this call or vocation is worthy of respect and sustained attention."[3] Over the course of drafting *Co-Workers*, those involved continued to struggle with this question of vocation. The final document ends with a frank admission: "The preparation of *Co-Workers in the Vineyard of the Lord* has already indicated a need for a more thorough study of our theology of vocation."[4]

Vatican II unambiguously affirmed the universal call to holiness and, in doing so, challenged the widespread assumption among Catholics that God's call belonged only to a select few. The recognition that *everyone* has a vocation loosened up the category. It freed vocation from a narrow identification with priesthood and religious life, thus making it possible for lay ministers to appropriate the language of vocation in coming to understand and describe their own experience. Still, despite this broadening, many of the older theological assumptions have remained in place. The very way in which the bishops responded to those early testimonials ("Is this a fourth vocation?") suggests the ongoing association in the Catholic consciousness between vocation and state of life. The deep sense of call to direct ministry experienced by many lay ecclesial ministers seems to be something more than the universal call to holiness (even as this ministry—like all ministries—is grounded in the baptismal vocation). But lay ecclesial ministry is not a state of life. It exists somewhere in between. Can we call this a vocation?

Lay ecclesial ministry represents a call to a new way of *doing ministry*, but it also represents a new way of *being a minister*. For here we have a significant, long-term, and full-time commitment to a position of ministerial leadership outside of the clerical state and distinct from religious life. However, it will not do to imagine lay ecclesial ministry as a new vocation alongside (or overlaid on top of) priesthood, religious life, and married life—if our primary association is that of a state of life. Our theological response will thereby founder if it expects a static status or the kind of lifelong commitment from the individual that mark these other venerable vocations. Lay ecclesial ministry is not a state of life but a living commitment. As a way of embodying a life of Christian service, lay ecclesial ministry has shown a remarkable freedom and fluidity. This reality calls for a theology of vocation to match, a theology articulated in more dynamic, developmental, and relational terms.[5]

In this essay, I propose an ecclesial theology of vocation as a way to talk about the call to lay ecclesial ministry. By an "ecclesial theology of vocation" I mean to highlight the way in which lay ecclesial ministers are called in, through, and on behalf of the ordered communion that is the church. In order to address the call to lay ecclesial ministry, we must first locate it within the broader context of *the call to ministry*—a term that I take to include all those actions that serve the mission of Christ. The call to ministry must itself be seen within the broader context of *the call to discipleship* that it serves. Thus the essay will move from discipleship to ministry to lay ecclesial ministry. But first let me say a bit more about the importance of an ecclesial theology of vocation.

Toward an Ecclesial Theology of Vocation

I suggested above that, for centuries, reflection on vocation within Roman Catholicism was constrained by a narrow identification with a few, ecclesiastically approved states of life. However, alongside this institutionalization of vocation was a further problem: the interiorization of God's call. Since at least the seventeenth century, seminary textbooks have spoken of the call to priesthood as a kind of "secret voice" whispered by God in the depths of an individual soul.[6] Neoscholastic theologians became increasingly preoccupied with vocation as a kind of supernatural grace hidden within. They debated the duties and obligations of such a call, parsed out its intersection with human freedom, and charted the various marks or signs that would indicate whether a young man truly "had" a vocation. In general, such an approach promoted a certain passivity in the church's vocational efforts. Those responsible for clergy formation were required to sit back and wait for a candidate to approach them and announce that he had heard God's call in his heart. Some went so far as to argue that, if it could be shown that this individual did indeed possess an inner call, his bishop would have no choice but to ordain him.

The problem with this conception of an inner call was not the notion that God speaks to the heart. The truth of God's presence within us is a cornerstone of Christian spirituality and the starting point for any authentic prayer. The problem, rather, was that this genuine spiritual insight was framed within a deficient theology of grace that reified God's call and reduced it to a kind of extrinsic force nudging some souls but not others. The neoscholastic separation of nature and grace made it impossible for theologians at the time to talk about the deep intimacy of God's call without presupposing a dualism that ultimately kept this call at a distance. Thus vocation became something *in* an individual that was separate *from* that individual—a supernatural addition to one's natural constitution, a kind of communiqué that could ask of a person anything. Such a notion too quickly separated God's call from the particular human being to whom it was addressed. It overlooked the distinctive constellation of gifts and abilities, experiences and associations, relationships and contexts that make every individual person a unique child of God.

Over the course of the twentieth century, Catholic theologians and magisterial statements largely abandoned the nature-grace dualism that had marred so much of post-Reformation Catholic theology. Today grace is seen not as some "thing" given to a few but as God's own life offered to all. Grace is nothing less than God's loving presence stretching out across the whole world and reaching deep into every human heart. This insight (which is largely a recovery of biblical themes and earlier theologies) has touched virtually every area of contemporary Catholic theology. But its implications for vocation have yet to be thought out.

This essay is a modest attempt to begin some of this thinking. The movement of God in the heart is still very important, for attention to the inner life remains an essential dimension of vocational discernment. But a broader and more generous theology of grace recognizes that discernment is a holistic, embodied, and relational process (something that the great spiritual masters of the modern period—from Ignatius of Loyola to Thomas Merton—recognized, despite the poverty of the theology they had to draw on). It is something that we do *with others* because God calls us *through others*. The soul is not so separate from the self or its surroundings. And an incarnational and sacramental sensibility suggests that God's call is never unmediated. Any experience of call, no matter how personal or powerful in the life of an individual, always comes to a person through another person—parents and mentors, pastors and teachers, prophets and friends. Indeed, we only know of the Christ because those first few followers of Jesus described their experiences to others, wrote them down, and passed them on.

Here we begin to enter into the realm of the ecclesial. For believers, our relationships to one another relate us to Jesus. Through baptism we enter into the body of Christ and join the people of God. Christ's call comes to us not only through our lives lived out in a grace-soaked world but also in a special and explicit way through the church. Drawing on the ecclesiological vision of the Second Vatican Council, Pope John Paul II offered us this lasting insight:

> Each Christian vocation comes from God and is God's gift. However, it is never bestowed outside of or independently of the Church. Instead it always comes about in the Church and through the Church because, as the Second Vatican Council reminds us, "God has willed to make men holy and save them, not as individuals without any bond or link between them, but rather to make them into a people who might acknowledge him and serve him in holiness." (I Will Give You Shepherds/*Pastores Dabo Vobis* [1992] 35)

This ecclesial vision of vocation is a far cry from the default individualism of contemporary society and the skewed introspection of past accounts of vocation. It invites us to reflect on the role of relationships in responding to God—an ecclesial theological foundation for the call to discipleship and the call to ministry.

The Call to Discipleship

We cannot speak about ministry—never mind lay ecclesial ministry—until we speak about what it serves: discipleship for the sake of Christ's mission. In doing so, I link together two notions as so intimately interrelated that they are virtually identified: the call to discipleship and the call to holiness. A certain gap may exist in our minds between these two notions, largely, I believe, because many of us tend to associate "holiness" with a particular kind of piety, usually an "otherworldly" piety focused on the individual believer. But holiness cannot be reduced to piety—otherworldly or not—because holiness is nothing less than what Vatican II called "the fullness of Christian life" and "the perfection of charity" (*Lumen Gentium* 40). To be holy is to grow in love (*caritas*) for God and for others. This is the heart of holiness and, at the same time, the goal of discipleship.

The call to be a disciple (literally, a "learner," a "listener") of Christ is a call to follow him; it is a call to be in relationship with Jesus. As the gospels repeat in dozens of different ways, to be drawn into relationship with Christ is to be drawn into relationship both with God and with other people. Love is the gospel name for this relationship. Thus we begin to see how discipleship and holiness are linked by the long arc of love: the call to discipleship *is* the call to relationship with Christ *is* the call to love God and neighbor *is* the call to holiness.

Vatican II's Constitution on the Church, *Lumen Gentium*, dedicated its fifth chapter to "The Universal Call to Holiness," a chapter that un-ambiguously affirms, "It is therefore quite clear that all Christians in whatever state or walk in life are called to the fullness of Christian life and to the perfection of charity, and this holiness is conducive to a more human way of living even in society here on earth" (LG 40). This claim would not be so remarkable were it not for the impression among Catholics, shaped by centuries of spiritual writing and ecclesiastical statements, that a life dedicated to the public embrace of the evangelical counsels was the superior path—even the exclusive path—to holiness. The council did not deny the value of the vows of poverty, chastity, and obedience, nor did it dismiss the role of religious life in the church; but it did remove any doubt that genuine holiness could be achieved in any walk or way of life. *All* are called to be holy.

One of the obstacles to affirming a broader call to holiness lay in the negative associations "the world" carried in many traditional Catholic spiritualities. Too often, the monastic impulse was distorted by translat-ing the "flight" from the world into an escape from the realm of sin. According to such a view, the monk or the virgin fled the sullying dangers of money, sex, and power (commerce, family life, and politics—another way of naming life "in the world") and so became free to dedicate himself or herself to the "higher things" of the spiritual life. Much of this attitude changed over the course of the twentieth century, as shifting conceptions of the nature-grace relationship and a renewed appreciation for lay activity seeped into the Catholic consciousness. In the "theologies of the laity" that developed on the eve of Vatican II, the layperson's place in the world was no longer seen as an obstacle to the exercise of charity but rather as the arena within which most of the baptized are called to respond to Christ and neighbor in love.[7]

What is interesting, however, is that *Lumen Gentium*'s chapter on the "universal call to holiness" emerged not out of this theology of the laity but out of conversations surrounding religious life. This is not to say that the relationship between a broader holiness and a more positive theology of lay secular involvement did not have its influence. Even before the council, Pope John XXIII made this link: "Let no one imagine that he must necessarily withdraw from the activities of temporal life in order to strive for Christian perfection, or that it is impossible to engage in such activities without jeopardizing one's human and Christian dignity" (*Mater et Magistra* 255).[8] Still, *Lumen Gentium* does not base the universal vocation to holiness on any convictions about the secular world. Instead, it grounds the universal call in a distinctly ecclesiological claim: "The church, whose mystery is set forth by this sacred synod, is held, as a matter of faith, to be unfailingly holy" (LG 39). The holiness of the church itself grounds the call to holiness of its members.

Chapter 5 originated as a totally different chapter on the "States for the Acquisition of Evangelical Perfection" that was part of a draft text *De Ecclesia* prepared in advance of the Second Vatican Council. When the draft *De Ecclesia* was rejected at the first session of the council, this chapter too was rejected. Members of the theological commission responsible for revisions argued that its exclusive focus on the superiority of consecrated life obscured the basic truth that all Christians are called to be holy.[9] At the insistence of Cardinal Leo Josef Suenens of Belgium, a new text was prepared by the theologian Gustave Thils on "The Call to Holiness in the Church."[10] This new text took its point of departure from the universal call to holiness, and sought to locate religious life within this broader context of general Christian charity.

When this revised chapter was brought up for debate at the second session of the council, it was still found lacking. While many bishops appreciated the broader and more inclusive treatment of Christian holiness, many felt that it still approached the issue in a way that was too individualistic. Writing shortly after the council, Friedrich Wulf summed up a repeated complaint: "the new text dealt solely with the sanctity and perfection of the individual, not with that of the Church as such, which is *essentially* holy, holy in the deepest source of her being, which is Christ."[11] As a result of these critiques, the chapter was further revised, precisely to bring out this ecclesial dimension. Thus the final text of *Lumen Gentium's* chapter 5 begins not with particular states of life or individual believers but with the church itself, which, the council claims, as a matter of faith, is "unfailingly holy." The universal call to holiness then flows out of this ecclesiological conviction. Because Christ loved the church, because he gave himself up for it, because he endowed it with the gift of the Holy Spirit, the church is holy. And because the church is holy, all those who belong to it, "whether they belong to the hierarchy or are cared for by it," are called to holiness. It is only within this ecclesiologically conditioned conception of holiness that the call to perfection of various groups and individuals—including married couples and parents, widows and widowers, single people, those who are poor or who suffer—is spelled out. The foundational vocation of the Christian, the call to holiness and discipleship, is not a solitary enterprise. According to the council, it always occurs in the context of community.

The Call to Ministry

Vatican II's treatment of the universal call to holiness points us to the common vocation that all disciples share. But vocation is also specific. It refers to the particularity of our diverse callings. Under the broad umbrella of the universal call to holiness, the language of vocation is used in several different ways. Drawing on the work of Marie Theresa Coombs and Francis Kelly Nemeck, Kathleen Cahalan helps to bring some clarity to the conversation by distinguishing three ways in which we speak of specific callings: vocation can refer to (1) *who* God calls us to be, (2) *how* God calls us to live, and (3) *what* God calls us to do.[12] The first speaks to our *self-identity*, reminding us that we are not generic beings but that each of us lives out the universal call to holiness in a unique way, thanks to our individual gifts, personalities, and experiences. The second speaks to our *state of life*, which remains the default mode for many Catholics in talking about vocation. The third speaks to our *ministry*, the particular way each of us is called to serve God and others, and so contribute to the mission of Christ and his church.

This typology helps us to recognize that, within the life of any individual, particular vocations are multiple and overlapping. What I feel called to do is likely rooted in my individual gifts and conditioned by my state of life, and I may be called to do many different things over the course of my life. In this section we will focus on the third way of speaking about vocation: what God calls me to do to contribute to the mission of the church—the vocation to ministry. The point I want to make is that, like the call to discipleship, the call to ministry is an ecclesial call—it comes to the individual in and through the church.

Vatican II used the word "apostolate" to refer to this broader contribution to the church's mission. Implied in the universal call to holiness and discipleship is a further call, the call to serve, celebrate, and spread the gospel—the call to the apostolate. Some authors today want to limit the word *apostolate* to a distinctively *lay* activity of Christian witness "in the world"—separate from the *ministry* that belongs to the ordained "in the church." But such a restrictive understanding of apostolate was foreign to the council. In the years leading up to Vatican II, Catholics used the word *apostolate* in a broad and undifferentiated way to refer to any activity that advanced the mission of the church. It was a word that—unlike "priesthood" or "clergy"—could be comfortably applied to both the laity and the ordained. The council followed this common usage, stating, at the beginning of the Decree on the Apostolate of Lay People: "Every activity of the mystical body, with this in view, goes by the name of apostolate, which the church exercises through all its members, though in various ways. In fact, the christian vocation is, of its nature, a vocation to the apostolate as well" (*Apostolicam Actuositatem* 2).

The most significant shift at Vatican II with regard to the apostolate was not the idea that the laity could join in it. This had been repeatedly affirmed over the first half of the twentieth century. Instead, the most significant shift was the council's recognition that the apostolate of the laity comes not from the hierarchy but from Christ himself. In 1927, Pope Pius XI had affirmed the lay apostolate in the form of "Catholic Action," giving this movement its classic definition as "the participation of the laity in the apostolate of the Church's hierarchy."[13] Compare this to Vatican II's Decree on the Apostolate of Lay People:

> Lay people's right and duty to be apostles derives from their union
> with Christ their head. Inserted as they are in the mystical body of

Christ by baptism and strengthened by the power of the holy Spirit
in confirmation, it is by the Lord himself that they are assigned to the
apostolate. (*Apostolicam Actuositatem* 3)

According to Vatican II, participation in the mission of the church does
not belong to the hierarchy, which is then beneficently parceled out to
the laity. It belongs to all members of the body of Christ by virtue of a
common baptism.[14]

If the source of our participation in the mission of the church lies in
baptism, then it is important to recognize that baptism is not a personal
endowment or private possession. It is an initiation into a community.
Prior to Vatican II, a number of theologians interested in promoting
greater lay involvement in the life and liturgy of the church turned to
baptism. In particular, they turned to Thomas Aquinas's notion of the
"character" imparted at baptism. Typically, seminary textbooks at the
time described this character as a kind of invisible imprint on the soul, a
"seal" that helped to explain why the three sacraments of baptism, confirmation, and ordination were never repeated. Aquinas, however, had
evoked a richer theological vision by describing this sacramental seal as
a participation in the priesthood of Christ.[15] That insight provided a rich
resource for proponents of liturgical reform. They argued that, by virtue
of the character imprinted at baptism (and confirmation), the laity share
in Christ's priesthood and so actively offer the sacrifice of the Mass along
with the ordained priest—an insight confirmed by Pope Pius XII's 1947
encyclical *Mediator Dei*. The argument was soon extended beyond the
liturgy to provide a theological rationale for the broader lay apostolate.[16]

The downside of this development, however, was that by describing character as an invisible mark on the soul, baptism continued to be
presented rather individualistically. Yet developments toward a more
ecclesial consciousness were already underway. And by mid-century,
Catholic theologians had begun to break out of this interiorized and
isolated treatment of the sacramental "character." The work of Edward
Schillebeeckx, Karl Rahner, and others pursued character not as an individualistic and invisible imprint on the soul but as a real relation with
the church, one diversely determined by baptism, confirmation, and
orders. Karl Rahner wrote,

The teaching of St. Thomas on baptismal character does not necessarily
contradict this view. It is sufficient to ask why through the baptismal
character a human being shares in the priesthood of Christ and how

this participation can be distinguished from the one that derives from grace. The answer must surely be that it belongs to a man in as much as he is a member of the Church and remains in relation to the Church.[17]

According to this developing consensus, participation in the church's mission does not come by way of personal entitlement. Rather it comes via one's presence and participation within the community. It was the discussion of "character" that opened up space, within the constraints of neoscholasticism, to make this shift from sacramental theology to ecclesiology. Through baptism and confirmation one becomes a member of the body of Christ, and as a member one is called to contribute to its life: one enters into a community with a mission and therefore takes up this mission. Throughout the documents of Vatican II, whenever baptism is mentioned, what comes to the fore is initiation into community. Baptism is less about the mark on an individual than about the relationship of the baptized to Christ, their entrance into the royal priesthood described in 1 Peter, and their incorporation into the church, the body of Christ and people of God.[18] The baptismal call to serve the mission of Christ comes *through* the community.

While Vatican II used the language of apostolate to describe broad participation in the mission of the church, in the years after the council, this language all but disappeared. In its place came "lay ministry." This terminological shift followed an appropriation by Catholics of ministry language then current among Protestant theologians. It had some papal support, particularly in Paul VI's letter *Ministeria Quaedam* (1972), which established the lay "ministries" of lector and acolyte. But what fueled the rapid and wide embrace of ministry language was a changing reality: lay Catholics began to take up activities in liturgy and in education that had until then been reserved to priests or nuns. If this history blurred the neat linguistic distinction that had held between clergy and laity, it was because more and more Catholics were active in the church and its communities. Those who saw in this movement the work of the Spirit and who sought to encourage such activity pointed to the broader ecclesiological themes of the council: the church as the whole people of God, baptism as an initiation into the community and its mission, and an expectation of active participation as the norm. A broad and inclusive appeal to "ministry" captured these themes in a forceful and positive way.

In a perceptive early essay, John Coleman pointed out that by the end of the 1970s the term "ministry" had become a pervasive catchphrase among Catholic religious professionals. He underlined the fact that the term was already so taken for granted that it was rarely defined. And he noted that it is precisely those things that are taken for granted that constitute the existing theological culture. "What we do not need to define itself defines our world and charts our view of reality."[19] Coleman called the term ministry a "motivational symbol" for active laity. Its use reflected a shifting view of life in the church and new expectations on the part of many American Catholics.

Thus *ministry* has become the way in which Catholics today talk about what Vatican II meant by *apostolate*. Avery Dulles points out that, even in official Catholic documents, "there has been a growing tendency to apply the term *ministry* to lay activities where the council would probably have used *apostolate*."[20] "Ministry" is simply how Catholics today name a broad participation in the mission of the church. This semantic shift is not uncontested, as some voices in the church want to limit the terms "ministry" and "minister" to the ordained.[21] While I take such a restrictive use of the terms as unfounded, I do recognize that the call to ministry is a specification (and thus a certain "narrowing") of the broader call to discipleship. To speak of Christian ministry is not to speak of every good thing that disciples do; rather, it is to speak of those activities that build up the body of Christ and serve its mission in the world by witnessing, celebrating, and advancing the reign of God. Moreover, within this definition, distinctions among ministries can still be made.

In what follows, we explore some of these distinctions in order to bring to light what is distinctive about the vocation to lay ecclesial ministry. We have seen how the call to discipleship and ministry comes *in* and *through* the church community. Now we turn to consider those who are called to serve *on behalf of* this church.

The Call to Lay Ecclesial Ministry

The bulk of this essay has been devoted to demonstrating the ecclesial context of vocation. According to the Second Vatican Council, we are called to holiness in the context of church communion; and we are called to mission and ministry through our participation in this communion. Baptism—as a fundamentally relational sacrament that initiates believers into the body of Christ—stands as the touchstone and criterion for any theology of vocation. We simply cannot understand the call to lay ecclesial ministry apart from this foundation.

Like all Christians, lay ecclesial ministers are called to lives of holy discipleship and to participation in the mission of the church. They too are baptized and thus called into a relationship with God that is oriented outward to relationship with others. However, the call to lay ecclesial ministry brings with it a further dimension, the call to minister on behalf of the church in a public and professional way. By virtue of their preparation, leadership, close collaboration with the ordained, and authorization, lay ecclesial ministers are called into a new set of relationships, a new position within the ecclesial community: they minister in the name of the church.

Another way to say this is to recognize that *every* contribution to the mission of the church—every ministry—is ecclesial, in the sense that it is rooted in baptism and flows through the church community. But not every ministry is ecclesial in the sense of serving formally and publicly in the name of the church. Lay ecclesial ministry is ecclesial in both senses. It is rooted in baptism, in the call to holiness and mission incumbent on every believer. *And* it involves a formal and public service on behalf of the church. *Co-Workers in the Vineyard of the Lord* evokes this twofold meaning when it explains that this ministry "is *ecclesial* because it has a place within the community of the Church, whose communion and mission it serves, and because it is submitted to the discernment, authorization, and supervision of the hierarchy" (11).

The *ecclesial* in lay ecclesial ministry, then, evokes a new set of relationships. Richard Gaillardetz describes lay ecclesial ministers as an example of an "ordered ministry" whose call to serve publicly in the name of the church entails an "ecclesial re-positioning."

> Clearly there are certain ministries in the Church which, because of their public nature bring about a certain "ecclesial re-positioning" or re-configuration. In other words, the person who takes on such a ministry finds themselves in a new relationship within the Church and the assumption is that they will be empowered by the Spirit in a manner commensurate with their new ministerial relationship. These ministers are public persons who in some sense are both called by the community and accountable to the community.[22]

"Ecclesial re-positioning" applies clearly to the ordained ministries of bishop, presbyter, and deacon who, through ordination, enter into a demonstratively new relationship within the ministerial structures of the church. But Gaillardetz's point is that an analogous repositioning occurs for the lay ecclesial minister. "This 'lay' minister, is called by the community, based on a recognised charism, to take a new public role in the Church. She is called to enter into a new ministerial relationship within the community. This new ministerial relationship may or may not be ritualised, but the repositioning is clear and obvious to those active in her community."[23] He goes on to argue that this new position becomes evident, for example, in the community's tendency to hold lay ecclesial ministers to a higher moral standard. "We recognise the possibility that their moral failings, because of their public character, might be a cause of scandal."[24] By framing "ecclesial" in such explicitly relational terms, we see more clearly how the "vocation" of the lay ecclesial minister is not some special state of life or particular function. Rather, this calling takes shape as a distinctive set of *relationships* within the ministerial life of the church.[25]

The public nature of the ministry is an important component of this "ecclesial re-positioning," but I would argue that the "place" of the lay ecclesial minister is also determined by (1) the minister's commitment to serve and (2) the church's recognition of her or his ministry.[26] In other words, the vocation of the lay ecclesial minister depends on a *call* that is both experienced by the *minister* and extended by the *community*. On the side of the minister, this call is first and foremost a call to serve, thus it primarily concerns Cahalan's third question: *What* does God call me to do? Without a doubt, the call to serve—to help others, to teach the faith, to facilitate worship, to walk with young people, to lead other ministers—is the core of the call to lay ecclesial ministry. Yet this call is not separate from the questions, *How* does God call me to live, and *who* does God call me to be? For the minister, *what* is done in service to the reign of God is shaped by and, in turn, shapes her way of living in the world, her lifestyle and lifelong commitments—just as the ministry draws on each individual minister's unique constellation of charisms and, in turn, draws that minister into the special relationship with Christ that constitutes his personal holiness. Identity, lifestyle, and service are wrapped up in the call to lay ecclesial ministry.

On the side of the community, the question of call is a little more complex. To say that lay ecclesial ministers serve in the name of the church demands some clarity on what we mean by "church." Historically, a certain dichotomy has entered into Western Christianity on this question. Since the earliest days of the Reformation, Catholics have tended to associate "church" with the *clergy*. Protestants have tended to associate "church" with the *congregation*. The implications for an "ecclesial call" follow from these differing ecclesiologies. Luther reacted vigorously to what he saw as the episcopal and papal absolutism of the Roman Church. He argued that, on the question of appointing ministers, it is the local congregation of Christians that is paramount: "Therefore, when a bishop consecrates it is nothing else than that in the place and stead of the whole community, all of whom have like power, he takes a person and charges him to exercise this power on behalf of the others."[27] Luther went on to tell the story of ten brothers who appoint one of their number to lead in the interest of all; or of a group of sincere laymen who are taken hostage and dropped in a desert somewhere. According to Luther, should this group elect one of its members to lead the prayer, this man "would be as truly a priest as though he had been ordained by all the bishops and popes in the world."[28]

Luther's position modulated over time, and the various Protestant churches emerging out of the Reformation took a variety of approaches to appointing and ordaining ministers— often involving some combination of episcopal oversight and local involvement of congregations. But Rome reacted strongly to Luther's challenge. The Council of Trent stated in no uncertain terms:

> The holy council further teaches that in the ordination of bishops, priests and other ministers neither the consent nor calling nor authority of the people or of any secular power or functionary is so required that without it the ordination would be invalid. On the contrary, it declares that those who are raised to the exercise of these ministries when called and appointed only by a secular power and functionary, and those who have the temerity to assume such office themselves, are to be regarded one and all, not as ministers of the church, but as thieves and robbers who have not entered by the sheepgate.[29]

Over the course of the modern period, *any* participation of the local community in the selection of its ordained ministers gradually disappeared within Catholicism. And in its official structures today, the Catholic Church still struggles to find ways to incorporate the whole people of God in calling forth ministers to serve.

This is unfortunate for at least two reasons. First, our earliest and best theology affirms a more holistic and comprehensive vision of vocational discernment rooted in a notion of the church as an ordered communion. The great Dominican ecclesiologist Yves Congar often pointed out that the modern divide between a Roman Catholic preoccupation with hierarchical institutions, on the one hand, and a Protestant fascination with a structure-less society of equals, on the other, would have seemed strange to the early church. Christ did not appoint a hierarchy that then created the church. Nor did he inspire a community that later elected its leaders.

In his gathering of disciples and choice of the Twelve, we see the birth of a church that from the beginning existed as an ordered communion, a structured community. As the church evolved over the course of the first millennium, the call to ministry came from *both* congregation *and* clergy. In his exhaustive ecumenical study of ordination rites from the third century to the present, James Puglisi argues, "In the early Church, the *vocatio* of the minister was mediated by the other Christians and ministers, according to the needs of the service of the Gospel, in a particular time and a specific place; in later times this *vocatio* no longer is seen as the business of the people as bearers of the Spirit, but rather a very personal reality."[30] The loss was not the institutionalization that Luther deplored; rather, the loss was an individualization and an interiorization of the whole process of vocation. Discernment became less and less something that the whole community did together; instead, it was something that the individual worked out alone with God. Puglisi continues, "All these changes tended towards the separation of the subject and the object, towards the progressive autonomy of the person of the minister in relationship to his ministry rooted in its ecclesial context, a disastrous direction which will result in the disarticulation of the Church as a concrete structure of communion."[31]

Puglisi is not suggesting that we replace sacramental ordination with congregational elections. Rather, the call of the community—what the early rites call *electio* or *vocatio*—reminds us that the process of calling forth ministers "includes a complex of actions and roles which inaugurate new, personal, and enduring relationships between the new minister, his Christian brethren, and God."[32] This point brings us to a second reason to encourage a more holistic and comprehensive process for calling forth ministers to serve: it works. If we turn from the experience of ordained ministry in the first millennium to the experience of lay ecclesial ministers today, what strikes us immediately is the breadth of the call. The rise of lay ecclesial ministry is one of the great success stories of the postconciliar period. This ministerial transformation and expansion was not the coincidence of a thousand points of light. Nor was it the result of some Vatican directive or a national pastoral plan. Instead it was—as the US bishops have said—the work of the Spirit, calling through the voices of many members. The whole church, clergy and community, played a role in calling forth these ministers. We hear this call in the words of the Second Vatican Council affirming the baptismal dignity of the people of God; we hear it in colleges and schools developing programs for lay ministry formation; we hear it in pastors and other leaders inviting and encouraging new roles on the parish staff; we hear it in small Christian communities and *Cursillo* groups lifting up leaders; we hear it in parishioners welcoming lay ecclesial ministers into their midst. If we were to return to the beginning of this essay and continue the conversation with those lay ecclesial ministers we met there, what we would hear, no doubt, are the many ways in which their personal call to ministry came to them *through others*: through the invitation of a pastor or a fellow parishioner, through the response of the children in the First Communion class or of the teens in the youth group, through the example of another lay ecclesial minister, through the needs of the community that nobody else was addressing. The call to lay ecclesial ministry is a call through and into relationships. It is a dynamic and communal process. It is an ecclesial vocation.

Conclusion: Ecclesial Discernment

What distinguishes the vocation to lay ecclesial ministry from the broader call to discipleship and the broader call to ministry is the call to serve publicly in the name of the church. Obviously, lay ecclesial ministers are not the only ones who minister in the name of the church, but they are the ones who so minister as *laypersons* in collaboration with the ordained, in positions of ministerial leadership, with the preparation and authorization appropriate to such a role (*Co-Workers*, 10). What does it mean to be called to serve in the name of the church? As the church and its leaders continue to promote and receive this vocation, our attention will increasingly be drawn in the direction of discernment.

Discernment cannot be reduced to an individual enterprise. If we are to take the ecclesial nature of vocation seriously, then we have to recognize that discernment is an ecclesial affair (see *Co-Workers*, 27–32). It is something that involves the whole church in calling forth ministers to serve. This recognition will require, first of all, continued reflection on the role of the bishop in calling lay ecclesial ministers. All ministry (understood broadly as participation in the mission of the church) finds its ultimate source in Christ, its ultimate empowerment in baptism. But those who minister "in the name of the church" take on a new relationship to the community, signified and further empowered by some form of authorization. At present, in most dioceses, the bishop is involved in authorization only indirectly: usually the pastor hires a lay ecclesial minister and, in doing so, authorizes this minister. The connection is further removed for those lay ecclesial ministers who serve outside of parishes in hospitals or prisons, schools or college campuses. If the bishop is to get more involved, it will be important to locate authorization within the broader ecclesial call—remembering that authorization does not *create* the call to ministry whole cloth, nor does it simply *confirm* a call already arrived from elsewhere. Instead, authorization is one element within a more organic and involved process of cultivating, recognizing, challenging, and celebrating the call to serve the reign of God. Thus any formal authorization is a designation, a *naming* of an ecclesial relationship that both already exists and, at the same time, is enhanced in the naming. But such a designation only makes sense within a broader communal context in which the whole church—the whole people of God—are involved in calling forth ministers to serve.

This brings us to the final, and perhaps most important, point. Ecclesial discernment of the call to lay ecclesial ministry cannot be reduced to two players: the individual minister and the bishop. Rather, it involves a number of agents through whom the Spirit of Christ works in the life of the local church: ministers and mentors, pastors and parishioners, formation programs, family ministries, professional ministry associations, universities, lay movements, religious networks, and diocesan offices. In a number of places, formal processes have been implemented and informal practices have appeared that help to foster broader ecclesial discernment. Dioceses and parishes partner to identify and sponsor individual ministers; Catholic colleges coordinate classes for ministry formation programs; campus ministers write letters of recommendation; pastors encourage volunteers to enter certificate programs; diocesan convocations draw lay ministers and ordained ministers into conversation. Much is being done, and lay ecclesial ministry would not exist were it not for the Spirit calling forth individuals in this broad and diffuse way. But much, much more needs to be done to expand the call to ministry—particularly in this time of ecclesial contraction—to strengthen the vocation of those laywomen and laymen who serve in the name of the church.

Notes

1. David DeLambo, *Lay Parish Ministers: A Study of Emerging Leadership* (New York: National Pastoral Life Center, 2005), 71.

2. Ibid., 72.

3. Lay Ecclesial Ministry: The State of the Questions, 27.

4. USCCB, *Co-Workers in the Vineyard of the Lord: A Resource for Guiding the Development of Lay Ecclesial Ministry* (Washington, DC: USCCB Publishing, 2005), 67.

5. The present essay draws on and develops my earlier work: *Ministries: A Relational Approach* (New York: Crossroad, 2003); "Wondering About Wineskins: Rethinking Vocation in Light of Lay Ecclesial Ministry," *Listening: Journal of Religion and Culture* 40 (2005): 7–22; "When the Church Calls," *America* 195 (October 9, 2006): 10–14; "The Vocation to Lay Ecclesial Ministry," *Origins* 37 (August 30, 2007): 177–82; "Theology of Lay Ecclesial Ministry: Future Trajectories," in *Lay Ecclesial Ministry: Pathways Toward the Future*, ed. Zeni Fox (Lanham, MD: Rowman & Littlefield, 2010), 67–83; and *Awakening Vocation: A Theology of Christian Call* (Collegeville, MN: Liturgical Press, 2010).

6. The interiorization of vocation is treated at length in *Awakening Vocation*, 47–90.

7. An important early study is Yves Congar, *Lay People in the Church*, trans. Donald Attwater (Westminster, MD: Newman Press, 1965).

8. Cited in Friedrich Wulf, "Introductory Remarks on Chapters V and VI," in *Commentary on the Documents of Vatican II*, vol. 1, ed. Herbert Vorgrimler (New York: Herder and Herder, 1967), 258.

9. Wulf, "Introductory Remarks," 256.

10. Jan Grootaers, "The Drama Continues Between the Acts: The 'Second Preparation' and Its Opponents," in *History of Vatican II*, vol. 2, ed. Giuseppe Alberigo and Joseph A. Komonchak (Maryknoll, NY: Orbis, 1997), 408–10. See Gustave Thils, "The Universal Call to Holiness in the Church," *Communio* 17 (1990): 494–503.

11. Wulf, "Introductory Remarks," 259–60. On the debate, see also Alberto Melloni, "The Beginning of the Second Period: The Great Debate on the Church," in *History of Vatican II*, vol. 3, ed. Giuseppe Alberigo and Joseph A. Komonchak (Maryknoll, NY: Orbis, 2000), 91–93.

12. Kathleen A. Cahalan, *Introducing the Practice of Ministry* (Collegeville, MN: Liturgical Press, 2010), 28. See Marie Theresa Coombs and Francis Kelly Nemeck, *Discerning Vocations to Marriage, Celibacy and Singlehood* (Collegeville, MN: Liturgical Press, 1994), 2–5.

13. Pius XI, "Discourse to Italian Catholic Young Women," *L'Osservatore Romano* (March 21, 1927): 14. For an extended treatment of Catholic Action, see Congar, *Lay People in the Church*, 362–99.

14. We will have to address the role of ordained leaders in coordinating this mission. The paragraph from *Apostolicam Actuositatem* cited above concludes, "It is for the pastors to pass judgment on the authenticity and good use of these gifts, not certainly with a view to quenching the Spirit but to testing everything and keeping what is good (see 1 Th 5:12, 19, 21)."

15. Thus for Aquinas, it was not just ordination that draws one into Christ's priesthood; in an analogous way, baptism and confirmation also draw believers into this priesthood. And he went on to describe character as a spiritual power

of the soul oriented to action—specifically action in divine worship. This action consists either in receiving divine things (a power granted in baptism and confirmation) or in giving divine things (the power granted in ordination). For a fuller treatment, see *Ministries: A Relational Approach*, 162–75.

16. An interesting early study of this development is the doctoral dissertation of Fr. Theodore M. Hesburgh, later president of the University of Notre Dame, titled "The Relation of the Sacramental Characters of Baptism and Confirmation to the Lay Apostolate" and reprinted as *Theology of Catholic Action* (Notre Dame, IN: Ave Maria Press, 1946).

17. Karl Rahner, *The Church and the Sacraments*, trans. W. J. O'Hara (London: Burns & Oates, 1974), 90. See also Edward Schillebeeckx, *Christ the Sacrament of Encounter with God*, trans. Paul Barrett et al. (New York: Sheed & Ward, 1963), 154–79.

18. A sampling of baptismal references underscoring the ecclesial include *Sacrosanctum Concilium* 6, 14; *Lumen Gentium* 7, 9, 10, 11, 14, 15, 21, 31, 32; *Gaudium et Spes* 22; *Ad Gentes* 7, 14, 15; *Unitatis Redintegratio* 2, 3, 22; *Apostolicam Actuositatem* 3; *Presbyterorum Ordinis* 5.

19. John Coleman, "The Future of Ministry," *America* (March 28, 1981): 243–49, at 243.

20. Avery Dulles, "Can Laity Properly Be Called 'Ministers'?" *Origins* 35 (April 20, 2006): 725–31, at 728.

21. This argument often follows in part on an overly restrictive reading of the 1997 Vatican instruction on lay collaboration. See Congregation for the Clergy et al., On Certain Questions Regarding the Collaboration of the Non-Ordained Faithful in the Sacred Ministry of Priests, *Origins* 27 (November 27, 1997): 397–409.

22. Richard R. Gaillardetz, "Shifting Meanings in the Lay-Clergy Distinction," *Irish Theological Quarterly* 64 (1999): 115–39, at 135. Gaillardetz describes "ordered ministry" as a reality broader than the ministry of the ordained (though inclusive of it) but narrower than Christian discipleship. See id., "The Ecclesiological Foundations of Ministry within an Ordered Communion," in *Ordering the Baptismal Priesthood: Theologies of Lay and Ordained Ministry*, ed. Susan K. Wood (Collegeville, MN: Liturgical Press, 2003), 26–51.

23. Gaillardetz, "Shifting Meanings," 135.

24. Ibid.

25. *Co-Workers in the Vineyard of the Lord* points toward just such a relational approach in the way it grounds lay ecclesial ministry in the communion of the triune God and develops its treatment of the relationships between lay ecclesial ministers and bishops, priests, deacons, and the lay faithful.

26. See *Ministries: A Relational Approach*, 128–50.

27. Martin Luther, "To the Christian Nobility of the German Nation (1520)," in *Luther's Works*, vol. 44 (Philadelphia: Fortress Press, 1966), 128.

28. Ibid.

29. Council of Trent, 23rd Session (July 15, 1563), in *Decrees of the Ecumenical Councils*, vol. 2, ed. Norman P. Tanner (London/Washington: Sheed and Ward/ Georgetown University Press, 1990), 743.

30. James F. Puglisi, *The Process of Admission to Ordained Ministry*, vol. 1, trans. Michael S. Driscoll and Mary Misrahi (Collegeville, MN: Liturgical Press, 1996), 203. Evidence of this early emphasis on the needs and the good of the community is found in those stories of individuals ordained even against their will. See Yves Congar, "Ordination *invitus, coactus* de l'église antique au canon 214," *Revue des Sciences Philosophiques et Théologiques* 50 (1966): 169–97.

31. Puglisi, *Process of Admission*, 1:206–7.

32. Ibid., 1:205.

Chapter 4

The Biblical Basis for Understanding Lay Ecclesial Ministry
A Consideration of Spiritual Gifts and the Body of Christ (1 Corinthians 12–14)

Charles A. Bobertz

Sacred theology relies on the written word of God, taken together with sacred tradition, as its permanent foundation. By this word it is powerfully strengthened and constantly rejuvenated, as it searches out, under the light of faith, all the truth stored up in the mystery of Christ.
—Dei Verbum 24

Beginning with *Apostolicam Actuositatem*, the Second Vatican Council's Decree on the Apostolate of Lay People (1965), and running through both the subsequent Vatican clarification of lay ecclesial roles within the church, *Ecclesiae de Mysterio*[1] (1997) and the United States Conference of Catholic Bishops' 2005 statement on lay ecclesial ministry, *Co-Workers in the Vineyard of the Lord*,[2] there has been strikingly little attention paid to the biblical basis for a theological understanding either of the general lay apostolate or the more specific role that has now come to be called lay ecclesial ministry. When attention is given to the biblical basis for this aspect of the church's life and practice, it is most often Paul's discussion of spiritual gifts in the ministry, 1 Corinthians 12:1-12, that is cited.

Interpretation of these verses centers on Paul's emphasis on the necessity of all the parts of the body working together for the good of the whole. In addition these verses are put forward as a primary biblical basis for a hierarchically ordered Catholic ministry within which lay ecclesial ministry must function.[3] One might expect, therefore, that a fuller exploration of the literary context and theology of this section of Paul's famous letter would serve to further inform and ground any discussion of the role and function of all Catholic ministry, but especially the relatively recent emergence of lay ecclesial ministry. Such is the objective of the present study.

Paul's metaphorical understanding of the Corinthian community in 1 Corinthians 12:1-12 is justly well known:

> Now concerning spiritual matters, brothers, I do not wish you to be ignorant. You know how, when you were pagans, you were constantly attracted to dumb idols and led astray. Therefore I would have you know that no one speaking by the spirit of God says, "Jesus is anathema." And no one is able to declare Jesus as Lord except by the Holy Spirit. There are varieties of gifts but the same Spirit; there are varieties of service but the same Lord; there are varieties of manifestations but the same God who manifests all of them in all people. To each person is given the manifestation of the Spirit for mutual care. For to one is given through the Spirit the word of wisdom; yet to another the word of knowledge according to the same Spirit; to another faith by the same Spirit; to another gifts of healing by the one Spirit; to another works of power; to another prophecy; to another discernment of spirits; to another a type of tongues; to another interpretation of tongues. Yet one and the same Spirit provides all of these things, distributing them to each individual as he wishes. For as a body is one and has many parts, all the parts of the body, being many, are one body, so also Christ.[4]

The use of this text in *Apostolicam* (1965) comes primarily in chapter 3, an exploration of the laity's call to sanctify and evangelize the temporal order. That the laity is given special gifts for this task, according to the will of the Spirit, is supported by an allusion to 1 Corinthians 12:7 and 12:11. Within this understanding the council document goes on to stress the middle section of 12:7, "*the [same] Spirit,*" namely, that the laity is given this particular gift from the one common Spirit for the particular task of sanctifying and evangelizing the temporal order.

With *Ecclesiae de Mysterio* (1997) the particular employ of 1 Corinthians 12 has changed, animating as it were a discussion of theological principles behind the *distinction* of common priesthood from ministerial priesthood. Here the focus is on the idea that a particular spiritual gift (ministerial priesthood) has been given to the church to "help the People of God to exercise faithfully and fully the *common priesthood* which it [the laity] has received" (1, my emphasis). In essence the emphasis is now on the first part of verse 12:7, "*to each person* is given the manifestation of the Spirit . . ." In this case the one Spirit has provided spiritual gifts with differing functions according to the ordered ecclesial context (ministerial or common priesthood). The spiritual gift of ministerial priesthood is given so as to order the spiritual gift of the common priesthood for the upbuilding of the entire church.[5]

Finally, *Co-Workers* (2005) examines in some detail what it terms "an ecclesiology of communion" in ministerial roles and underscores the point of "diversity in unity" in order to emphasize that all the different ministerial functions within the church serve what Paul terms mutual care or common good (*sympheron*). In other words, the emphasis in *Co-Workers* has been placed on the final section of verse 12:7, "the manifestation of the Spirit *for the common good*."

Considered together these major church documents each employ a reading of 1 Corinthians 12:7 to underscore three different emphases in Paul's admonition that serve to support three different aspects of the contemporary church's description of the potential role of the gifts of the Spirit in lay ecclesial ministry: (1) the one Spirit, (?) given as gift to function differently with respect to articulated ecclesial roles, and (3) to serve the common good. Such careful and nuanced reading of these verses in support of different aspects of the church's understanding of lay ecclesial ministry within a broader understanding of the church's ministry as a whole offers the enticement to explore more fully the historical and literary context of not only these verses but also the whole of the letter within which they occur. My goal here is to understand better the biblical basis upon which the church's ministry must be built.

At the beginning of 1 Corinthians the reader is made aware that Paul's primary concern in the letter is an increase in factionalism within the church at Corinth (1:11). Corinthian partisanship appears to be based on church members having been baptized by particular apostolic figures (Paul, Apollos, and Kephas [Peter], 1:12). In particular, certain spiritual powers (gifts), given as a result of baptism, have been attributed as a benefaction or favor from the apostle who performed the ritual, thus creating relationships between particular apostles and members of the community.[6]

What Paul confronts here, and throughout the letter, is the customary ancient social practice of forming factions within a social network of patron-client relations.[7] Patrons provided benefactions to clients and in return enjoyed the expectation of support and loyalty in the religious, social, and political affairs of the ancient city-state. In the case of the Corinthians, their apparent association of powerful spiritual gifts with baptism by particular apostles seems to have led to the creation of these sorts of factions within the church at Corinth: "I belong to Paul," or "I belong to Apollos," or "I belong to Kephas," or "I belong to Christ" (1:12).[8] Paul's task in this letter, then, is to move the Corinthians' understanding of spiritual gifts away from the notion that they are personal benefactions granted from an apostolic patron to the idea that all such experiences and abilities are granted from the one Spirit of God manifest in the community to the gathered body of Christ understood as a whole community.

Yet a more complete understanding of the source of the benefactions, spiritual gifts (*pneumatika*), would not be enough to overcome the factionalism present in the Corinthian church. Paul had also to communicate a different understanding of the Spirit itself—and here again he confronts widely held expectations of power and "natural" social ranking in the ancient context. For Paul the ritual of baptism and the inbreaking of spiritual gifts is linked indelibly to the cross and death of Christ (1:23; Rom 6:3; Phil 2:8) and this includes not just the death itself but the manner of the death, humble, despised, and even foolish in the eyes of the world (1:27-28). The Corinthians, on the other hand, understand the gifts to function as they normally would in the ancient social context, to increase the social status of the benefactor and for *him* to provide wisdom and power now enjoyed by his clients. For these Corinthians the link between spiritual benefaction and the cross as humiliation and foolishness is all but forgotten.

Paul's paradoxical juxtaposition of spiritual power emerging from the humble death of Christ is also linked to his understanding of resurrection, an understanding presumed throughout the entire letter. The resurrection for Paul constitutes the *body* of Christ, the church (*ekklēsia*) animated by the *Spirit* of God within the ritual assembly (Lord's Supper). Yet this assembly also remained within a temporal world subject to God's full redemption in the immediate future.[9] Hence what happens in the body has eternal significance in the world. In Paul's understanding the body of Christ resurrected is not separated from the Jesus who died humbly on a cross but, rather, incorporates perfectly the reality of how

God works within the world. He raises the lowly and humbles the proud and thereby transforms the world itself in the resurrection of Christ. In other words, the spiritual gifts manifest in the experience of resurrection within the ritual assembly are not ones that draw individuals away from the temporal world to enjoy higher spiritual realms. Rather, these spiritual gifts animate the *body* of Christ, the gathered church within the world. The gifts assist that body, the community, to place itself in eternal right relationship with God by manifesting the social pattern of the cross itself.

In the cultural context of the letter it appears that some of the Christians in Corinth understood resurrection as an already accomplished *spiritual* event in which one participates through ritual incorporation. That is, in the experience of resurrection one leaves the world, the *body*, for a true spiritual home (4:8). In this understanding spiritual gifts would not animate the *body* of Christ as part of this world but function as ecstatic experiences that move one from the world toward exclusively divine existence.[10]

To comprehend more fully Paul's understanding of the Spirit of God animating the resurrected *body* of Christ in the world, we might first look more carefully at the Corinthians' understanding of the resurrection, most evident in 1 Corinthians 15 and Paul's understanding of the Eucharist, especially 1 Corinthians 11:17-34. These sections of the letter form the context immediately post and prior to the more substantive discourse on spiritual gifts in 1 Corinthians 12–14.

The context for Paul's claim at chapter 15, to have witnessed personally the resurrection of Christ, is his awareness that there are some in Corinth who deny the resurrection of the dead (15:12). While the basis for this denial is not entirely clear, many scholars point to the possibility that these Corinthians actually denied a future *bodily* resurrection in favor of emphasizing a spiritual resurrection already manifest in the grant of powerful spiritual gifts within the community (realized eschatology).[11] In response Paul affirms both a spatial and temporal dimension in his understanding of resurrection: he argues for the resurrection *body* (15:35-50), manifest in the community ("the body of Christ"), and the connection between the past body (the cross of Christ) and future of this body (15:20-28; 1 Thess 4:16-17). This connection is the crucial moment of Paul's position vis-à-vis his Corinthian opponents. Jesus Christ was raised (11:16-17), the transformation of the body that begins the transformation of the ecclesial body and body of creation (11:20; Rom 8:19-21). But just as the resurrection of Christ—the manifestation of spiritual power and gifts—is tied to the self-gift of his body on the cross, so also now the manifestation of resurrection in the ecclesial body—spiritual power and gifts—is tied to the bodily ethical life of the community. The self-gift on the cross leads to resurrection, humility, and forbearance, marking the present resurrection life of both Christ and his body the church. The community must enact the pattern of Christ, cross and resurrection, in order to become continually what Christ now is. Hence what Paul says about the nature of the communal resurrection in chapter 15 acts as a capstone to the entire letter: how the Corinthians act *in the body* (for example, in sexual conduct discussed in chapters 5–7) is directly linked to the manifestation of resurrection life (for example, spiritual gifts) both now and in the ongoing life of the community.

Immediately preceding Paul's discussion of the spiritual gifts in chapter 12 is Paul's treatment of the issues surrounding the practice of the ritual meal in 1 Corinthians 11:17-34. The historical context of the issues cited by Paul concerning conduct at the "Supper of the Lord" (11:20), described in 1 Corinthians 11:17-34, has been successfully illuminated by Gerd Theissen.[12] In general Paul's remonstrance to the Corinthians concerning their ritual meal practices has to do with the articulation of honor and social status within ancient public meals. In simple terms, ancient public meals provided by patrons and benefactors to celebrate events were primary occasions for the public display and recognition of social honor and status from clients.[13] Within the world of clients, not only would the patron (provider) of the meal, and those of high social status whom he invited, be accorded the *places* at table of overall privilege, such persons would also be publicly and obviously served a more sumptuous meal. Those of lower social status would be seated at a lower place and would be served food of less quantity and quality.

In the case of Christian "public" meals taking place within this social structure of private house churches there was, at least for Paul, a conflict between the accepted social norm of discrimination (for example, 11:21, "one is hungry while another is drunk") and the sacred character of the Christian ritual meal grounded in the *crucified* and resurrected *body* of Christ. For Paul this sacred quality of the meal as the body of Christ called for particular mutuality and forbearance (11:33) unlike outside meals (11:22).[14]

What later Catholics would come to know as the institution of the Eucharist (11:23-26) is provided by Paul here within this overall social context. The key word here, of course, is *body*, for Paul's recitation of the passion and Last Supper fits his overall understanding of the eschatological body present in the meal at Corinth. In literary structure Paul creates a rhetorical sandwich of sorts. He leads up to this recitation of the meal tradition with an admonition not to dishonor (*kataphroneite*) or shame publicly (*kataischynete*) those who have no food or drink at the Lord's Supper, followed immediately by a rhetorically obvious return to the tradition of the passion and Last Supper shared with the Corinthians:

> For I received from the Lord what I also delivered to you, that the Lord Jesus on the night when he was betrayed took bread, and when he had given thanks, he broke it, and said, "This is my *body* which is for you. Do this in remembrance of me." In the same way also the cup, after supper, saying, "This cup is the new covenant in my blood. Do this, as often as you drink it, in remembrance of me." For as often as you eat this bread and drink the cup, you proclaim the Lord's death until he comes. (11:23-26)

> Whoever, therefore, eats the bread or drinks the cup of the Lord in an unworthy manner will be guilty of profaning the *body* and blood of the Lord. (11:27)

Following this recitation of tradition, at verse 27, Paul deliberately returns to his consideration of current meal practices in Corinth.[15] Whatever the actual manner of eating the bread and drinking the cup was (11:26), it is clear that the particular eating and drinking took place within the larger ritual structure of a quasi-public meal. But it is also clear by Paul's specific citation to the earlier tradition that "eating the bread and drinking the cup" locates the most sacred moment of the ritual as the act that articulated the presence of the eschatological body of Christ within the ritual ("this is my body"). Hence Paul's reference to eating the bread and drinking the cup in an "unworthy manner" (*anaxiōs*) in 11:27 specifies that the bread ("body") and wine ("blood") articulate a particular understanding of the ethical conduct of the eschatological body present in the ritual gathering.[16] Here a certain reality—this ritual supper as an enactment of the eschatological body of Christ—depends on whether the necessary understanding of the body as self-gift is being enacted: "This is my *body* which is *for you*." So also the citation to memory in the drinking of the cup, "Do this, as often as you drink it, in remembrance of me," is a call to make present "the night when he was betrayed," the night in which Jesus gave of himself, dishonored rather than honored, shamed rather than shaming. In other words, the present reality of the ritual *body* is bound up with the ethical conduct of Jesus in the passion;

the resurrection *body* now is part of the temporal body as a single reality that guides the ethical conduct of the meal.

One might think of Paul's "logic" here in the converse: *if* those of lower social status, parts of the *body*, are honored with food and drink, *then* the meal enacts the eschatological *body* of Christ because it enacts the passion *body* of Christ. Hence it is this present reality of the eschatological body, rightly understood, that ensures both physical and spiritual salvation, for when the body of the passion and resurrection does not exist (because weaker parts of the body are not honored or are shamed), then some members get weak and sick and some even die (11:30; cf. 6:18).[17]

So it is when Paul considers the Lord's Supper, he intimates that the ritual and ethical life of the community, the resurrected *body* gathered at the supper of the Lord, is *simultaneously* in time and the completion of time. What matters is not so much the passing of time, a *future* temporal eschatology, but the relation of all that is now to that which is its completion or goal (*telos*) outside of time itself. The cosmos is, as it were, in the midst of a transformation of the creation toward its proper and eternal status, restored to proper relationship with God (11:29-30; Rom 8:19). To put this in Christian ritual terms from 1 Corinthians 11:23, it matters what Jesus did "on the night he was betrayed" because his activity in the body led to the completion of the body in resurrection, animated by the Spirit of God. That act of self-gift, now again enacted in the meal ritual and commensurate practices at Corinth, is what enacts the completion of the Corinthian body in resurrection, animated by the Spirit of God. This is the subject of the next three chapters of 1 Corinthians and so brings us to the center of our study.

1 Corinthians 12–14

This discussion of the completion of the eschatological body in self-gift brings us full circle to a more careful consideration of Paul's discussion of the eschatological body and spiritual gifts in 1 Corinthians 12–14, more particularly the connection between Paul's discussion of spiritual gifts (12:1-11) and their manifestation within the eschatological body of Christ (12:12-31). Two things strike the reader of the letter here: first, the context from chapter 11, a discussion of proper ritual performance within the social context of the Lord's Supper, has not changed. The one spirit called upon here is the same spirit that animates the attention to social status at the ritual meal. Hence it is quite possible that the reversal called for by Paul, to honor those parts of the body that would not normally be honored in the Greco-Roman meal context (12:23), applies here to the distribution of spiritual gifts as well. In this context the expectation would likely be that social superiors, alluded to by Paul earlier in the letter,[18] would not only get the choicest food and place at table but the choicest spiritual gifts as well. Paul's expression here, "You know how, when you were pagans, you were constantly attracted to dumb idols and led astray" (12:2), might well be a reference to meals with those idols, meals in which the ordinary expectations of social status and honor were enacted. Here Paul signals a sort of cruciform counterattack on such an idea, emphasizing the relationship between the true (real) Spirit of God and the seemingly counterintuitive distribution of spiritual gifts to those lower in social status and honor. For Paul there is a profound relationship between the one Holy Spirit (12:3) and the exercise of gifts, human ritual activities animated by the Spirit that build up the eschatological body of the church. Amidst the great diversity of gifts is the unifying feature of their foundation in the Spirit of God, which is manifest only in the event of the cross. Such is the import of the reference to the curse and proclamation recited in 12:3, which contains an obvious allusion to Deuteronomy 21:22-23:

> Therefore I would have you know that no one speaking by the spirit of God says, "Jesus is anathema." And no one is able to declare Jesus as Lord except by the Holy Spirit. (12:3)

> If a man guilty of a capital offense is put to death and you hang him on a tree, his corpse shall not remain on the tree overnight. You must bury it the same day; anyone who is hanged is a curse of God. You shall not defile the land which the LORD, your God, is giving you as a heritage. (Deut 21:22-23, NABRE)

No one who affirms that the curse of Deuteronomy applies to Jesus crucified speaks with the Spirit of God; only the person who affirms that the curse has been reversed and Jesus exalted as Lord speaks with that same Spirit. Hence the exaltation of Jesus by God is the eschatological reversal par excellence. Here the cursed one has become Lord, animated in resurrection by the Spirit of God, and as such God's Spirit will always and everywhere consist of that same reversing quality as it is continually manifest in the community. As a result, Paul enumerates what might have been considered the most coveted and powerful gifts in Corinth—miracles, prophecy, the speaking in and interpretation of tongues—*last* on his list of spiritual gifts, even while the more mundane gifts, wisdom, knowledge, and faith, are listed first (12:7-12).

But there is more. The Spirit of God that is manifest in the spiritual gifts for the purpose of animating the realized eschatological body of Christ gathered at meal takes as its starting point God's animation of the body of Christ from the cross. The single and paradigmatic eschatological reversal of the messiah (Christ) crucified and respirited by God in resurrection becomes the called-for pattern of spiritual animation of community practice and identity.[19] It is the foundation for the practice of all particular roles and responsibilities within the gathered assembly. It is the idea that the entire *body* of Christ—all of its parts and not just the spirit or mind of Christ—was on the cross and that these parts, animated by the Spirit of God, were (and are) in a relationship of interdependence within that body. So in the ecclesial body of Christ the more mundane roles and practices of community life, teaching, helping, prophesying, evangelizing, etc. (12:28), are animated by the self-same Spirit of God that animated Christ's body from the cross. Put simply, a cruciform incarnational model, how God creates and sustains a right relationship with the world, is to understand the relationship between God and the creation on the basis of the paradigmatic event of the cross as self-gift ("my body which is *for you*"). This is the Spirit of God realized and enacted within the Christian community in its spiritual gifts—now enlivening the body of Christ, the new creation, within the world.

Moreover, it is almost startling to realize how Paul understands this incarnational dynamic of communal life as the goal of Christian life itself. He gives no hint in this letter that the spiritually animated "body of Christ," the local church (*ekklēsia*) in cruciform practice, is anything but the eternal body of Christ in right relationship with the Spirit of God. In other words, this reality is not some sort of temporary situation from which the individual or community—animated by the Spirit of God—will eventually move to a kind of pure spiritual existence. Indeed it is the Corinthian opponents who have divorced spiritual gifts from community practices. It is they who have made the mistake of recognizing the Spirit of God *without* its necessary connection to the cruciform *body*. In response, Paul in chapter 12 communicates an understanding of the *eternal* body of Christ, the community animated by the Spirit of God already manifest in the dynamic, gifted and giving, of the ritual gathering itself.

1 Corinthians 13

In chapter 13, Paul uses an earlier and traditional hymn concerning love (*agapē*) as the bridge between his articulation in chapter 12 of the relationship between the Spirit of God and the roles and practices of the church and a fuller exhortation concerning speaking in tongues (*glōssē*) and prophesying (*prophēteuōn*) in chapter 14. Literary analysis—the sudden shift to the first person and the way in which the text is set apart between 12:31 (*"earnestly desire* the higher gifts") and 14:1 (*"earnestly desire* the spiritual gifts")—as well as the inclusion of subjects and practices not previously mentioned (e.g., 13:3, charity and martyrdom) point to the fact that the hymn is part of an earlier Christian tradition used and modified by Paul. As a rhetorical bridge, he uses this hymn both to summarize a cruciform incarnational understanding of the quality of relationship at the heart of the church (love as self-gift), and to point forward to how his more specific teaching on the spiritual gift of tongues should be understood in chapter 14.

The placement of the hymn here between chapters 12 with its focus on the body of Christ and 14 with the focus on spiritual gifts of tongues and prophecy allows Paul to articulate an understanding of *agapaic* love centered on the self-gift found within the cross of Christ as that which forms the relationship between the body and its animation by the Spirit. The paradox here is not located simply in the ignominious death of God's Christ but, more important, in the attitude of Christ associated with that death. The hymnic exhortation here is about Christ:

> Love is patient and kind; love is not jealous or boastful; it is not arrogant or rude; *love does not insist on its own way*; it is not irritable or resentful. (13:4-5)

It parallels Paul's other well-known use of a hymn, Philippians 2:5-11: "though he [Christ] was in the form of God, did not count equality with God a thing to be grasped" (Phil 2:6). In other words, what is crucial is not the fact that there are indeed different roles and statuses within the churches but the self-giving love with which those roles and statuses are enacted. Christ was indeed in the form of God, the highest status, but did not seek such status. His attitude was one of love toward others, of emptying himself to the extent of an ignominious death on a cross and, *on that basis*, was given his higher exaltation in authentic resurrection (Phil 2:11).

So also here, on both sides of the hymn to love Paul exhorts the Corinthians "to earnestly seek" (*zēloute*) the higher gifts (12:31; 14:1). In English "to seek earnestly" has the connotation of honest and persistent effort. In Paul's discourse, however, the seeking itself is filled with irony, for to seek earnestly after a spiritual gift in order to realize higher status within the community is also to seek with the attitude of Christ on the cross, the one who did *not* seek status but rather emptied himself in love. Christ was exalted on the basis of *not* seeking equality with God (Phil 2:6) and *because* he was willing to act as self-gift upon the cross. So also in Corinth, Paul exhorts those of high status (socially or ritually gifted) to seek earnestly for higher gifts with this same cruciform attitude. They should seek only with love (*agapē*) in the manner of cruciform self-emptying that matches the attitude of Christ and so gives life to the community.

1 Corinthians 14

This ironic mode of status seeking now forms the basis of Paul's contention with, and exhortation toward, certain spirit-filled members of the Corinthian community. Chapter 14 is primarily a discussion of the relationship between the claims of communal status put forth by those with the spiritual gift of *glossolalia* (tongues) and the authority of Paul within the community (14:18). Here the irony is turned toward the building up and sustaining of the community. Spiritual gifts that only aggrandize the self instead of serving others within the body of Christ are not practiced out of love. They are selfish rather than self-gift (*agapē*). Prophecy must benefit the community; tongues must be interpreted by one who understands in order to edify the community and draw in the stranger (14:4-5). Paul himself could claim great status as a superior speaker in tongues but, on the conscious model of Christ on the cross, would rather have little or no status from the gift in order to give himself in love to the community following the pattern of Christ (14:18-19).

Finally a word should be said about the employment within ritual of the spiritual gifts discussed here by Paul. The potential for anarchy in such practices, for example, many speaking in tongues at once, is noted. In response to this threat to community identity, Paul proposes that such practices be ordered by the conscious exercise of the gifts, even in ecstatic utterance, toward community needs and building up the church. Here Paul moves beyond any description of the necessary relationship of God with creation, that is, the Spirit of God in relation to the body of Christ the church, and on to the principle inherent in the ordered body itself. The body of Christ, the church in the world as the new creation, is so because each person as part of the body gives of herself or himself to benefit the body as a whole. The Spirit of God is in relation to an ordered and harmonious creation because *the body* enacts the selfless cruciform love of Christ. The order of creation, therefore, the order that was intended by God from the beginning and that is enacted within the church gathered, is marked by the attitude and action of the self-gift of the cross. The spiritual power of the resurrection—witnessed in the outpouring of spiritual gifts—is not a result of the cross (as in "Christ died so now we can enjoy spiritual power") but manifest *within* the movement and attitude of Christ on the cross. The historical event of Jesus' passion is not divorced from the faith event of the resurrection of the Christ; rather the former is constitutive of the latter. This is an order of creation in which diversity is manifest for the purpose of self-gift, in other words, a creation that internally manifests the external love that God has for it.[20]

So now, given Paul's sense of the eschatological body (chap. 12) animated by love as self-gift (*agapē*; chap. 13), which constitutes the intended order of creation in the ritual identity and practice of the community (chap. 14), we may return to the contemporary church's understanding of lay ecclesial ministry rooted in 1 Corinthians 12:4-7:

> There are varieties of gifts but the same Spirit; there are varieties of service but the same Lord; there are varieties of manifestations but the same God who manifests all of them in all people. To each person is given the manifestation of the Spirit for mutual care.

The recent manifestation of lay ecclesial ministry in the church is an outpouring of the one Spirit articulated in different ecclesial roles to serve the common good. As contemporary ecclesial documents such as *Co-Workers in the Vineyard of the Lord* specify, lay ecclesial ministry in the Catholic Church is the contemporary and continual exercise of spiritual gifts first experienced in the earliest Christian churches. As such, these gifts, as with all the diverse gifts of ministry given to the church, are bound up specifically with the self-gift of Christ on the cross. Paul's critique of his opponents' self-serving attitude about spiritual gifts is as timely now as it was then: to create factions or to seek status on the basis of spiritual gifts is to fundamentally misunderstand the Spirit of God. His letter to the Corinthians teaches us how these gifts are to be exercised in a church that claims to be, and is in fact, the body of Christ as self-gift, the eternal creation animated by the one *cruciform* Spirit of agapaic love and so in right relationship with God. Indeed our discussions of who is commissioned or authorized in ministry, or how to articulate these ministries within canon law—necessary as these are for the proper ordering of the church's ministry—must always proceed within a context set by Paul's understanding of the true nature of the gifts and the proper exercise of ministry on behalf of the church.

It is also the case that the mutual care of the community—what the community needs from the exercise of spiritual gifts—might well change over time. The need for certain spiritual gifts might diminish (exorcists and exorcisms might become fewer, for example) while others emerge (for example, the gift to understand modern tax structures or the gift to be able to honestly listen to victims of abuse) but the cruciform attitude with which these roles are performed and gifts exercised must not change. Our development of descriptions and rituals to acknowledge and celebrate this new outpouring of the Spirit should therefore always focus on the cruciform nature of the resurrected *body* of Christ. The purpose of new descriptions and ritual practices cannot have as a result the creation of factions within the church as they did so long ago in Corinth; rather they must bring forth unity founded in the cross of Christ. In ritual and practice we should heed Paul's admonition to seek earnestly the spiritual gifts for the building up of God's church.

Notes

1. *Ecclesiae de Mysterio*: On Certain Questions Regarding the Collaboration of the Non-Ordained Faithful in the Sacred Ministry of the Priest by Eight Dicasteries of the Holy See.

2. USCCB, *Co-Workers in the Vineyard of the Lord: A Resource for Guiding the Development of Lay Ecclesial Ministry* (Washington, DC: USCCB Publishing, 2005).

3. *Apostolicam Actuositatem* 3: "The holy Spirit sanctifies the people of God through the ministry and the sacraments and, for the exercise of the [lay] apostolate, gives the faithful special gifts besides (see 1 Cor 12:7), 'allotting them to each just as the Spirit chooses' (1 Cor 12:11)." *Ecclesiae de Mysterio* 1: "For the building up of the Church, the Body of Christ, there is a diversity of members and functions but only one Spirit who, for the good of the Church, distributes His various gifts with munificence proportionate to His riches and the needs of service (cf. 1 Cor 12, 1-11)." *Co-Workers*, 20: "An ecclesiology of communion looks upon different gifts and functions not as adversarial but as enriching and complementary. It appreciates the Church's unity as an expression of the mutual and reciprocal gifts brought into harmony by the Holy Spirit. An ecclesiology of communion recognizes diversity in unity and acknowledges the Spirit as the source of all the gifts that serve to build up Christ's Body (1 Cor 12:4-12, 28-30).

For 'to each is given the manifestation of the Spirit for the common good' (1 Cor 12:7)."

4. Unless otherwise indicated, all Bible translations are my own.

5. The warrant here bears emphasis: the spirit of ministerial priesthood is to serve the spiritually gifted mission of the laity within which lay ecclesial ministry plays a vital role.

6. Paul refers to this factionalism as "being with" one apostle, or even to Christ (1 Cor 1:12).

7. For further discussion see Charles A. Bobertz, "Religious Bodies and Organizational Forms: Christianity," in *Religions of the Ancient World: A Guide*, ed. Sarah Iles Johnston (Cambridge: Harvard University Press, 2004), 323–24.

8. Paul therefore downplays his own role in baptizing converts in order to emphasize the nature of Christian spiritual power grounded, ironically, in the weakness of Christ crucified (1 Cor 1:14-16).

9. This understanding is quite clearly expressed in Rom 8:19-23.

10. Wayne Meeks, *The Writings of St. Paul*, Norton Critical Edition, 2nd ed. (New York: Norton, 2007), 24–25.

11. Some scholars would argue that this notion fits well with general conceptions of ancient Hellenistic dualism in which the fate of the corporeal body is of no consequence. Rather it is the spirit (which has occupied the body for a time) that is the object of resurrection and therefore salvation. See the discussion in Dale Martin, *The Corinthian Body* (New Haven: Yale University Press, 1995), 6–7 and esp. n. 13. Martin argues, however, that a modern Cartesian dualism, body distinct from soul/spirit, has been read back into the ancient sources, including 1 Corinthians. The ancients, he argues, thought in terms of a material hierarchy ranging from the heavy stuff of the body to the ethereal (though still physical) stuff of the soul.

12. Gerd Theissen, "Soziale Integration und Sakramentales Handeln: Eine Analyse von 1 Cor. XI 17-34," *Novum Testamentum* 24 (1974): 179–205; see also Wayne A. Meeks, *The First Urban Christians: The Social World of the Apostle Paul* (New Haven: Yale University Press, 1983), 140–63.

13. Examples would include personal birthdays, dates marking the foundation of cults, or the visit of an imperial official. For extensive discussion along with examples from contemporary Greco-Roman sources, see Charles Bobertz, "The Role of Patron in the *Cena Dominica* of Hippolytus' *Apostolic Tradition*," *Journal of Theological Studies* 44 (1993): 170–84.

14. The letter suggests that there was another sort of tension surrounding the provision of Lord's Suppers by patrons within house-churches. Would the patron of such meals, most likely the owner of a house-church, be expected to invite the entire local assembly to the Lord's Supper? In ordinary circumstances the patron would have the social privilege of inviting whomsoever he or she chose and feeding those persons in a manner commensurate with their public social status. Would a consideration of such social norms help to illuminate Paul's

statement at 11:19 as ironic in intent: "For there must be factions among you in order that those who are genuine among you may be recognized" (11:19)? Clearly for Paul the only true faction is the faction of Christ. See Carolyn Osiek, "The Patronage of Women in Early Christianity," in Amy Jill-Levine and Maria Mayo Robbins, eds., *A Feminist Companion to Patristic Literature* (London: T&T Clark, 2008), 173–92.

15. See Jerome Kodell, *The Eucharist in the New Testament* (Wilmington: Glazier, 1988), 22ff.; John Koenig, *The Feast of the World's Redemption* (Harrisburg: Trinity Press International, 2000), 54–59.

16. I would note here that Paul does not understand his admonition in light of the passion tradition he quotes here but rather the passion tradition in light of the situation in Corinth, where some, in Paul's estimation, have failed to understand what that tradition means for contemporary church practice.

17. See below, the discussion of 1 Cor 12:23.

18. 1 Cor 4:8: "You are already satisfied; you have already grown rich; you have become kings without us! Indeed, I wish that you had become kings, so that we also might become kings with you."

19. The theological implications here are important but beyond the scope of this essay. The Spirit of God that animates the body of Christ from the tomb—following the self-gift of the cross—is the self-same Spirit of the original creation. Creation itself finds its authentic identity, its very animation, in the Spirit of God as self-gift. As the (new) creation of God the communal body of Christ gives witness to the authentic realization of God's Spirit in the world.

20. What this means for a renewed understanding of the gospel narratives is quite clear: the depiction of Jesus' historical action moving toward the cross is the basis upon which spiritual power (e.g., miracles) is present within his ministry. The ministry of Christ, teaching and action toward the cross, is a claim for the intended cruciform order of creation itself.

Chapter 5

Vocation and Authorization of Lay Ecclesial Ministers
Lessons and Insights from Early Conversations about the Identity of the DRE

Hosffman Ospino

For nearly half a century Catholics in the United States have been engaged in a very exciting conversation about the role of laypeople as ministers in the church and their contributions to the church's evangelizing mission. In this essay we explore one particular instance of that reflection from a historical perspective, namely, the conversation about the identity of the Catholic director of religious education (DRE), and how such conversation serves as a reference point to advance contemporary reflections about the vocation and authorization of lay ecclesial ministers. Our main goal is to draw a number of helpful lessons and insights from this history to address questions of vocation and authorization of lay ecclesial ministers. In these pages the reader will encounter a variety of perspectives to key concepts such as "ministry" and "professionalization." We must state from the very beginning that these terms are highly debated in the literature about ecclesial ministry. Not one definition wins the day; yet, the various definitions available share common elements that allow for a fruitful conversation. This variety of perspectives reflects the complexity of issues related to the identity and role of the DRE that have emerged throughout the years, questions that now we encounter again as we reflect on the identity and role of the lay ecclesial minister.

Let us begin with three scenarios:[1]

> Christina Smith received a master's degree in religious education in the early 1990s from a prestigious Catholic university in the northeast. She has worked since then as a director of religious education in two parishes. Christina is widely known in her diocese and in several national organizations for her vast experience and remarkable dedication to ecclesial service as a religious educator. Her personal experience as a committed Christian woman, mother, and wife and her ministry are intimately intertwined. She recently moved with her husband and three children to become the new director of religious education at St. Catherine of Siena Parish under a three-year contract. The job at her previous parish ended when a new pastor arrived and regretfully informed her that he was giving the position of DRE to someone with whom he had worked for several years and knew very well.[2] For Christina her ministry is more than a job; it is her vocation and fulfillment. She is glad to be able to serve in the new parish.

> Sonia and Cristobal Gomez migrated from Nicaragua three decades ago. Both served as *Delegados de la Palabra* (Delegates of the Word) in their native country. Because of the social circumstances in which they lived, they were not able to complete formal education beyond high school. Soon after their arrival in the United States, they became the leaders of the religious education program in Spanish at St. Paul's Parish, where nearly 80 percent of the population is Hispanic. As the years passed, they increased the amount of time given to their ministry. They currently spend nearly forty hours a week (sometimes more) and many of their personal resources in this service, yet they do not receive a salary or employment benefits from the parish. All pastors at St. Paul's have been very pleased to count on such faithful volunteers. Members of the parish see the Gomezes as the "official" DREs. They have trained dozens of leaders (two young men have gone to the seminary and four women joined religious congregations), accompanied many couples on their journey toward the sacrament of marriage, prepared thousands of children and youth to receive the sacraments of initiation, and been instrumental in inviting many lukewarm Catholics back into practicing their faith. They know that through their work they are serving the mission of the church.

> Father Charles Wilson was recently ordained and assigned as the parochial vicar for St. Julia's Parish. One of his main responsibilities

as a young curate is to oversee the parish's efforts for adult faith formation, something that he enjoys doing as part of his proper service to the people of his community in the ministry of the Word.[3] Father Wilson understands his role as an expression of his ministry as an ordained priest.[4]

The above scenarios encapsulate the experience of three bodies of baptized people committed to the church's educational ministry in different ways in Catholic communities of faith around the United States. The nature of their work and how they do it are the objects of vibrant conversations among theologians and pastoral ministers whose shared hope is to define in clear terms what ecclesial ministry means today. For centuries, to speak of ministry meant almost exclusively a reference to the work of those who were ordained. In the last decades, particularly under the impulse and wisdom of the Second Vatican Council, US Catholics have pioneered the exploration of wider and deeper perspectives about ministry. Among them is a growing appreciation of the gift of lay ecclesial ministry in the church.

If ministry is understood as *"the public activity of a baptized follower of Jesus Christ flowing from the Spirit's charism and an individual personality on behalf of a Christian community to proclaim, serve, and realize the kingdom of God,"*[5] then Christina, the Gomezes, and Fr. Wilson without a doubt are doing some sort of *ministerial* work in the church. All three participate in one way or another in the church's educational ministry, which is an actualization of the ministry of the Word. But the question that brings us together in this reflection is not to determine their level of ministerial commitment but their identity as ministers in the life of the church with particular attention to the experience of the laity. For this the use of two lenses is helpful: vocation and authorization. Let us look at the ministry of these three groups of ministers with each lens and see what questions emerge.

From the perspective of *vocation*, Christina, the Gomezes, and Fr. Wilson share a sense of calling to pastoral service in the church. Regularly, conversations about vocation point to priesthood or religious life, which makes things easier in the case of Fr. Wilson. He felt the calling, an ecclesial authority acknowledged it, and he was ordained. For the Gomezes and for Christina there is no ordination. How do the community and the institutional structures then recognize their vocation? Christina holds a degree in religious education and has dedicated her life to service in the church. Does being hired to serve as a DRE mean an acknowledgment of her vocation to lay ecclesial ministry? If so, how is this acknowledgment affirmed and incorporated into the church's ministerial structure? The Gomezes are neither ordained nor hired but their calling to ministry is recognized and affirmed by what could be understood as an extraordinary exercise of *sensus fidelium* on the part of members of the church at various levels. Is this a form of vocational recognition that the church as a whole must pay closer attention to in today's context? How and what will such recognition entail? Unless we have clearly defined institutional channels to acknowledge and affirm the vocation of all lay ecclesial ministers, laypeople formally involved in ministry will constantly find themselves in the uncomfortable situation of "proving" the authenticity of their calling to the ecclesial community that they already serve in ministerial and professional ways.

From the perspective of *authorization*, Christina, the Gomezes, and Fr. Wilson understand themselves as serving *in*, *to*, and *on behalf of* the ecclesial community. As an ordained minister, Fr. Wilson received the faculties from his bishop and thus has official authorization to indefinitely exercise his ministry in the church—except if his faculties are suspended for a particular reason. Since the one who authorizes the ordained is also ordained, one could assume that authorization in this case is somehow a power-sharing exercise on a common level—that of the ordained. Is this so? Is this the only way to look at authorization when we talk about ecclesial ministry? Christina and the Gomezes are not ordained: who then authorizes them? Does authorization in their case mean power-sharing at different levels? Christina is formally hired by a pastor and is subject to the terms of a contract. Is the contract simultaneously a legal and an ecclesial expression of authorization? What if there is no contract? Is her authorization as a lay ecclesial minister temporary or indefinite as that of Fr. Wilson? The Gomezes are not exactly aware of how the idea of authorization works; they have never asked for authorization and frankly do not seem interested in doing so. Can they be rescinded the implicit authorization from their faith community to lead the religious education efforts as volunteers? Should they be formally authorized by an ecclesial body? In what ways will authorization change the Gomezes' labor conditions (e.g., salary, benefits, accountability)? Will they qualify for authorization?

The Development of the Ministry of the DRE

Protestant Beginnings

The emergence of the role of DRE in the United States dates back to the turn of the twentieth century in the context of Protestant Christianity.

At the time, three major conversations coincided: "concern for the character of the young, the hope presented by a new educational psychology and an enlightened Biblical scholarship, and the desire to match the public school in the quality of education provided."[6] In some sense the development of the DRE was a response to the signs of the times both in the various Christian communities and in the larger society. The Sunday School movement was perhaps the most widespread effort to organize the educational ministry in Protestant communities.[7] However, its model of reliance on volunteer teachers under the oversight of the clergy and its emphasis on a schooling model were found wanting. The DRE movement emerged as a "new profession" that encouraged religious educators to look beyond mere content, be conversant with emerging theories in the fields of education and psychology, and develop new forms of professional leadership in Christian communities. Soon the movement was perceived as progressive.

One of the key concerns of the new profession was to define the nature of its own professionals—not an easy task. DREs would bring to their faith communities a new set of concerns, methodologies, and standards.[8] At first the understanding of what it meant to be a DRE reflected that of professional teachers outside ecclesial contexts. In fact, many of the first DREs were former teachers and school administrators hired by faith communities.[9] The expectation was that these professionals would bring the best of their experience into the emerging profession. The DRE was to be professionally trained in fields such as education, psychology, Sacred Scriptures, and theology.[10] Though many ordained ministers worked as DREs, ordination did not play a defining role. It was assumed that "one ordained without the proper training could not be a Director of Religious Education."[11]

Setting high professional and formation standards was the beginning. DREs soon established national, regional, and denominational organizations that helped them discuss key issues about the new profession and envision ways to strengthen it. The largest and still existing among these organizations was the Religious Education Association (REA) founded in 1903. In 1906 the REA began publishing the *Journal of Religious Education*, which currently serves as the main outlet for scholarship and reflection about the field in the English-speaking world.

The emphasis on the professional character of the ministry of the DRE from the beginning led to key questions such as, is the DRE a vocation? Who can be a DRE? What is the role of the DRE in the structure of the faith community? Who authorizes the DRE? In 1920 Norman Richardson wrote that the DRE is "not a vocation born in a day, to flourish for a few hours, only to vanish at nightfall."[12] Perhaps the most significant challenge that the profession of DRE faced was the ecclesial communities' poor understanding of what it really was.[13] In the 1930s and 1940s some communities struggled to differentiate so much the role of the DRE from that of the ordained minister making the former an almost strange presence within the community. The DRE was defined as the specialist in religious education and the pastor as the specialist in preaching and administration. Such definitions revealed a struggle for equality of status that soon led to conflicts and jealousies. Many pastors did not accept the idea that expertise and authority went hand in hand. The tension was solved when directors acknowledged the pastor as the head of the faith community.[14] In other communities the DRE assumed so many tasks that this person came to be perceived as a "jack-of-all-trades." Still other communities hired poorly trained DREs based on watered-down standards determined by whoever was in charge of leading the faith community. Whether absent or radically affirmed, professionalism as a distinctive mark of the DRE was perceived as the key to define the identity of the DRE. Lack of clarity about professional standards and misunderstandings about the role of the DRE in the community became sources of disillusionment and despair for many.[15]

In the 1950s and 1960s a new development moved the conversation about the profession of the DRE in a different direction that offered hope and a sense of revival. The office of the DRE was not set over or against that of the pastor but as someone who works in collaboration as part of a ministry team.[16] Directors recognized the leadership of the pastor in the community and the pastor affirmed the professional/ministerial gifts of the DRE. This was indeed a change of mentality in both camps. Furthermore, during this period of time DREs explored the idea of research, which led to scientific approaches to their work as well as engagement in theological conversations at various levels.[17] While in the first half of the century the work of the DRE was defined primarily by its concern for good teaching and good administration of religious education programs, fifty years later the DRE had assumed the responsibility of also being a theologian.[18] The vision of the DRE as an enabler took root, someone whose efforts and guidance helped "others to grow toward their full potential as committed Christians and as members of the church."[19]

In the 1970s and 1980s Protestant religious educators returned to the question about the nature of the field.[20] One gets the impression that thinkers during these years realized that too much time and energy were spent on the person and responsibilities of the DRE that for a moment they lost sight of the nature of the profession. Another way of reading the shift is that by better articulating the nature of the profession, the better one understands those who are called to it and their mission.[21]

Three periods then marked the development of the role of the Protestant DRE during most of the twentieth century. All three periods focused in one way or another on issues related to vocation and authority:

> In the first period, the question was one of authority. Which one had jurisdiction over the other, and in what areas? This was the burning question from the beginning of the profession until 1930. In the second period, the problem was seen to be a matter of personality characteristics. What kind of a person should attempt to work in a multiple staff ministry? This was the concern during the years from 1930 to 1950. It was only in the third period, the years following 1950, that the concept of "team ministry" developed. What was seen as the central task of the church, and how could pastors and directors work together to accomplish it?[22]

The Catholic Experience

Catholics were aware of the conversations about the DRE as a professional, yet it would take six decades before they joined such interactions and contributed with their own perspectives. For nearly four centuries the Confraternity of Christian Doctrine (CCD) was the structure within which the church's catechetical ministry was organized in many parts of the world. CCD directors were mostly priests. Laypeople assisted the work of CCD directors primarily as volunteer teachers. Questions of vocation and authorization were rather clerical concerns. In the 1960s, around the time of the Second Vatican Council (1962–65), building on the success of events such as the international catechetical weeks, Catholics in the United States engaged in conversation about what it meant to be a DRE in the Catholic world. Catholics were simultaneously faced with the advantage of decades of reflections accumulated by Protestant DREs and the specific challenges that were unique to the Catholic context. Questions about vocation and authorization soon came to the fore, though with a new perspective.

Four main factors shaped the particular development of the DRE as a professional/minister in the Catholic context. First, the Second Vatican Council provided a new language to talk about the role of the laity in the life of the church. Laypeople began to participate in the mission of the church in new ways, many assuming offices and responsibilities previously reserved to the ordained. This was revolutionary in many ways. Second, vowed religious, mostly women, accessed programs of higher education in significantly large numbers and soon assumed key positions of leadership in the church. Laypeople, seminarians, vowed women and men, and priests shared academic contexts formally studying the theological and ministerial disciplines. Around the time of the council, hundreds of former nuns, priests, and seminarians found themselves working in parishes and other ecclesial institutions as DREs. Their previous experience significantly informed their ministry and for them it was not too difficult to navigate the ecclesial structures. However, all these groups soon realized that there was an urgent need for fresher language to talk about ministry, a language that until then was framed around the experience of priests and vowed religious. Third, Catholic universities developed graduate programs of religious education that attracted hundreds of students. Catholic DREs could choose from Catholic or Protestant programs for their formal training. Fourth, by the middle of the twentieth century the two major efforts through which the church advanced its educational mission in the United States, namely, the CCD and the Catholic parochial school system, experienced signs of decline and made way for new initiatives. The CCD practically disappeared as a system and attention shifted significantly from almost exclusive attention to children to a growing interest in adult faith formation. Hundreds of Catholic schools closed and the remaining opened their doors to non-Catholic and non-Christian students. Since the vast majority of Catholic children and youth did not attend Catholic schools, more resources were allocated to parochial programs of religious education.

These factors altogether facilitated a growing participation of the laity in the church's educational mission beyond traditional roles, not merely as assistants to the clergy but as active pastoral agents; empowered many Catholic women to exercise ministerial leadership beyond the context of holy orders or vowed religious life; expanded the view by engaging voices outside Catholic circles and focusing on issues beyond Catholic internal affairs; encouraged the emergence of a new language to name the ministerial work of the laity in the church as something more than that which is not the work of the clergy; and inspired renewed conversations about the church's commitment to Christian education.

The new pastoral leaders were called DREs and CREs (Coordinators of Religious Education). Other related titles were also used by parishes and dioceses throughout the country. At first most of these ministers were vowed religious and priests specialized in the art of Christian education or catechesis, yet in less than two decades the number of laypeople hired by parishes as DREs outgrew that of vowed religious and ordained DREs. Their presence in the parochial ministerial structure raised some important questions: where did they stand vis-à-vis the clergy and the rest of the community?[23] Did they have any autonomy and if so, did such autonomy derive from some form of ecclesial authorization or from their professional competencies? Were they responding to a particular calling as DREs or was their vocation the actualization of something much bigger? In some sense, these questions echoed those of Protestant educators and their communities about the identity of the DRE in the first decades of the twentieth century. More questions would emerge as most of these pastoral leaders would be primarily laypeople who rapidly began to assume other pastoral responsibilities in the life of the faith community.

Catholic DREs worked alongside clergy in the organization of parochial and diocesan programs of religious education. Their expertise was necessary at an ambiguous time: millions of Catholics grew interested about their faith and wanted more than the basic answers provided by the Baltimore Catechism, yet millions more Catholics embraced an attitude of indifference about the life of the church and the content of the faith. We can say that the identity and the role of the DRE were shaped in response to the particular circumstances of the moment. Parishes and dioceses established support structures for the work of DREs and various organizations at national, regional, and local levels served as catalysts to address emerging issues and further visions. Journals such as *The Living Light* and *PACE* (Professional Approaches for Christian Educators) served as outlets for reflection and professional development.

Not long after their emergence, Catholic DREs embarked in a process of self-analysis about their role in the life of the church and their future. The language driving the conversation was largely that of professionalization: is the DRE a professional minister or a religious education professional assisting the church's mission? Though scholars and practitioners agreed on the idea of professionalism, what became a source of tension was the discussion of whether the DRE was primarily a professional minister or primarily a professional educator.[24] Each perspective would yield particular insights about vocation and authorization.

Professional Ministers or Professionals in the Ministry of the Church?

The literature focusing on the professional identity and role of the Catholic DRE is quite abundant and it would take more than a few paragraphs to summarize the different conversations that dominated during the early years. I hereby present three major arguments and briefly analyze how each addressed issues of vocation and authorization.

Professional ministers of catechesis. The use of ministerial language to name the work of the catechist was inspired in great part by the 1972 apostolic letter *Ministeria Quaedam,* in which Paul VI reformed the traditional minor orders and introduced the idea of officially installed ministries for the laity. One such envisioned ministry was that of catechist.[25] Catholic DREs and CREs in the United States received this proposal with hope, yet with a sense of caution, as an affirmation of their work, particularly at the level of leadership that they already exercised in the life of the church.[26]

A number of religious education scholars rapidly emphasized the identity of the DRE as a catechist. Catechists are called and especially commissioned by the church, are indispensable for the church's work of evangelization, are witnesses to Christ, and can sometimes supply for the priest although without being his substitute.[27] An obvious consequence of this characterization would be to think of the DRE as a minister. Catechesis is an ecclesial activity and those who advance it do so as part of the church's mission. Furthermore, catechesis is not the responsibility of one individual but of the whole ecclesial community.[28] According to Berard Marthaler, "the position of the director of religious education is not just another job. It is first and last a ministry."[29]

The vocation of the DRE as a minister emerges within the context of the church. Such vocation has a double aspect: it is communal insofar as it is recognized by the community and individual because it is the person who hears it first in the heart.[30] Because of the nature of his or her calling, the DRE participates in a unique way in the ministry of the Word in the ecclesial context.[31] Thus, professionalization is desired and welcomed but not as something more important than the primacy of Christian witness and ecclesial commitment.[32]

The language of "officially installed ministry" for lay ministers called to be catechists provided a window of opportunity to explore the issue of authorization of the DRE. If the model was that of the already approved ministries of lector and acolyte, then the installation of the DRE would require a ceremony presided by a bishop or a priest, be celebrated in the presence of the community, and attend to the noble simplicity of the liturgy.[33] The installed DRE would participate in the church's ministry of the Word in an officially recognized way, work with other ministers in the church as coworkers in the same evangelizing mission, and acknowledge the particularity of his or her own ministry.[34]

Professional educators in the ministry of the church. The argument emphasizing the ministerial dimension of the identity of the DRE was not the only one. A number of religious education scholars and practitioners, without denying the ecclesial and pastoral dimensions of the work of the DRE, focused primarily on professionalization from the perspective of expertise in the field. In 1980 the National Conference of Diocesan Directors of Religious Education (NCDD) issued a statement defining the DRE as someone "with a master's degree in theology, religious education or an approved equivalent, and at least three years of administrative or teaching experience, who has demonstrated skills in organization, would be a professional, salaried, full-time member of the parish staff."[35] This statement perfectly captures the spirit of this second position.

The professional religious educator working in the church was defined as someone who significantly enhanced the church's educational ministry with skilled perspectives and training. Stephen Nevin proposed that the coordinator was a theological resource person, a master teacher, and an organizer or manager.[36] As a religious educational professional, the DRE's identity is defined primarily by the profession; he or she remains in conversation with other professional religious educators in the church and beyond, and does not see himself or herself as church officer.[37] The professional DRE seeks to work in the parish as part of a team that privileges horizontal, collaborative structures of service over hierarchical structures of power.[38] The DRE coordinates the educational activity of the faith community in light of his or her expertise.

This understanding invited awareness of the new possibilities and challenges regarding the professional contributions of DREs who do not see themselves as official ministers in the life of the church.[39] On the one hand, the existence of professional religious educators would require the existence and stability of a profession. The question was whether such profession could actually exist without the direct support—and oversight—of the institution that hired the professionals who ascribed to it. Autonomy would represent a cost. On the other hand, professional religious educators were aware of their potential to enrich and transform the church's educational ministry by incorporating the insights from the disciplines and theories with which they were engaged. The question was whether the ecclesial communities were open to developing practices and spaces to embrace the advice of these professionals without considering them suspect or intrusive, yet valuing their expertise. If Maria Harris was correct when she estimated that the majority of DREs were not expecting to be ordained, and I believe that such is the case today as well, then the issue was about the authentic incorporation of a body of mostly lay professionals living their baptismal call to the fullest and contributing directly to an essential dimension of the church's evangelizing mission: education.[40]

The vocation of the professional religious educator from this perspective would be understood in light of the standards established in the larger realm of the (secular) professions. Vocation would then be the embrace of a set of values that directs the professional to make specific social and ethical commitments and to place his or her gifts at the service of the common good.[41] Vocation here is primarily personal awareness and commitment, though lived in a particular community. The supernatural dimension of vocation that the language of ministry would privilege was rather secondary. Nonetheless, because the professional religious educator was a baptized person guided by the gift of faith, the Christian calling to holiness was actualized in his or her professional practice. In the case of the DRE such professional practice is performed in an explicitly ecclesial context.

As a professional, the DRE would establish a contractual relationship with the institution or community that required his or her service and expertise. The contracting parties were autonomous to negotiate issues related to qualifications, expectations, and responsibilities. The authority of the DRE was thus exercised in light of the standards of the profession and the terms of the contract with the ecclesial community where he or she served.

Professional educators and ministers. Each of the above perspectives had its strengths and limitations and most of the time they were not perceived as mutually exclusive. One third argument vis-à-vis the question of professional character of the DRE sought to affirm the relationship between the idea of the DRE as minister and that of the DRE as an education professional—yet preserving the necessary distinctions. Maria Harris suggested that the ideal would be to "keep both education and ministry distinct but related as legitimate professions for the DRE."[42] For Harris neither ministry nor education rigidly defined the identity of the DRE yet both offered an abundance of resources for this professional to shape his or her service to the faith community.

It seems that at the heart of this argument—some kind of *via media*—was the definition of the profession rather than that of the professional. Institutions tend to define in specific terms the activities that identify their mission and channel the incorporation of professionals to advance such mission. In the case of the church, her educational activity is shaped by the commitment to evangelization: the church exists to evangelize (*Evangelii Nuntiandi* 14). Religious education is a pastoral activity that has its specific goals, ecclesial and educational, that require the wisdom of the professional field of education to be effective. The DRE emerged as the professional who would embrace this specific mission of the church and freely decide whether he or she wanted to contribute to the advancement of such mission. This perspective left open the possibility for the DRE to serve the ecclesial community in specifically ministerial ways (e.g., ordained, vowed religious, installed catechist) or contribute out of one's own expertise and professionalism without being named an official minister. It would be up to the DRE to decide how to live his or her baptismal vocation and serve the faith community in what Harris called an adult, that is to say, a responsible and informed decision.[43] The church was thus not to impose "ministerial" categories upon all laypeople to participate in her evangelizing mission. However, the possibilities to serve in that mission, especially when such participation required assuming pastoral responsibilities that entailed the well-being of the larger community of faith, and the channels of institutional authorization validating that service had to be defined with clarity.

What Do We Learn from the Earliest Conversations about the Identity of the DRE to Better Understand Issues of Vocation and Authorization in the Context of Lay Ecclesial Ministry Today?

The above brief historical overview serves as a tool for theologians and practitioners engaged in reflection about lay ecclesial ministry in the twenty-first century to compare developments, revisit questions, and learn valuable insights. According to recent statistical studies, the largest body of laypeople working in parishes as lay ecclesial ministers is directly involved in the church's educational ministry as religious educators.[44] Because of such significant presence, reflections about the vocation and authorization of lay ecclesial ministers are and will largely be enriched by developments in the understanding of the role of religious educators in the life of the church.

Lessons and Insights about Vocation
The reflection about the vocation of the DRE in the Catholic context evolved in the midst of a major transition vis-à-vis those who identified

with this particular role: from mostly vowed religious and clergy to mostly laypeople. But the transition did not happen overnight. In the early years the ranks of DREs who were neither consecrated nor ordained were filled largely with former vowed religious, priests, and seminarians. The prevalence of the experience of these voices so closely related to the worlds of vowed religious life and ordained priesthood in some sense biased the reflection about vocation to ministry among DREs who had not participated or were not fully familiar with such experience. The transition demanded a shift in language and perspective about vocation particularly for two reasons: (1) laypeople actively serving as DREs in the church's educational ministry needed to name the uniqueness of their vocation in positive terms[45] without feeling that theirs was a watered-down or a second-class alternative to the more traditional vocations to ministry, and (2) DREs were seriously engaged in reflection about the nature of their vocation as professional religious educators whose context and locus was the evangelizing mission of the church.

One key question with which DREs particularly wrestled, then, was whether their vocation needed to be named in ministerial terms and be assigned some ecclesial ranking. It seems that the language of lay ecclesial ministry has been effective in addressing the first concern: the vocation of the layperson involved in ecclesial ministry. However, many reflections about lay ecclesial ministry often take for granted that all laypeople professionally working in ecclesial contexts, including DREs,[46] are ministers in one way or another and that their work is to be defined in ministerial terms. Such "ministerialization" (if the term is allowed) of the work of laypeople in the church may potentially blur the differences between the general expectation of practicing one's baptismal vocation in the everyday when one serves in an explicitly ecclesiastical context (e.g., a secretary in a parish) or one closely related to it (e.g., a nurse in a Catholic hospital) and the explicitly ministerial roles within the life of the church that require more elaborate levels of authorization and accountability. Also, it says little about the status of laypeople who are fully collaborating in the church's evangelization mission yet do not meet the standards set by ecclesiastical offices to be recognized as ministers.

> Insight 1: The conversation about the vocation to lay ecclesial ministry must begin with an affirmation of our baptismal calling in the church and how such calling is actualized in distinct yet intimately related ways as part of the church's one mission: evangelization.

Insight 2: When addressing issues related to the vocation to lay ecclesial ministry—and to ordained ministry—it is important to affirm
the possibility of vocations to particular ministries: a call within
the call.

Insight 3: Many lay ecclesial ministers serve the church as professionals in a particular field besides ministry or theology (e.g., education, counseling, social work, management). While the ecclesial
community is the appropriate body to recognize the authenticity of
the specific vocation to ministry, there must be sufficient dialogue
with the professions to determine competencies.

Insight 4: Reflections on lay ecclesial ministry must consider the
ministerial (see note 5) and professional dimensions of this vocation as well as the various possible perceptions/understandings
of these dimensions by different communities within the church.

Insight 5: The definition of the vocation of the lay ecclesial minister
must take into consideration the multiple realms within which this
person's life unfolds. The lay ecclesial minister is often required
to be accountable to several vocations within the church: family,
ministry, profession.

Lessons and Insights about Authorization

Catholic DREs from the very beginning had clarity about the hierarchical organization of the church and the role of the DRE was rarely defined
as antagonistic to that of the clergy. Furthermore, the Second Vatican
Council provided a truly dynamic language and a new framework to talk
about the various members of the people of God in advancing the mission
of the church.[47] All laity and clergy are members of the same people of
God and all participate in the church's mission with the gifts (charisms)
received from the abundance of the Holy Spirit (cf. LG 12).

The language of authorization evolved in the midst of the tensions
that emerged in defining the identity of the DRE: a minister, a professional, both? The understanding of authorization would depend on
where one stood in this conversation. If the DRE was defined primarily
as a minister, then authorization and supervision came from ecclesiastical sources. If the DRE was defined primarily as a professional, then the
person needed to meet the standards of the profession and find his or her
place in the life of the church. More often than not, Catholic DREs found
themselves inquiring about whether there was actually a profession, a
question that Protestant DREs had been considering for more than half
a century, and whether the church was prepared to embrace the work of

professionals who did not explicitly identify themselves as ministers but were fully committed—in terms of time, skills, and resources—to advancing the church's educational mission. If DREs had the freedom to choose whether to be ministers or professionals or both, a new set of questions needed to be addressed: were the DREs authorized as individuals who could change locations and choose the extent of their work according to their professional (or ministerial) interests? Was the authorization of the DREs valid only within the context of a particular faith community? This further raised questions about the length of the authorization: permanent or temporal? How would temporality be determined?

Insight 1: The authorization of ministers in the life of the church is rooted in the nature of the mission that they share as coworkers rather than in a multilevel transfer of power.

Insight 2: The role of the DRE is intimately related to the church's evangelizing mission and thus possesses a communal dimension. Such communal dimension does not suppress the individual identity of the DRE as a professional (professional minister or professional educator or both) but affirms it in ways that allows it to flourish in the context of the life of the church.

Insight 3: The church in the twenty-first century must continue to reflect about the development of structures of authorization for baptized lay professional women and men participating in the church's educational ministry, particularly in contexts when such service is not defined in ministerial terms.

Insight 4: Religious educators/catechists serving ministerially in the church should be appropriately installed. On the one hand, it is possible to envision a somewhat universal ritual of installation for these ministers such as in the case of lectors and acolytes, which would provide a sense of unity and official recognition—and a more unified theological reflection about this ministry. On the other hand, we must remain attentive to those particular churches that have already developed rituals of installation and commissioning of catechetical ministers and the reflections that have led them to such development.[48]

Insight 5: We need more theological and pastoral reflection about installed ministries for laypersons professionally/ministerially involved in the church's evangelizing mission who are not on the path to ordained priesthood. This is an urgent task given the flourishing of lay ecclesial ministry in the United States.

Insight 6: The early discussions about professionalism among DREs were helpful to ponder about issues of authorization of the DRE as a minister and/or a professional. Theologians and religious educators have a unique opportunity to return to these conversations now in light of recent developments about lay ecclesial ministry.

Insight 7: Further research and reflection must explore the reality of DREs and laypeople who do not meet standards of professionalism established by local churches, faith communities, and centers of formation yet are doing work equivalent to that of officially recognized lay ecclesial ministers. How does the church acknowledge their contributions to the mission of evangelization? *Co-Workers in the Vineyard of the Lord* speaks of professional competence (5, 12) and professional skills (56). What is the context in which our ecclesial communities define professionalism? Our church must draw from her prophetic and pastoral tradition to affirm the role of those who collaborate in the work of lay ecclesial ministry but presently do not qualify to be recognized as such.

The first two decades of reflection about the Catholic DRE yielded rich insights about issues related to the vocation and authorization of this specialized lay ecclesial ministry. The key catalyst in the conversation was the question of professionalization. In the subsequent decades the intensity of the conversation significantly faded. Many parishes fortunately still count on the presence of professional DREs whose training and experience continue to enrich the church's educational mission. However, parishes are increasingly hiring DREs with limited formation in the fields of education and theology. How does their presence and work shape the conversation about professionalism? In many communities laypeople who are not professionally recognized lead educational initiatives that are vital for the evangelizing mission of the church. Are they also lay ecclesial ministers? If not, how can the church recognize and affirm their pastoral work? Focusing on the particularity of specific ministries gives us the opportunity to ask these questions.

In many communities pastoral associates are responsible for tasks previously overseen by DREs; a growing body of general pastoral ministers is assuming the tasks performed by DREs and pastoral associates, including complex administrative responsibilities. Since most of these ecclesial leaders are laypeople, this reality points to a rapid evolution of lay ecclesial ministry in the United States. At the same time we are confronted with two challenges. On the one hand, many questions related to specific ministerial/professional roles in the church such as the DRE remain unaddressed.[49] The lack of further reflection on these questions and concerns weakens their impact in the evangelizing mission of the church. On the other hand, the accumulation of undifferentiated responsibilities among lay ecclesial ministers poses the risk of this body of pastoral agents becoming "jacks-of-all-trades." The conversation about vocation and authorization of lay ecclesial ministers will significantly depend on how we address these two challenges.

Conclusion

Let us return to our friends at the beginning of this essay, Christina, the Gomezes, and Fr. Wilson. They represent three bodies of ecclesial leaders who will always be present in our faith communities. We can agree that all of them are directly involved in the church's educational mission in some ministerial capacity. We can also agree that they are living their baptismal identities, each in a particular way. We could even say that all serve their faith communities at some level of professionalism.

The previous analysis places us in a better position to reflect about Christina's identity as a DRE. Based on the brief vignette, we can infer that she meets the criteria of a professional religious educator and that she defines her service in the church in ministerial terms. She knows that she has a vocation; she understands her role in the church and the importance of her ministry and her three-year contract in the new parish is what we could call a "visible" sign of her authorization.

The reflection is less helpful when we think of Fr. Wilson. Matters of vocation and authorization in his case are mostly addressed from the perspective of his ordained priesthood. His service in the church as a religious educator flows from his vocation and authorization as an ordained priest.

The Gomezes are in some sort of a "ministerial limbo." Their pastoral service in the church reveals a commitment that is evidently beyond regular expressions of apostolic life to which every Christian is called (cf. AA 2–4), but they are not explicitly authorized as ministers by an ecclesial authority. Nevertheless, they enjoy the recognition and affirmation of the community in which they serve and the tacit approval of the pastor of their parish who is pleased with their work as volunteers. According to the literature on lay ecclesial ministry and that on the identity of the DRE, they are neither *ecclesial ministers* nor *professional religious educators*. What are they?

The above analysis offers us a twofold challenge as we continue to study the theology and praxis of lay ecclesial ministry in the twenty-first century. On the one hand, it is imperative that we return to those questions that are unique to each particular ministry performed by women and men identified as lay ecclesial ministers and as professionals in ministry. The more clarity we have about those questions and concerns, the better we can address issues of vocation and authorization. On the other hand, we need further clarity about the vocation and authorization of laywomen and laymen who are considered neither lay ecclesial ministers nor professionals in ministry, yet their service to the church's evangelizing mission closely mirrors that of the people called ministers.

Notes

1. These vignettes draw from real situations observed by the author in different contexts throughout the country. Names of persons and institutions are fictional.

2. The length of assignments of lay ecclesial ministers and other professionals involved in ministry in the church is regularly defined by a temporary contract. *Co-Workers in the Vineyard of the Lord* suggests, "When a lay ecclesial minister enters the service of the Church, it is often hoped that they will continue in such service over time. As pastors change, these lay ecclesial ministers can both offer support to the departing pastor and help to orient the new pastor and assist him and the people of the parish in building new relationships. *It may be desirable in some situations that the term of a lay ecclesial minister conclude, even if subject to renewal, when the pastor's term of office comes to an end*" (USCCB, *Co-Workers in the Vineyard of the Lord: A Resource for Guiding the Development of Lay Ecclesial Ministry* [Washington, DC: USCCB Publishing, 2005], 64, my emphasis).

3. Cf. *Code of Canon Law*, c. 757. John P. Beal, James A. Coriden, and Thomas J. Green, eds., *New Commentary on the Code of Canon Law* (New York: Paulist Press, 2000).

4. "The special role in the diocesan catechetical mission that [priests] exercise arises directly from the Sacrament of Holy Orders, which constitutes priests as educators in the faith" (*National Directory for Catechesis* [USCCB, 2005], 221–22). See also Congregation for the Clergy, *General Directory for Catechesis* (USCCB, 1997), n. 224.

5. Thomas F. O'Meara, *Theology of Ministry*, revised ed. (New York: Paulist Press, 1999), 150, original italics.

6. Dorothy Jean Furnish, *DRE/DCE: The History of a Profession* (Nashville, TN: Christian Educators Fellowship, 1976), 19.

7. For a helpful history of the Sunday School movement, see Robert Lynn and Elliot Wright, *The Big Little School —200 Years of Sunday School* (Birmingham, AL: Religious Education Press, 1971).

8. Cf. Furnish, *DRE/DCE*, 16.

9. According to Dorothy Jean Furnish, a "1926 survey showed that 51 percent of the DRE's had had previous salaried teaching experience, and 30 percent had had previous salaried supervisory experience, while only 27 percent came from experience in 'the ministry' " (Furnish, *DRE/DCE*, 19).

10. In 1914 the constitution of the Association of Church Directors of Religious Education indicated that "to be an active member, a director was required to have had a four years' college course or its equivalent plus a full three years' theological course in a seminary, with a course in religious education; or in addition to the college course, two years of study in an approved School of Religious Pedagogy" (ibid., 34).

11. Ibid.

12. Norman E. Richardson, *Religious Education As a Vocation: Occasional Papers*, XX, n. 1 (Chicago, IL: Northwestern University, 1920), 20. Cited in Furnish, *DRE/DCE*, 37.

13. Cf. Edna Baxter, "The Parish Minister of Christian Education," in *Religious Education* 4, n. 4 (July–August 1959): 343.

14. Cf. Furnish, *DRE/DCE*, 78.

15. Cf. ibid., 38.

16. Cf. ibid., 83.

17. Cf. ibid., 60.

18. Cf. ibid., 84–85.

19. Louise McComb, *D.C.E.: A Challenging Career in Christian Education* (Richmond: John Knox Press, 1963), 12. Cited in Furnish, *DRE/DCE*, 92.

20. See, for instance, Jack L. Seymour and Donald E. Miller, *Contemporary Approaches to Christian Education* (Nashville, TN: Abingdon Press, 1982).

21. Such seems to be the main idea behind Donald G. Elmer's book *Revisioning the DRE* (Birmingham, AL: Religious Education Press, 1989).

22. Furnish, *DRE/DCE*, 75.

23. Cf. Joseph C. Neiman, *Coordinators: A New Focus in Parish Religious Education* (Winona, MN: St. Mary's College Press, 1971), 49.

24. The word professional means commitment. Thomas O'Meara argues that *professional ministry* is service that requires preparation, long-term commitment, and institutional recognition. Cf. O'Meara, *Theology of Ministry*, 185.

25. Cf. Paul VI, "Ministeria Quaedam," *Acta Apostolicae Sedis* 64 (1972): 529–34. See also Edward P. Hahnenberg, *Ministries: A Relational Approach* (New York: Crossroad Publishing, 2003), 183–93.

26. In 1973 the US Bishops' Conference moved toward the establishment of the ministry of religious education for laypeople—as well as the ministry of music—but no permission has been granted from Rome. Cf. Alan F. Blakley, "Decree

on the Apostolate of Lay People," in *Vatican II and Its Documents: An American Reappraisal*, ed. Timothy E. O'Connell (Wilmington, DE: Michael Glazier, 1986), 155. Only the ministries of lector and acolyte have been recognized as officially installed ministries for laymen, mainly as part of the process of formation toward the reception of the sacrament of holy orders.

27. Mary Charles Bryce cites these characteristics building on the work of Bishop Jan Van Cauwelaert. Cf. Mary Charles Bryce, "The Status and Installation of Catechists," in *The Living Light* 10 (Spring 1973): 130–31.

28. Cf. Berard L. Marthaler, "Ministry of a DRE?," in *The Living Light* 14 (Winter 1977): 512–15.

29. Ibid., 518.

30. Cf. Bryce, "Status and Installation of Catechists," 131–32. See also Marthaler, "Ministry of a DRE?," 518.

31. Cf. Marthaler, "Ministry of a DRE?," 513.

32. Ibid.

33. Cf. Bryce, "Status and Installation of Catechists," 133–35.

34. The 1971 *General Catechetical Directory* distinguished four forms of the ministry of the Word: evangelization or missionary preaching, catechetical, liturgical, and theological. Cf. GCD 17. The 1997 *General Directory for Catechesis* defines these forms also as functions of the ministry of the Word and names them in this way: announcement or missionary preaching, pre- and post-baptismal catechesis, liturgical, and theological. The Directory further asserts that these forms often assume more than one function, thus highlighting their interrelated character. Cf. GDC 52.

35. "NCDD Statement on the DREs," *The Living Light* 17, n. 1 (Fall 1980): 247.

36. Cf. Stephen Nevin, "Parish Coordinator: Evaluating Task and Roles," *The Living Light* 9, n. 1 (Spring 1972): 48–56. Cited in Maria Harris, *The D.R.E. Book: Questions and Strategies for Parish Personnel* (New York: Paulist Press, 1976), 3.

37. Cf. Kieran Scott, "The Director of Religious Education and Professionalization," *PACE* 14 (1983): 3.

38. Cf. Harris, *D.R.E. Book*, 32.

39. For a good analysis of the issue of DREs and professionalization, see Scott, "Director of Religious Education and Professionalization."

40. Cf. Harris, *D.R.E. Book*, 189.

41. Cf. Scott, "Director of Religious Education and Professionalization," 5.

42. Maria Harris, "DREs in the U.S.: The First Twenty Years," *The Living Light* 17, n. 1 (Fall 1980): 258. See also Harris, *D.R.E. Book*, 120.

43. Cf. ibid., 258.

44. In 2005, 41.5 percent of those identified as lay ecclesial ministers worked specifically as religious educators. Cf. David DeLambo, *Lay Parish Ministers: A Study of Emerging Leadership* (New York: National Pastoral Life Center, 2005), 22. However, the same study indicates that the second largest category of lay ecclesial ministers, namely, general pastoral ministers, are highly responsible

for educational tasks: 48 percent are involved in the catechumenate (RCIA), 47 percent work in adult religious education, and 35.5 percent are engaged in sacramental preparation. Cf. DeLambo, 90.

45. On the idea of a positive theology of the laity at the Second Vatican Council and the theological movements leading to this perspective, see Edward P. Hahnenberg, *Awakening Vocation: A Theology of Christian Call* (Collegeville, MN: Liturgical Press, 2010), 34–44.

46. Such is the assumption in the three largest studies about lay ecclesial ministers in the United States: DeLambo, *Lay Parish Ministers* (2005); Philip J. Murnion and David DeLambo, *Parishes and Parish Ministers* (New York: National Pastoral Life Center, 1999); Philip J. Murnion, David DeLambo, Rosemary Dilli, and Harry A. Fagan, *New Parish Ministers: Laity and Religious on Parish Staffs* (New York: National Pastoral Life Center, 1992).

47. *Lumen Gentium* beautifully refers to all the baptized as members of the people of God participating, though each according to the call received, in Christ's priestly, prophetic, and kingly ministry (LG 9–13).

48. In 2008 the archbishop of Mexico, Cardinal Norberto Rivera Carrera, officially instituted the permanent ministry of catechist in his archdiocese. He invoked the power given to him by the Code of Canon Law, c. 157: "Unless the law explicitly establishes otherwise, it is for the diocesan bishop to provide for ecclesiastical offices in his own particular church by free conferral." He approved *ad experimentum* for a period of five years the requirements for laypeople to receive this ministry. Some of these requirements include the following: to be baptized and confirmed; to be at least sixteen years old; to have received formal catechetical training for at least three years; the candidate will put in writing to the bishop or the episcopal vicar the intention to receive this ministry; the catechist will indicate whether he or she wants to exercise this ministry for one, two, or three years and in what area of catechesis he or she hopes to serve; a formal file will be opened in the catechist's parish, which will become a permanent record. More information about this experience is at http://www.vicariadepastoral. org.mx/proyectos /7a_semana/hojas/7_semana_04.htm (web site in Spanish). It is too early to assess the impact of this decision. However, the institution of the permanent ministry of catechist in this particular church has become an opportunity to reflect about the wider issue of lay ecclesial ministry in the church in Mexico. I am grateful to Rev. Eduardo Mercado Guzmán, director of the Catechetical Commission of the Archdiocese of Mexico, for sharing with me some observations and resources about this initiative.

The experience in the Archdiocese of Mexico is deeply rooted in the reflections and recommendations of the *General Directory for Catechesis* on the vocation to the ministry of catechesis and the need for this ministry to be permanent in the particular church:

> The vocation of the laity to catechesis springs from the sacrament of Baptism.
> It is strengthened by the sacrament of Confirmation. Through the sacraments

of Baptism and Confirmation they participate in the "priestly, prophetic and kingly ministry of Christ." In addition to the common vocation of the apostolate, some lay people feel called interiorly by God to assume the service of catechist. The Church awakens and discerns this divine vocation and confers the mission to catechize. The Lord Jesus invites men and women, in a special way, to follow him, teacher and formator of disciples. This personal call of Jesus Christ and its relationship to him are the true moving forces of catechetical activity. "From this loving knowledge of Christ springs the desire to proclaim him, to 'evangelize,' and to lead others to the 'Yes' of faith in Jesus Christ." To feel called to be a catechist and to receive this mission from the Church acquires different levels of dedication in accordance with the particular characteristics of individuals. At times the catechist can collaborate in the service of catechesis over a limited period or purely on an occasional basis, but it is always a valuable service and a worthy collaboration. The importance of the ministry of catechesis, however, would suggest that there should be in a Diocese a certain number of religious and laity publicly recognized and permanently dedicated to catechesis who, in communion with the priests and the Bishop, give to this diocesan service that ecclesial form which is proper to it. (GDC 231)

49. For instance, should we take for granted that the DRE is a minister? What kind of academic formation must the DRE have? What kind of theological and ministerial formation must the DRE have? In what ways does the DRE belong to a profession? Does that profession actually exist? What is the role of the DRE in the ecclesial community vis-à-vis clergy and lay ecclesial ministers? How does the DRE further the church's ministry of the Word in today's context? What competencies are demanded of DREs working in culturally diverse contexts?

Part III

Authorization of
Lay Ecclesial Ministers

Chapter 6

A Theology of Authorization of Lay Ecclesial Ministers

Susan K. Wood, SCL

What Is Authorization?

Authorization is one of several elements that characterize lay ecclesial ministry, namely, (1) a personal call; (2) ecclesial discernment and recognition of a genuine charism; (3) formation, possibly requiring significant education, appropriate to the demands of the ministry; (4) ecclesial authorization; and (5) some liturgical ritualization of assuming this ministry.

Co-Workers in the Vineyard of the Lord defines authorization as "the process by which properly prepared lay men and women are given responsibilities for ecclesial ministry by competent church authority."[1] Authorization, then, is the act of giving someone a mission to perform a ministry in the name of the church. The key elements to explore within the definition of authorization are (1) the source of authorization, (2) the mission implied in authorization, and (3) what it means for a lay ecclesial minister to serve "in the name of the church."

This essay is an effort to determine when and what kinds of hierarchical authorization are needed to exercise certain types of ministry in the name of the church. It also explores the relationship between authorization and the other components of lay ecclesial ministry and places authorization within the theological context of the communion of the church.

Vocation, occurring as the first of the above elements, is related to authorization, one of the last of the elements, in the following manner. The

discernment for lay ecclesial ministry requires the participation of the ecclesial community since it is in their name that ministry is given. Necessary
components of vocational discernment include personal qualities such as
human development and maturity, professional and academic preparation,
ministerial skills, and ecclesial identity demonstrated by participation in
the communal and sacramental life of the church. The community tests
the personal discernment of the individual to ascertain that the personal
desire for ministry is accompanied by the appropriate human and spiritual characteristics essential for this public service and that the individual
has acquired the necessary formation and education to be an effective lay
ecclesial minister. Thus vocation to lay ecclesial ministry has both a personal
and an ecclesial dimension. A person must be called by both God and the
ecclesial community. These are not two separate calls unrelated to each
other, for God calls through the discernment of the community. It may be
that a person falsely mistakes a personal call to a more intense Christian
discipleship and service for a vocation to lay ecclesial ministry. Communal
participation in vocational discernment helps to sort out these various calls.
The authorization by the bishop or the commissioning pastor or minister
represents the ratification that this communal discernment has occurred.
When authorization is ritualized in a context of prayer, this emphasizes
the spiritual dimensions of ministry at the same time that the relationship
between the lay ecclesial minister, the community gathered in prayer, and
the authorizing minister becomes visible to all present.

A theology of authorization requires that lay ecclesial ministry be
distinguished from other kinds of service or discipleship in the church.
The lay ecclesial minister generally exercises leadership responsibility
for some area of ministry, usually within a relationship of coordination
and direction of others in the community. Lay ecclesial ministry is also
stable, extending over a significant period of time, rather than an occasional service in the church.[2] These characteristics will be important
when we examine several case studies of ministry to determine whether
they are, in fact, lay ecclesial ministries. We will also see that the level
of authorization does not necessarily correspond with whether or not a
given ministry is, in fact, a lay ecclesial ministry.

What Does Authorization Confer?

The Ability to Minister "in the Name of the Church"

Authorization confers the ability to minister as a representative of
the church so that the ministry rendered is the church's ministry rather

than the ministry of an individual member of the church. While it is true that the church is the people of God and not just the hierarchy, the ministry of an ecclesial lay minister represents the whole people of God or the people of God of a particular diocese or parish and not just an individual Christian. This topic will be discussed in more detail later in the essay where it is argued that "ministry in the name of the church" is a more helpful descriptive of lay ecclesial ministry than "public" as opposed to "private" ministry.

A Mandate for Service in a Particular Place and for a Particular Duration of Time

Authorization can also be said to confer the mandate to serve particular people in a particular place for a particular duration of time. Authorization entrusts to the laity a specific task in the church. These may range from various ministries to ecclesiastical offices.[3] Examples of the latter include such specific positions as diocesan chancellor, tribunal judge, or finance officer. A person may graduate from a school of theology or complete a lay formation certificate, but this person is unable to exercise ministry for a particular portion of the people of God without authorization. This precise service constitutes a true responsibility recognized by the local church and is for specific duration, although this duration may be renewable. Arguably, the *power* of lay ministry lies in the ecclesial status, graces, and charisms received sacramentally in baptism and confirmation, while the *exercise* of these charisms in certain ecclesial situations is ecclesially authorized by commissioning, appointment, or installation.

A Relationship of Communion with the Bishop and Local Pastor and, through Them, with the Church

Authorization establishes a relationship of communion with the bishop and local pastor. Communion has been a dominant image of the church since the Final Report of the Extraordinary Synod of Bishops in 1985 stated, "The ecclesiology of communion is the central and fundamental idea of the Council's documents."[4] The dimensions of communion are threefold: communion with the apostolic past, the essence of the apostolicity of the church; communion within the parish, diocese, or universal church; and communion among these levels of ecclesiality. Each level is served by an ordained minister responsible for communion within that level—the pastor for the parish, the bishop for the diocese, and the Bishop of Rome for the universal church. Communion among these levels is represented and facilitated by communion among the ministers serving them.

The category of communion as a descriptor of the church implies that the church is fundamentally relational. A parish cannot exist apart from the diocese, and the diocese must be in communion with the universal church through hierarchical communion with the Bishop of Rome. No local church exists in isolation but only in communion with other churches. There is absolute interdependence among all the churches as there is among the members of the churches.

Within the church diversity is coordinated within unity through a ministry of unity exercising authority as a part of the community, not standing above the community as a self-contained isolated authority. Authority in the church is personal, communal, and collegial. The ordained ministers exercising authority in the church are selected through ecclesial discernment and authorized through prayer to the Holy Spirit and the laying on of hands. They exercise authority in the church in a relational manner. This collegiality is embodied in the college of presbyters and the college of bishops. Lay ministers participate in this relational ministry by being in communion with the ordained ministers responsible for communion and by cultivating collegial relationships with their co-workers, both lay and ordained.

A ministerial principle corresponds to the relational character of the church. Ministry serves the communion of the church and contributes toward building it up. No minister functions in isolation but only in communion with other ministers. Thus lay ecclesial ministers must be in communion with other lay ministers, their pastor, their bishop, and with the Bishop of Rome. Obstacles to this ministerial principle include the phenomenon of fiefdoms and lone rangers where ministers protect their turf and work in isolation rather than collaborate with other ministers, disengagement from official church teaching or from presence to a faith community, and compartmentalization where a minister's personal life is in dissonance with that person's public ministerial identity. All these violate the ministerial principle of communion.

Authorization creates a bond of communion between the authorizer and the minister and empowers the minister to actually engage in the ministry over which the authorizer exercises oversight. This is why the local church, not the formation program or school that educates the lay ecclesial minister, is the proper agent of authorization. Authorization is an ecclesial act distinct from preparation and certification. Lay ministry preparation (education and formation), certification (testimony that the minister has achieved a certain level of competency and has met certain standards), and authorization (ecclesial appointment) are distinct processes and can be done by different individuals or groups. For instance, a school may prepare, a professional organization may certify, and a bishop may authorize. Authorization establishes an ecclesial relationship, although, unfortunately, a letter of appointment, a form of authorization, may not be seen as creating an ecclesial relationship either by the person hiring a lay ecclesial ministry for a "job" or by the person being hired.

Accountability to Church Authority and the People Served

Authorization establishes lines of responsibility and accountability within the organizational life of the church. The bishops and their assistants, the priests, have the responsibility of discerning, judging, and ordering the charisms given by the Spirit and consequently ordering and coordinating the various ministries and apostolates of the laity (AA 23–24; LG 32). From the perspective of the ministry, the new set of roles and responsibility of lay ecclesial ministry require ecclesial authorization and coordination. From the perspective of the minister, the lay ecclesial minister needs to be acknowledged, affirmed, and supported through public recognition and clarity about their rights and responsibilities.

Even though lay ecclesial ministers are accountable to the person who authorizes, he or she is also accountable to those who receive ministry. Thus authorization is not simply a way to ensure accountability to one's employer or superiors or to church authority. Assurance through authorization is one form of accountability to those who receive ministry so that they know that the church is ministering to them through this person and that this minister has the prerequisite qualifications for ministry and is in communion with the church.

Lay Ecclesial Ministry as Distinguished from Christian Service of All the Baptized

Lay ecclesial ministry, the responsibility of only some of the baptized, must also be differentiated from Christian service and discipleship, which is the co-responsibility of all the baptized.[5] All the baptized are incorporated into Christ and the church, his ecclesial body. United to Christ, they participate in his triple function as priest, prophet, and king and thus share in the mission of the entire body within an organized and differentiated participation or communion. All are co-responsible for proclaiming the Gospel according to the vocation and charisms proper to each one. In this sense, the church is entirely ministerial.[6] This is the coresponsibility of all the baptized, who exercise this ministry by virtue of their baptismal faith and the charisms they have received. However, within this common responsibility for service and discipleship of all the baptized, some are called and authorized for a ministry in the name of all the others, to act in the name of the church as a whole, and not just under their own responsibilities.

The Source of Authorization

The etymological root of the word "authorization," as also the word "authority," is "author," indicating the source from which the mission arises. The source of all mission and ministry in the church is the triune God. The Decree on the Church's Missionary Activity from Vatican II situates the missionary identity of the church in its origin in the mission of the Son and the Spirit within the Trinity (*Ad Gentes* 2; see also *Co-Workers*, 17–18). Since the church by its very nature is missionary, lay ecclesial ministers, by the very fact of being *ecclesial* ministers, are required to also be missionary. That means the lay ecclesial minister is sent by the Son and empowered by the Spirit to do the work of the church in continuing the mission of Christ in the world.

The sacramental source of this mission is baptism as the foundation or font of mission and ministry. Baptism is administered in the name of Father, Son, and Spirit. By assuming the identity of Christian in baptism, one assumes responsibility for continuing the mission of Christ in bringing about the reign of God. The anointing with chrism at baptism is a sign of the identity of the baptized as priests, prophets, and kings and brings with it the responsibility for helping sanctify the world, witness to faith through word and life, and work for the reign of God. While all Christians have this responsibility, the lay ecclesial minister does not just engage in these activities as an individual Christian but does them "in the name of the church" in such a way that his or her ministry is an instrument for the church carrying out its mission corporately.

Concerning lay ecclesial ministry, the question is whether lay ecclesial ministers receive their authorization from their sacramental reception of baptism and confirmation, or whether their authorization by the bishop is juridically received as a participation in his ministry, which finds its sacramental basis in his sacramental ordination. As we will see below, the answer to this question depends on the particular ministry. Some tasks undertaken by lay ecclesial ministers are proper to the laity (e.g., directors of youth ministry, directors of religious education) while other tasks belong properly to the ordained (e.g., celebrating baptisms, witnessing marriages, pastoral responsibility for parishes).

Authorization may take various forms depending on the stability and ecclesial validation that accompanies the ministry, the person who authorizes, and whether the authorization is accompanied by a ritual within a prayer service or liturgy, or is a letter of appointment.

The Mission Implied in Authorization

The word "mission" means a "sending out." One never sends oneself; one is sent. Authorization is the source of that sending. To speak of authorization is to speak of the source of the authority of one who is sent. As we have seen, this source is trinitarian in the missions of the Son and the Spirit, sacramental in the sacraments of baptism and confirmation, and ecclesial in the authority of the bishop or his representative. We are baptized into the mission of the church.[7] This mission is not something added on to the church but the very reason for the church's existence as "the expression and fulfillment of God's love for the world."[8] The church begins with Jesus gathering a community of followers to continue his mission to serve, proclaim, and realize the reign of God with the empowerment of the Spirit. The Pastoral Constitution on the Church in the Modern World proclaims, "Proceeding from the love of the eternal Father, the church was founded by Christ in time and gathered into one by the holy Spirit" (GS 40). According to the council, the church has a secular mission, the transformation of the world into the family of God (ibid.).

The recognition of the secular mission of the church is important in the context of this discussion of lay ecclesial ministry for two reasons. First, it demonstrates that ministry that contributes to the mission of the church is consonant with the secular character of the laity (see LG 31). Second, as Richard Gaillardetz notes, "the firm orientation of all the baptized as those bound together in a common mission . . . serves as a vital corrective against any tendency to allow practical distinctions between the church *ad intra* and the church *ad extra* to turn into a dichotomizing separation."[9] This is particularly important since it underscores the appropriateness of the laity serving the church *ad intra* as lay ecclesial ministers and, conversely, emphasizes that all church ministry, ordained and lay, is fundamentally oriented toward the church's mission to the world.

In France the document that offers hierarchical authorization to a lay ecclesial minister is called a *lettre de mission*, "letter of mission" or perhaps better rendered in English as "missioning letter," indicating that the person authorized is both sent and has a mission to perform. While there is no consistent term for the document that confers the hierarchical authorization, dioceses should at all costs avoid such terms as "letter of certification" since certification by professional organizations that standards and competencies have been met is different from hierarchical authorization, which is an ecclesial, not a professional, act. Preparation may be the work of a theological school and certification a function of a professional society, but authorization must always be an act of an official representative of the church. On the other hand, ecclesial authorization should indicate its richer theological meaning and not simply be the hiring of a lay ecclesial minister for a "job." Even though someone hired may receive a letter of appointment, a form of authorization, both the person hiring and the person being hired may not see this as creating an ecclesial relationship. The French term *lettre de mission* has the advantage of incorporating the language of mission, of implying that someone is being *sent* for the ministry of the church, and of invoking the trinitarian source of ministry, the missions of the Son and Spirit sent by the Father.

Ministry "in the Name of the Church"

In contradistinction from the "all" who are baptized and service the church out of the charisms of their baptism, there is the collaboration of the "some." These include the ordained, who are the sacrament of Christ the head, and those laypersons who have the required personal and spiritual qualities, who have the necessary theological and pastoral formation, and who are entrusted with offices and ecclesial charges that they exercise according to the law of the church. They are sent by the church to exercise their ministry "in the name of the church." The canonist Alphonse Borras explains the juridical meaning of "in the name of the church":

> The expression "in the name of the church" has a precise juridical meaning. First of all, it signifies that it is not only in his own name, as an individual, that the baptized acts. It signifies especially that the individual engages the Church *in another way*. Henceforth, it is no longer under his exclusive personal responsibility that he is engaged and that he engages the Church; it is with official support in an *authorized* manner.[10]

Borras finds the distinction between the co-responsibility of all and the collaboration of some to be critical. This distinction helps explain the title of the Vatican document On Certain Questions Regarding the Collaboration of the Non-Ordained Faithful in the Sacred Ministry of Priest,[11] although Bernard Sesboüé observes that the language of "collaboration" remains extrinsic and material compared to the language of "participation."[12] While this document wishes to avoid applying the name "minister" to laypersons and does not address the new ecclesial identity given to laypersons associated in a stable manner with pastoral ministry, it nevertheless still uses the term "ministry" for the ecclesial functions assumed by laypersons, noting that there are two kinds of ministry in the church, ordained ministries arising from ordination and baptismal ministries arising from Christian initiation and the universal priesthood.[13]

While the French literature speaks of authorization to minister "in the name of the church," the USCCB document *Co-Workers in the Vineyard of the Lord* instead says that lay ecclesial ministers "are authorized by ecclesiastical authorities to carry out certain ministerial responsibilities in public service of the local church" (54). This shift in language represents a change in the drafting process of the document. The fourth draft of the document had described authorization as "authorization of the hierarchy to act in the name of the Church." The sixth draft revised it to read "in the name of the local church." The seventh draft and final wording is "authorization of the hierarchy to serve publicly in the local church."[14]

One can only suppose that a possible reason for this change was to distance the description of lay ecclesial ministry from that of ordained ministry, which is "in the name of the church." However, there are undoubtedly times when a distinction between "private" and "public" ministry is not so clear, the first being the individual service required of all the baptized and the second the authorized service of some. For instance, an individual may sponsor a radio talk show or a television series with the purpose of evangelization. This is a very public activity on the part of that individual arising from various charisms received in baptism. However, unless this ministry is authorized "in the name of the church," it is not lay ecclesial ministry even if the director of the show exercises leadership in a relationship of supervision and coordination of others and the show is broadcast worldwide.

The essential and differentiating question should be, whose ministry is it? The answer for lay ecclesial ministry must be "the church's ministry." The issue is not whether the ministry is public or private, but whether it is ministry of an individual, exercised on the basis of his or her personal responsibility, or the ministry of the church. Authorization is a designation to engage in the ministry of the church through a relationship of communion with its ordained representative.

Nevertheless, ecclesial authorization involves more than simply issues of authority and governance. At root it is a question of identity. Identity answers the questions, Whose work is this, and who is present in this ministry? The answer must be, the church, for lay ecclesial ministry is performed "in the name of the church."

The research on this issue shows that episcopal conferences within different countries have developed a practice, language, and theology of lay ecclesial ministry independently of one another. This duplication of efforts, while providing for the particular needs of the local church in different cultural contexts, is not helpful in the long run since episcopal conferences have much to learn from one another.

Election and Reception of Lay Ecclesial Ministers

One aspect missing from this account of authorization is the role of election and reception by the community. The community, of course, exercises a role in an individual's discernment of a vocation to lay ecclesial ministry. Nevertheless, even once the vocation is discerned, there is an active role of reception and election without which authorization would seem to be a top-down hierarchical action divorced from the life of the community. Worse yet, it could be conceived as an arbitrary imposition of a lay ecclesial minister on a particular community.

The need for a reciprocal action on the part of the community that corresponds to the act of authorization was evident in the discussion of authorization at the 2011 Collegeville National Symposium on Lay Ecclesial Ministry. The Hispanic community, in particular, spoke of the role of their communities in the designation of lay ecclesial ministers. Because of the network of close relationships, it was inconceivable to them that a person outside this network of relationships would simply be dropped into their midst. Initially they proposed that the community authorizes its lay ecclesial minister. However, the problem with this model "from below" is that such an action on the part of the community does not create a bond of communion with the pastor or bishop. A need exists for both hierarchical communion and communion with the people served.

Further conversation suggested that authorization as described in this essay would work if it were accompanied by an act of reception on the part of the community. This would seem to involve some kind of participation of the community in the selection of an individual for service to that community. This is analogous to the process or rite of election in ordained ministry. In the *Apostolic Constitutions*,[15] for example, the election of a bishop by the entire people preceded his ordination. The people presented a candidate for ordination. Election by a church, however, was never sufficient, for one was only consecrated bishop through the ordination rite. This election of a candidate for ordination "was understood as the means by which God's choice of a person for a particular ecclesiastical office was discerned and made manifest."[16] Today we do not practice this tradition of election in the church, although vestiges remain in the rite of ordination and in the practice of discerning the vocation and aptitude of seminarians throughout their preparation for ordination.

Authorization of lay ecclesial ministers and ordination are not the same thing, although both are ecclesial acts. Nevertheless, the history of ordination rites gives us an insight into the reciprocal character of the selection and designation of an individual for ecclesial service. The community does not authorize a lay ecclesial minister, but this does not prevent it from presenting a candidate to the bishop or his representative for authorization or from formally receiving this individual once authorized. Both the presentation for authorization and the reception of the lay ecclesial minister can be ritualized in a para-liturgical ceremony as described by Zeni Fox in this volume of essays. It is possible for a community to work out a discernment process by which it can identify candidates for authorization. This process of identification of candidates and the reception of authorized lay ecclesial ministers requires good communication between the bishop or his delegate and the community.

Questions of Ministerial Identity and Authorization: Various Case Studies

Within the variety of services and ministries within the church today, several questions help sort out what constitutes a lay ecclesial minister and the variety of possible authorizations provided various ministries. The key questions are as follows: Is the ministry a lay ecclesial ministry within the present operative definition? Does this ministry exercise leadership responsibility for some area of ministry, usually within a relationship of coordination and direction of others in the community? Is this a stable ministry or an occasional service? Is there official ecclesial authorization by the bishop or his representative? Is this service in the name of the church? Three cases studies will show significant variations in how these criteria interrelate.

Case Study #1: Installed Ministries of Lector and Acolyte Compared with Other Lectors and Extraordinary Ministers of Communion

Authorization does not in and of itself make an activity a lay ecclesial ministry. Lectors and acolytes provide a good example of ministers that may receive two kinds of authorization for ministry, one installed and the other commissioned, when neither constitutes a *lay ecclesial ministry*.

Paul VI's apostolic letter *Ministeria Quaedam* (August 15, 1972) eliminated the minor orders preceding ordination and provided for the installation of laymen to the ministries of acolyte and lector, requiring these installed ministries for men ordained to the diaconate. Canon 230 implements *Ministeria Quaedam*, which eliminated the tonsure, the minor orders, and the subdiaconate from the Latin Church, and stipulates, "Lay men who possess the age and qualifications established by decree of the conference of bishops can be admitted on a stable basis through the prescribed liturgical rite to the ministries of lector and acolyte." The bishop presides over the rite of installation, which is a liturgical service. However, in the United States the same *function* is most often exercised by lectors and acolytes who are laypeople who are not installed in these ministries and who may or may not even be formally commissioned for them by the pastor. Thus the *installed* ministries, which are also lay ministries, receive a very high level of authorization (by a bishop at a liturgical rite) compared to the service of the vast majority of lectors and acolytes in a typical parish (possibly commissioned by a pastor, but not always or necessarily, in a para-liturgical rite, if any).

Neither are the installed ministers clerics, although in practice they continue to be steps toward admission to the diaconate or priesthood. They are ordinary ministers, not extraordinary ministers. The authorization is through installation. The form of installation is a liturgical rite presided over by the appropriate bishop or major superior of a clerical religious institute or society of apostolic life. Installed lectors and acolytes acquire a stability in ministry that extends beyond a particular liturgical celebration. Thus an installed minister may change from one parish or community to the next without needing an additional installation ceremony.

Installed ministries have not been widely implemented, possibly due to the fact that they are restricted to men. Canon 230 §3 makes provision for these ministries to be supplied by other laypersons: "When the need of the Church warrants it and ministers are lacking, lay persons, even if they are not lectors or acolytes, can also supply certain of their duties, namely to exercise the ministry of the word, to preside over liturgical prayers, to confer baptism, and to distribute Holy communion, according to the prescripts of the law."[17] This provision is not restricted to men. In distinction from extraordinary eucharistic ministers, lay lectors are not generally considered to be extraordinary, although canon 230 §2 states that laypersons can fulfill the function of lector in liturgical actions by temporary designation.[18] *Ministeria Quaedam* allowed episcopal conferences to request the installation of laity in other ministries, but despite a preliminary request for two formally instituted lay ministries appropriate to the US context, none were eventually established.[19]

Neither the installed ministries of acolyte and lector nor the ministry of other acolytes and lectors would be identified as lay ecclesial ministries insofar as these people do not exercise leadership for an area of ministry within a relationship of coordination and direction of others in the community. It is no small wonder, then, why there may be confusion regarding not only the identity of lay ecclesial ministers but also the various kinds of authorization they receive!

Case Study #2: Lay Ecclesial Ministry as Extraordinary Ministry Supplying for the Lack of a Sufficient Number of Ordained Clergy

A special instance of lay ecclesial ministry is those that supply for the lack of a sufficient number of clergy such as parish life coordinators who assume the direct pastoral care of a community in the absence of a resident pastor under the directives of canon 517 §2.[20] Parish life coordinators provide a ministry that is considered to be extraordinary and temporary since the norm is for an ordained priest to provide the pastoral care of a parish.[21] A parish life coordinator exercises a ministry that differs from many other lay ecclesial ministries in that this ministry may also be an office.[22]

In the case of parish life coordinators, those persons appointed to direct the pastoral care of a community under the provision of canon 517 §2, the ministry is a participation in the ministry of the bishop, analogous to a priest making the bishop present and undertaking his duties and concerns in the individual local congregations of the faithful that they serve (see LG 28). In this it differs from those ministries that properly belong to a layperson by virtue of baptism. Even when this ministry is performed by priests, priests are identified as "prudent cooperators of the episcopal college and its support and instrument," who make the bishop present in a sense in each local assembly of the faithful (ibid.). Although all lay ministry necessarily arises from baptism, the fact that this ministry is closely related to the ministry of the bishop, the ministry assumed by parish life coordinators cannot be founded on baptism *alone* but is a status received on account of having been missioned. That is, the *powers* of this ministry arise from baptism, but the *exercise* of this ministry is the result of having been missioned.[23] Parish life coordinators are by this fact cooperators of bishops, alongside of priests.[24] Those sacramental functions beyond the powers provided by baptism, such as confection of the Eucharist or the absolution of sins, are beyond the powers of lay parish life coordinators because these powers must arise from the sacrament of ordination, not baptism.

Yet another argument for the identity of parish life coordinators as participators in episcopal ministry arises from the nature of the parish. A parish exists as a necessary unit in the hierarchical structure of the church given the fact that dioceses are too large to function as congregations. Because the church is a hierarchically constituted society (LG 20), the parish is also constituted hierarchically; an ordained pastor serves the unity of this ecclesial unit in hierarchical communion with other pastors in the presbyterium and with the bishop, who in turn is in communion with all the other bishops and the Bishop of Rome. Even when the pastoral care of souls in a parish is entrusted to a parish life coordinator, a priest, who through his sacrament of orders possesses the power to sacramentally represent the community in hierarchical communion with the bishop, is appointed to direct that pastoral care. This is a function of sacramental representation, not a function of practical pastoral leadership.

Since it is an anomaly for a parish to be without a resident pastor, parish life coordinators represent an extreme instance of an "extraordinary" minister. They exercise leadership that requires the coordination of others, minister out of a vocation that is ecclesially discerned, receive the appropriate formation and education for their tasks, and are authorized by the local bishop to assume these responsibilities. Although extraordinary, they exercise a true lay ecclesial ministry.

Case Study #3: Lay Ecclesial Ministry as Ordinary Lay Ministry "in the Name of the Church"

A final category of lay ecclesial ministry is that of lay ministry that is neither clearly supplying for a deficiency of priests in what is normally a priestly ministry, for example, the care of a parish in the absence of a residential priest, nor an occasional extraordinary ministry of acolyte or lector, but rather a lay ecclesial ministry that is ordinary and that, while being recognized as service in the name of the church, clearly and unambiguously arises from baptism and confirmation. These forms of lay ecclesial ministry represent a development in the ministerial life of the church, which may be permanent and which may represent a diversification of ministry reflecting the nature of the church as a ministerial community.[25] Examples from the life of the church would be catechists, directors of liturgy, directors of faith formation, parish administrators where understood to be those charged with overseeing the material goods of the parish, etc. The parish pastor is the person who most often calls them to service in the church. They are true collaborators with him in his pastoral charge of the parish. The bishops and their assistants, the priests, order and coordinate the various ministries and apostolates of the laity (AA 23–24; LG 32). They also have the task of discerning, judging, and ordering the charisms given by the Spirit (LG 12, 23–24; AA 3).

Insofar as the service of these people is characterized by a personal vocation ecclesially discerned and affirmed, a pastoral charge for leadership in the church with a relationship of coordination and direction of others in the community, authorization by the appropriate ecclesial authority, and appropriate formation, they can be considered as lay ecclesial ministers. Their ministry requires structures and a process of accountability to the church.

These "ordinary" lay ecclesial ministers have a different relationship to the bishop than the case of the parish life coordinators described above. It would not be as accurate to describe that relationship as a "participation" in the ministry of the bishop, for the bishop does not assume all ecclesial ministry in his person even though he does have the responsibility of overseeing all ecclesial ministry. The ministries within this category do not function as a substitute for pastoral leadership in the form of "headship" in a community. While the bishop has the authority to oversee and authorize this more ordinary ministry, it does not substitute for the presence of the bishop in the way that the ministry of a pastor is described in *Lumen Gentium* 28.

The question must be asked whether lay ecclesial ministry is a stopgap measure to tide the church over during some decades of priest shortage, or whether it represents an organic development in the ministerial life of the church. Without a doubt, *de facto* the laity is performing tasks that were traditionally assumed by priests in recent centuries. However, it must be asked theologically and *de jure* whether all these tasks necessarily had to be assumed by priests or should be assumed by them in the future if they do not intrinsically arise from this pastoral ministry of presiding over the community and its Eucharist.[26] Louis-Marie Chauvet asks whether a differentiated co-responsibility among priests, deacons, and laity is only valuable in a crisis situation, or whether it belongs to the very nature of the church. He suggests that rather than being a transitory phenomenon, it may be a passage toward a form of the church other than what we have been habituated to according to a Gregorian or Tridentine model.[27] I would agree with him and add that the restoration of the catechumenate program has revitalized the church as a ministerial community. The diversity of ministries necessary for the evangelization, reception, formation, and support of newly converted Christians requires a plurality of ministerial models with an associated plurality of authorizations.

Notes

1. USCCB, *Co-Workers in the Vineyard of the Lord: A Resource for Guiding the Development of Lay Ecclesial Ministry* (Washington, DC: USCCB Publishing, 2005), 54.

2. National Conference of Catholic Bishops, Subcommittee on Lay Ministry, Lay Ecclesial Ministry: The State of the Questions (USCCB, 1999), 8.

3. See canon 228, which must be interpreted within the context of canons 129, 145, and 274 §1 on lay sharing in ecclesiastical jurisdiction, the elements of an ecclesiastical office, and eligibility for offices requiring orders or jurisdiction. For relevant literature, see J. Beal, "The Exercise of the Power of Governance by Lay People: State of the Question," *Jurist* 55 (1995): 1–92.

4. The Final Report, "The Church, in the Word of God, Celebrates the Mysteries of Christ for the Salvation of the World" (National Catholic News Service), II, C, 1.

5. The French literature on the subject distinguishes between *tous* (all) and *quelques-un* (some). See Hervé Legrand, "Le role des commmunautés locales dans l'appel, l'envoi, la reception, et le soutien des laïcs reçevant une charge ecclesial," *La Maison-Dieu* 215 (1998/3): 9–32; and Alphonse Borras, "Petite grammaire canonique des nouveaux ministères," *Nouvelle Revue Théologique* 117 (1995): 240–61, 242.

6. Borras, "Petite grammaire canonique," 242–43.

7. See Susan K. Wood, "Convergence Points towards a Theology of Ordered Ministries," in *Ordering the Baptismal Priesthood*, ed. Susan K. Wood (Collegeville, MN: Liturgical Press, 2003), 256–67, 257.

8. Richard R. Gaillardetz, "Ecclesiological Foundations of Ministry in an Ordered Communion," in Wood, *Ordering the Baptismal Priesthood*, 26–51, 29.

9. Ibid., 31.

10. Borras, "Petite grammaire canonique," 244. My translation; italics in the original.

11. Signed by five dicasteries on August 15, 1997, and approved by John Paul II *in forma specifica*. For a critical commentary, see Bernard Sesboüé, *Rome et les laïcs: Une nouvelle pièce au débat: L'Instruction romaine du 15 août 1997* (Paris: Desclée de Brouwer, 1998), as well as his book, *N'ayez pas peur! Regards sur l'Église et les ministères aujourd'hui,* coll. Pascal Thomas, Pratiques chrétiennes 12 (Paris: Desclée de Brouwer, 1996); and the view by Alphonse Borras, "L'Église et les ministères aujourd'hui: A propos d'un livre récent," *Nouvelle Revue Théologique* 119 (1997): 98–103.

12. Sesboüé, *Rome et les laïcs,* 71.

13. On Certain Questions, art. 1.

14. Amy Hoey, RSM, "Concepts and Language of *Authorization* and *Vocation*," in "USCCB Documents on Lay Ecclesial Ministry," white paper for the Collegeville Symposium, December 2008, p. 10.

15. The *Apostolic Constitutions* is a fourth-century pseudo-apostolic collection of eight treatises on early Christian discipline, worship, and doctrine, intended to serve as a manual of guidance for the clergy, and to some extent for the laity.

16. Paul Bradshaw, *Ordination Rites of the Ancient Churches of East and West* (New York: Pueblo, 1990), 22. See also Hervé-Marie Legrand, "Theology and the Election of Bishops in the Early Church," *Concilium: Election and Consensus in the Church,* ed. Giuseppe Alberigo and Anton Weiler (New York: Herder and Herder, 1972), 40–41.

17. Canon 230 §3 allows laypersons to act as lectors or ministers of the Eucharist (c. 910 §2), baptism (c. 862 §2), or of the Word (c. 759) or to preside over liturgical prayers as established by law. Code of Canon Law, Latin-English Edition, New English Translation (Washington, DC: Canon Law Society of America, 1999).

18. Although the document On Certain Questions criticizes the habitual use of extraordinary ministers of Holy Communion, it does not mention lay lectors (art. 8).

19. See "New Lay Ministries for the U.S.?," *Origins* 3 (Nov. 29, 1973): 262.

20. The Center for Applied Research in the Apostolate (CARA) identified thirty-six job titles for these ministers, identifying the most common as pastoral administrator, administrator, parish life coordinator, and pastoral coordinator. See Special Report, "Understanding the Ministry and Experience: Parish Life Coordinators in the United States" (Summer 2005), http://www.emergingmodels. org/doc/reports/PLC%20Special%20Report-FINAL.pdf, accessed September 6, 2011. Barbara Anne Cusack and Therese Guerin Sullivan, SP, prefer the designation "parish director" in *Pastoral Care in Parishes Without a Pastor: Applications of Canon 517, §2* (Washington, DC: Canon Law Society of America, 1995), xii.

21. According to CARA, in 2011 3,249 US parishes were without a resident pastor, 469 of which a bishop had entrusted the pastoral care to a deacon, religious sister or brother, or other layperson. Worldwide, 49,631 parishes were without a resident pastor, 3,106 of which a bishop had entrusted their pastoral

care to a deacon, religious, or other layperson. See http://cara.georgetown.edu/CARAServices/requestedchurchstats.html, accessed September 6, 2011.

22. See canon 145. See the discussion in Jon P. Beal, James A. Coriden, and Thomas Green, eds., *New Commentary on the Code of Canon Law* (New York: Paulist Press, 2000), 200.

23. This is analogous to the conversation surrounding the power of jurisdiction of bishops at Vatican II, where a similar distinction was made: bishops receive the *power* to bless, lead, and teach from ordination, but the *exercise* of that power depends on their union with the episcopal college through the person of the pope. No one would say that bishops receive the *power* to minister from the pope even though they cannot *exercise* that power without his hierarchical authorization. See "The Hierarchical Structure of the Church with Special Reference to the Episcopate," by Karl Rahner, Aloys Grillmeier, and Herbert Vorgrimler, in *Commentary on the Documents of Vatican II*, ed. Herbert Vorgrimler, vol. 1 (New York: Herder and Herder, 1967), 186–230.

24. Bernard Sesboüé, "Les animateurs pastoraux laïcs. Une prospective théologique," Études (September 1992): 259.

25. See Susan K. Wood, "Presbyteral Identity within Parish Identity," in *Ordering the Baptismal Priesthood*.

26. See Louis-Marie Chauvet, "Les ministères de laics: Vers un nouveau visage de l'Église?," *La Maison-Dieu* 215 (1998/3): 33–57, 50.

27. Ibid., 51.

Chapter 7

A Canonical Wish List for the Authorization of Lay Ecclesial Ministers

Lynda Robitaille

What Difference Does Authorization Make?

What difference does authorization make? Another way of looking at that same question is expressed by Edward Hahnenberg: "How can we help clergy and laity work together?"[1] If authorization is done well and is well understood in the community, then clergy and laity will be able to work together because everyone will know his or her role, and the community's needs will be met.

Lay ecclesial ministry is generally well accepted as a reality, but it remains at the discretion of the diocesan bishop or pastor. What difference authorization would make would be to bring stability to lay ecclesial ministers. The rights and duties of the ministry/role would be clearly outlined in the authorization, as would the lines of accountability, expectations for the ministry, the duration of the ministry, etc. Authorization is an essential element in a lay minister's ecclesial ministry (as in every minister's ministry). In addition to making the situation clear to the person authorizing and the person being authorized, authorization makes it clear to the community what the bishop's intention is with regard to the lay ecclesial minister's ministry.

The key is the recognition of the call by the church, namely, authorization. How should/could authorization look in practice and what it means for the individual and for the church community will be our focus here. A layperson may feel called to lay ecclesial ministry, but it is the community through the bishop who discerns whether and how to accept that call. The call is not to be exercised solely because of the layperson's desire to serve. Rather, that desire must be recognized and then exercised in communion with those responsible for ministry in the church, namely, the diocesan bishop and pastors. Once the call to serve as a lay ecclesial minister is recognized, there should be some stability to the call and its exercise. It should not matter who is diocesan bishop, or who is the pastor, whether the layperson is able to exercise his or her vocation to lay ecclesial ministry.

What is authorization? *Co-Workers in the Vineyard of the Lord* reminds us that authorization

> is the process by which properly prepared lay men and women are given responsibilities for ecclesial ministry by competent Church authority. This process includes the following elements: acknowledgement of the competence of an individual for a specific ministerial role . . . appointment . . . to a specific position . . . along with a delineation of the obligations, responsibilities, and authority of that position . . . ; and finally an announcement of the appointment to the community.[2]

The more clearly authorization is done, the better for all concerned. Sharon Euart comments, "Whether real or perceived, the lack of clarity regarding who is responsible for what, canonically and pastorally, and the blurring of roles and responsibilities often result in confusion and misunderstandings on the part of staff and faithful."[3] She continues:

> The development of job descriptions and the correct assignment of functions in the areas of education, pastoral services, worship, and administration are crucial to maintaining clarity regarding the responsibilities of those in parish leadership. In identifying lines of accountability, position descriptions can preclude or at least minimize the blurring of roles and functions between clergy and laity.[4]

The purpose of this article is to make concrete proposals regarding the authorization of lay ecclesial ministers.

Introduction

There are many stories of positive experiences of lay ecclesial ministry, which highlight pastors or diocesan bishops who encourage and support lay ecclesial ministry. Then there are stories about problems with lay ecclesial ministry, about diocesan bishops that did/do not support it, did/ do not agree with it; about pastors that did/do not support it, did/do not agree with it.[5] More difficult still are the stories of lay ecclesial ministers who had a positive encouraging experience under one diocesan bishop or pastor, only to have the newly appointed bishop or pastor change the lay ecclesial minister's role, or terminate the ministry.[6] The consequence? That there was/is no stability to lay ecclesial ministry, nothing to depend on. In some places lay ecclesial ministry is accepted and encouraged; in others it is not. Some lay ecclesial ministers find their role to be fulfilling and according to their expectations because they have a good relationship with the pastor or the bishop; others do not. If the lay ecclesial minister's service depends on the "whim" of the diocesan bishop or the pastor, there is a problem. It is not just that a lay ecclesial minister can serve in one parish but not in another; that one pastor will work with a lay ecclesial minister but the next will not; that lay ecclesial ministry is accepted under one diocesan bishop but not the next. It is also unjust when a lay ecclesial minister is given duties beyond his or her role. If lay ecclesial ministry is recognized as being important for the church, then such ministry needs to be protected with canonical norms to promote its stability, to give confidence to the ministers and those who are served by them. We take to heart Ladislas Orsy's exhortation: "Authentic canon law . . . is not petty nuisance and it is not divine ordinance. It is a necessary human instrument, in a divinely founded community, to bring good balances into the operations of the group. . . . No community, not even a community of God's children, can function without good order."[7] It is time to begin to regulate lay ecclesial ministry at all levels.

Norms are needed regarding expectations for what level of education/formation is required for such ministry, what kinds of pay scales for what roles, how long a lay ecclesial minister serves, how a lay ecclesial minister transfers parishes or dioceses, etc. In addition, norms should address how lay ecclesial ministers work with and relate to the other ministers in the diocese, namely, the diocesan bishop, pastors, parochial vicars, religious, other lay ecclesial ministers, etc.

Will legislation restrict the growth of lay ecclesial ministry? Not if it is done with an openness to such growth. The need for the legislation is clear, to promote the "re-ordering" of the lay ecclesial minister's "relationship to the community of faith."[8] Jim Coriden encourages leaders "to try new and different arrangements . . . to find 'what serves the people best' . . . A supple and adaptive approach may be preferable to locking in on a single, permanent policy."[9] He speaks of lay ministers being " 'repositioned' within the church and in relationship to its other ministers."[10] This essay is an attempt to begin looking more deeply into common legislation that will help growth and stability.

Role of Canon Law in This Discussion

Canonists speak of the very real relationship between theology and canon law. Law takes theological principles and puts them into practice, into the lived reality of the church community. Cardinal Castillo Lara writes, "The law is only a *means*, an *instrument*." Law in the church should exist only insofar as it is necessary.[11] Alphonse Borras reminds us the law is the mediator between a theoretically professed ecclesiology and ecclesial practice.[12] What I hope to do in this chapter is to give some concrete suggestions for making the principle of authorization for lay ecclesial ministry more of a lived reality in the universal church, as well as in each of our dioceses. To do this we must consider norms that would be helpful for the universal church, for episcopal conferences, and for individual dioceses.

The theologians in the first Collegeville Ministry Seminar gathered in August 2001, and the results of their discussions were published in 2003.[13] In the canon law presentation, Elissa Rinere reviewed the "developments" in lay ministry and stated that she assumed "that at some future time these developments will have to be articulated in law."[14] It is my premise that the time has come to legislate. Lay ecclesial ministry exists in the church and is recognized as being vital and important for the life of the church. We have moved beyond the question of whether lay ecclesial ministers only exist because of a shortage of priests to the recognition that there is something worthwhile in itself of lay ecclesial ministry. Lay ecclesial ministry is here to stay. As Roch Pagé stated, "regardless of the reasons which led to the full-time involvement of lay persons and their participation in the exercise of the bishop's pastoral office, it is better to presume that they are here to stay and, therefore, we should act accordingly."[15] Anne Asselin argued that we must develop an institutional form for this new category of ministers.[16] Tom Green suggested, "Bishops should . . . facilitate the emergence of lay leadership in response to new pastoral needs."[17] Euart adds, "there is little doubt that lay ecclesial ministry will continue to develop and flourish in the church through the working of the Holy Spirit."[18] How, then, should that ministry be recognized and promoted in canon law?

Lay ecclesial ministry needs to be recognized through structures that will help implement it in the life of each diocese. Structures need to be put in place not to confine lay ecclesial ministry but to give it stability in the life of the church, to make it clear that this is not something that is the whim of twenty-first-century North Americans, but that it is an essential part of building up the church community. As Coriden argues, "lay ministry . . . cries out for recognition and structural incorporation into the entire pattern of the Church's ministries."[19]

To Answer Before Proceeding

Do all the theological questions about lay ecclesial ministry need to be answered before we can legislate? In my opinion, no. There are many areas legislated in the life of the church that still leave room for development of the theological and canonical understandings. The same can happen in this area.

Is it too soon to legislate? I do not think so. In my opinion, it is now time to legislate on all levels (universal, regional, and diocesan) so that the law can better reflect the reality that is developing. This will give stability to the development of lay ecclesial ministry and give guidelines for the future.[20] As Hahnenberg pointed out in 2007, "we are called" to think through "realistic steps and concrete recommendations that are workable."[21] Coriden wrote, "Canonical discipline can and should recognize the full reality of what is actually happening 'on the ground,' namely that thousands of lay women and men have been and presently are exercising the power of governance."[22] More recently, Coriden argued, "A theological vision for the structural incorporation of these ministries is key . . . Happily, such a theology already exists, it is readily accessible . . . and it already commands a consensus in North America and beyond. This theologically guided task of ministerial integration is the logical next step after *Co-Workers in the Vineyard of the Lord*."[23] We also echo the words of Jim Provost, who explained that we need "legislation which will provide order, structure, and clear lines of responsibility . . . the development of this body of law gives the impression that a new form of ministry is developing, rather than a temporary replacement."[24] As Anne Asselin stated, "lay ministry must be formally recognized as an essential ministry and given the appropriate framework and structures."[25]

Context

Lay ecclesial ministry, like all ministry, is exercised in the diocese, under the leadership of the diocesan bishop. Tom Green speaks of the role of the diocesan bishop:

Despite their limitations, the code and the Directory stress the common sacramentally-grounded mission of all believers and the special
ecclesial service that bishops especially provide for others in the name
of Christ. Ecclesial ministry is to be exercised in a way that highlights
interrelatedness, interdependence, and shared experience comparable
to the life of the Trinity. Such a common mission precedes all differences of functions, charisms, and ministries. The bishop is an integral
part of a network of relationships within the diocese, actively focusing
its diverse resources for mission and coordinating various apostolic
enterprises to preclude a wasteful duplication of efforts.[26]

Green highlights that "two key Directory principles of episcopal governance are communion and collaboration. The bishop is to share his
apostolic burden with others."[27] Nevertheless, it is also true that one can
read canon law as though the diocesan bishop is the presence of Christ for
the particular church and all ministry belongs to the diocesan bishop.[28]
However, the diocesan bishop cannot exercise all pastoral roles on his
own. Others help him to fulfill his role. All who minister (priests, deacons, religious, and laity) share in the diocesan bishop's ministry. They
each share in different ways in this ministry, but the fact is that they are
all capable of sharing in it. That is the starting point of the proposals here.

Lay Ecclesial Ministers in the Church?

What, then, is the place in the church of individual lay faithful who
have discerned the Lord's call to ecclesial ministry? Based on their baptism and confirmation, they respond to follow that call within the community that is the church. In order to minister in the community, these
people (like all ministers) must be recognized by the church hierarchy
and authorized to minister. The US bishops call them "lay ecclesial ministers."[29] In so doing, the US bishops recall the 1997 instruction *Ecclesiae
de Mysterio*: "The application of 'ministry' to the laity is not something
to be confused with ordained ministry nor in any way construed to
compromise the specific nature of ordained ministry."[30]

Ministry can be understood in both a broad (generic) and narrow
sense. *Co-Workers* uses the term in the broad sense. *Ecclesiae de Mysterio*
uses it in the narrow sense: ministry connected with the sacrament of
orders. Those who are ordained have a special prerogative to minister,
to publicly exercise a function in the church for the good of the faithful.
Can laypeople "minister"? Can laypeople publicly exercise a role in
the church for the good of the faithful?[31] Answers to that question will
depend on whether one is speaking in the narrow sense of ministry that

has to do with ordination, or in a broader sense. This is an area where there is still much theological discussion. For the purposes of this chapter, I will use "ministry" in the broad sense, and I will not enter into the discussion of lay ecclesial "ministry" in the narrow sense. It is my contention that it is time for legislation regarding lay ecclesial "ministry" in the broad sense. I agree with Jim Coriden that "the lay ecclesial ministry explosion has already reshaped the ministry in American parishes . . . it still needs to be integrated into a theological vision and canonical formulation of ministry."[32]

Lay ecclesial ministers receive a call from Christ; the diocesan bishop recognizes that call and enters into a relationship with the lay ecclesial minister, who then functions in a diocese in a public manner. The lay ecclesial minister is committed on a part-time or full-time basis, temporarily or permanently, to this ministry. In order to pursue this ministry, the layperson needs to be called, that is, needs the authorization of the diocesan bishop. The ministry is public, exercised "in the name of the church."

Which specific ministries are lay ecclesial ministries? There is no definitive canonical list of lay ecclesial ministries. However, canonists do give us an idea of the possible ministries that could be considered, such as, catechist, moderator of an association, expert or advisor in councils, censor, chancellor, vice-chancellor, notary, financial officer, member of a diocesan finance council, administrator of an ecclesiastical juridic person, assessor, auditor, defender of the bond, promoter of justice, advocate, procurator, judge, expert, teacher of the sacred sciences, and those who work in parishes—presiding over liturgical prayer, conferring baptism, participating in the exercise of the pastoral care of a parish, assisting at marriages, presiding at funerals.[33] Principals of Catholic schools and teachers at Catholic schools could also be included.[34]

Another list of who lay ecclesial ministers are was highlighted by the USCCB's Subcommittee on Lay Ecclesial Ministry in its document Lay Ecclesial Ministry: The State of the Questions from 1999:

> The subcommittee identifies director of religious education, pastoral associate, youth minister, campus chaplain, hospital chaplain, and director of RCIA as lay ministries that need authorization from the hierarchy and require the supervision of bishops. Also included in the listing of lay ministries that require authorization are music director, social justice director, business manager, bereavement ministry coordinator, and principal of a Catholic school. According to the subcommittee, the term "lay ecclesial minister" is to be used only in reference to those laypersons who have "received the necessary

formation, education and training . . . Lay ecclesial ministers . . . occupy a formal and public role in ministry. This role must be conferred
upon them by competent ecclesiastical authority.[35]

Co-Workers does not give a list of positions; rather it highlights: "A diocese must first identify those roles that, in the judgment of the diocesan
bishop, are so essential to collaborating in the pastoral care of people
that diocesan policies are needed to ensure that those who are given
these roles have the appropriate education, formation, experience, and
ecclesial recognition to meet the needs of the community" (56).

John Huels gives us a way to focus the issue by reflecting on the
meaning of office in canon law.[36] Based on his work, I suggest that legislation begin with those lay ecclesial ministries that should be offices.

Lay Ecclesial Ministries as Ecclesiastical Offices

Canon 145 of the 1983 Code of Canon Law defines an ecclesiastical
office:

> §1. An ecclesiastical office is any function constituted in a stable man-
> ner by divine or ecclesiastical ordinance to be exercised for a spiritual
> purpose.
>
> §2. The obligations and rights proper to individual ecclesiastical of-
> fices are defined either in the law by which the office is constituted or
> in the decree of the competent authority by which the office is at the
> same time constituted and conferred.[37]

Offices can be created by ecclesiastical authority and in their creation,
ecclesiastical authority should outline the rights and obligations that go
along with the office. Canons 146–96 regulate ecclesiastical offices, how
they are obtained and how they are lost.

Huels reminds us that under the regime of the 1917 Code, offices
could only be held by clerics; that is no longer the case under the 1983
Code. He asks the question whether offices should be created for laypersons in parishes and diocesan administration. In my opinion, yes,
many of the positions held by laypersons should be true ecclesiastical
offices. Huels asks questions that would follow upon lay ecclesial ministries being called "offices": "Do persons in such positions act *in nomine
Ecclesiae*? Is the parish and diocese civilly and canonically liable for their
conduct in office?"[38] If laypersons are indeed exercising ecclesiastical
offices, then, yes, they have the rights and duties that come from those

offices. It would be best for all concerned if the offices, as well as the ensuing rights and duties, be recognized and legislated.

Huels traces the history of the concept of office beginning with the 1917 Code where offices were understood as a service performed "for a spiritual purpose" by a cleric. Thus, it would not be possible for a layperson, a noncleric, to hold an ecclesiastical office. What we can take from the 1917 Code's understanding is what Huels calls the *"objective stability"* of an office, meaning that it exists whether or not there is a person holding the office at a particular moment in time (ibid., 399). The office exists because it is recognized to fulfill a pastoral need. This is an important point for lay ecclesial ministries: ministries might arise because of a particular need that can be fulfilled by a specific person. However, after some time the ministry should not be regarded as person-specific. It needs to be established as an office that should regularly be filled. Turning to an example, in one parish the parochial vicar was moved and no one replaced him. The pastor could not fulfill all the ministerial roles himself and so encouraged a layperson in the parish to pursue studies in theology and then to take on roles in the parish. This was a way for the layperson to help out, to exercise his or her baptismal calling in a new way. The role was not yet stable and would depend on the whim of the pastor. Should the pastor feel that he could undertake all roles, or that he would prefer to work with someone else, the layperson would no longer be needed. However, if that layperson were to be authorized by the diocesan bishop to function publicly in that parish in a specific office, the role is different. When the office is stable and not person-dependent, it is recognized that this role is not only helpful but also necessary. The persons of the pastor and the layperson no longer matter; for the good of the community, they need to make the roles work.

An analogy might be helpful. Canon 519 explains, "The pastor (*parochus*) is the proper pastor (*pastor*) of the parish entrusted to him, exercising the pastoral care of the community committed to him under the authority of the diocesan bishop in whose ministry of Christ he has been called to share." Noteworthy also is canon 545 §1: "in order to carry out the pastoral care of a parish fittingly, one or more parochial vicars can be associated with the pastor. As co-workers with the pastor and sharers in his solicitude, they are to offer service in the pastoral ministry by common counsel and effort with the pastor and under his authority." The offices of pastor and parochial vicar are important for the care of the faithful. Can we learn something from the relationship between pastor and parochial vicar for the relationship between pastor and lay ecclesial minister? The bishop determines whether it is necessary to have an office of parochial vicar in a particular parish. If he deems it necessary, then for the good of the faithful the pastor and the parochial vicar work together. In a similar way, the bishop could determine that certain offices should be exercised by lay ecclesial ministers for the benefit of the faithful, and he could establish those offices. To continue the analogy, canon 547 makes it clear that "the diocesan bishop freely appoints a parochial vicar." Even though there is encouragement for the diocesan bishop to consult with the pastor and the dean (*vicar forane*), it is not obligatory. In other words, the decision whether or not to appoint a parochial vicar is the bishop's, not the pastor's. It should be the same for the decision to appoint a lay ecclesial minister to an office in a parish.

Anne Asselin reminds us that the ministries should be clear so that the priest can exercise his ministry as pastor, as guide as the *repraesentio Christi capitis Ecclesiae*, so that the deacon can exercise his role toward the "poor" of the community, to inspire them, motivate them, and form them, and so that the layperson can also fulfill his or her role as a baptized person who has been sent in a mission proper to him or her.[39] She then asks, do the structures in our present parishes permit such a collaboration?

Should all ministries be offices? Many roles exercised by laypeople—even in a stable manner for spiritual purposes—should not be considered offices. On the difference between established ministries and offices, Huels explains that there is a distinction to be made between a *munus* and an office (*officium*), namely, that an office is a kind of *munus* and that all *munera* are not offices. An office has stability in law and is granted in a formal manner (by canonical provision). *Munera* are not given by canonical provision and Huels gives examples, such as the liturgical roles of acolyte and lector, which are *munera* but not offices.[40] For Huels, it is essential to make distinctions between offices and other ways to serve in the church, even those that seem to be stable and for the spiritual good of people. The example he gives is the extraordinary minister of communion who is in a stable position that is not an office, even though it has a spiritual purpose.[41] Thus, it would be important to distinguish the different offices and other *munera* and forms of service in a diocese in order to clarify what are true ecclesiastical offices. One important criterion, according to Huels, is that an officeholder in the diocese is appointed by the diocesan bishop (ibid., 426). Thus, in Huels's view, the instituted liturgical ministries should not be offices. An essential point is that the person who holds an office fulfills it "*on behalf of a public juridic person."* The office holder "is not acting in a private, personal capacity but for the public good of the church community. The purpose of the office is to serve a public juridic person and further its mission" (ibid., 413). This is essential for understanding what public roles should be offices; or better, who serves in the name of the church?

Should lay ecclesial ministries be considered offices, the benefit would be stability, as John Beal points out: "The hallmarks of an ecclesiastical office are the continuance of the function in question beyond the tenure of any individual who carries it out."[42] Alphonse Borras reminds us that canon 145 §2 of the Code permits the competent authority to create ecclesiastical offices. Borras explains that a diocesan bishop or a conference of bishops could create ecclesiastical offices, and that it is precisely at this level that what is happening in lay ecclesial ministry should be evaluated.[43] He concludes by stating that it is particular law (episcopal conferences and diocesan bishops) that has the responsibility to systematically categorize lay ministries.[44]

Legislating offices. Huels notes that both particular and universal law can regulate offices and their rights and obligations.[45] How are offices legislated? Huels enumerates different ways of establishing offices, especially through general executory decrees, which are decrees of executive power (c. 31), and through singular administrative decrees. Here Huels distinguishes that a singular decree would be used to create a new office that is being established for a specific person. In other words, the singular decree is best used when the legislator is not yet certain that the office will continue beyond the tenure of the first person to hold the office.[46] This raises an important point. If it is clear that the office will continue beyond the first officeholder, a general executory decree may be used to create the office, and then the officeholder will be named to the office by a separate singular administrative decree (canonical provision); if the long-term viability of the office is not clear, a singular administrative decree will suffice.[47] It would be important before creating offices to establish whether this is a trial, to benefit a particular person, or whether this office is determined to be useful on a stable basis. This, then, is a long-term project. When creating new offices, the first step would be to establish the office for a particular person, as a singular administrative decree. This provides the stability the person needs to work well in the role. Yet, it also provides the flexibility that when the person leaves the office, it is over. The diocesan bishop will need to reevaluate the situation and determine, did the office serve the good of the church community?

Is it something he would like to see filled on a long-term basis? If so, then he can either issue another singular administrative decree creating the office for a specific person and thus continue the experiment, or the diocesan bishop can issue a general executory decree and create the office on a stable basis. In this latter case, the bishop would also have to issue a singular administrative decree to name the person to that office (the canonical provision) (ibid., 416).

Citing canon 146, Huels explains that canonical provision is required for someone to obtain an office (ibid., 423). Normally canonical provision is done in writing, following the regulations regarding decrees (cc. 51, 37, as well as 156). Whether this is done by means of a decree, a letter of appointment, or an employment contract, it should be clear what is happening (ibid., 424). Yet Huels dislikes the use of an employment contract instead of an ecclesiastical decree: "Free conferral is not a bilateral agreement between two equal parties but the act of a superior authority who makes a provision . . . intended for the public good in meeting specific needs of the ecclesial community. . . . The provision of office is an important public matter that must be documented and recorded" (ibid., 425). Thus, the appointment to an office in the church has both civil and ecclesial consequences.

Huels outlines his understanding of the offices necessary to establish in a diocese, highlighting offices in the curia (c. 470) and the tribunal (cc. 1420, 1421, 1435), deans (c. 553 §2), all important collegial offices such as the college of consultors (c. 502 §1) and finance council (c. 492 §1); offices whose end is pastoral care, such as the pastor (c. 522), and those with similar functions, that is, the parochial vicar (c. 547), chaplain (c. 565), rector of a church, parish deacon, and the person with care of the community as outlined in canon 517 §2 (ibid., 428). Where Huels has a very strict interpretation is that he states that other appointments should not be appointments to offices, thus, for example, extraordinary ministers of communion, and "most lay ministers can be empowered for their service simply by delegating them the necessary faculties without appointing them to office."[47] Huels also sees a distinction in canon 805, which speaks of the appointment or approval of teachers of religion in schools: "Approval is not the same act as appointment. Thus, the school principal or pastor would present the names of the religion teachers, and the bishop would approve them" (ibid., 427–28).

Although Huels has presented a good beginning for legislation for lay ecclesial ministers, it does not go far enough. He has given us a good basis for determining whether a ministry should be an office or not, and he gives us canonical groundwork to build upon, yet he considers many ministries fulfilled by laypersons can be done without legislating these ministries as offices. To begin, let us consider which ministries should be considered helpful as ecclesiastical offices, and then encourage bishops to establish them first by singular administrative acts to see how they work, and then by general executory decrees. This would encourage dioceses to fill such offices and recognize their long-term value for the life of the dioceses. In those situations where it is necessary still to establish the long-term value of certain ministries, let people be appointed to those offices by singular administrative decrees. With such decrees they will have stability of the rights and obligations inherent in the offices during their terms, but the offices will cease when their terms have ended, and the value of the offices can then be evaluated. Huels encourages approving teachers, and "assigning" people a *munus* rather than appointing people to ecclesiastical offices.[49] This seems to brush off the necessity of stability and authorization for such lay ecclesial ministers. I would encourage appointing lay ecclesial ministers to offices rather than *munera*. It is time to encourage stability of lay ecclesial ministers in offices, so that the expectations for their roles are clear, and so that their rights and obligations can be protected.

Let us turn now to what kinds of structures could be legislated at different levels: the universal church, regions (episcopal conferences), and then local dioceses, understanding that it is in the local church, the dioceses, where the majority of the work needs to begin.

Structures for the Universal Church

Roch Pagé notes, "the Code does not seem to have anticipated the rapid growth of lay involvement in pastoral structures. The least we can say is that it is very cautious."[50]

All ministry in a diocese centers around the diocesan bishop. He should have the greatest say in terms of structures in his diocese. However, there are structures that should not be left solely to authority at the local level. The fact that lay ecclesial ministers exist and can be called to cooperate in the ministry of the diocesan bishop needs to be addressed in the universal law of the church. Some of it has been addressed, as is clear from offices alluded to in the Code, namely, those in the diocesan curia (c. 470), such as chancellor and vice-chancellor (c. 482), notary (c. 483), diocesan finance officer (c. 494), and member of the diocesan finance council (c. 492); and in the tribunal, such as judge (c. 1421), defender of the bond and promoter of justice (c. 1435), assessor (c. 1424), auditor (c. 1428), as well as the office of the person named in canon 517 §2. That lay ecclesial ministers may hold these offices is clear from the Code. Their rights and duties are also outlined in the Code.

Coriden has suggested changes to the universal law that would facilitate an openness to lay ecclesial ministry. Perhaps some of his suggested changes to canons 129, 274, 564, and 1421 could be considered, among others.[51]

Structures for Episcopal Conferences

The US bishops published *Co-Workers in the Vineyard of the Lord* in 2005. The subtitle clearly indicates that this document is *A Resource for Guiding the Development of Lay Ecclesial Ministry*. This was a great step in the recognition of lay ecclesial ministry. However, it is clear from the title and the disclaimer at the beginning that it is only a "resource," and that it "does not propose norms or establish particular law" (6). It now seems to be time for the bishops to work together on some binding laws envisioning the structure of lay ecclesial ministry in the United States and elsewhere. We recall that the practice of lay ecclesial ministry in the United States started from the "bottom up": "It was not the result of a national plan. Rather . . . parishes and then dioceses began to recognize how necessary and how right it was for lay women and men to be entrusted with responsibilities of ministerial leadership."[52] It is time to recognize that reality and to structure it and give it stability.

At the level of the episcopal conference as well as of the diocesan bishop, the offices enumerated in the Code should be recognized explicitly as offices. Other than these offices, what lay ecclesial ministries should be considered offices? Some suggestions: on the diocesan level, directors of offices in the Curia such as, head of religious education, head of youth ministry, head of any specialized ministry for the diocese, director/moderator of the tribunal, superintendent of schools, director of religious education. On the parish level, director of religious education, youth minister, pastoral associate, director of RCIA, director of marriage preparation, director of any specialized parish ministry. What of campus chaplains and hospital chaplains? Would principals and teachers at Catholic schools be included?

As noted above, each of these offices should have a title, as well as an outline of the duties of the ministry. In addition, the qualities required for the person to obtain the office, the duration of the office, and the terms of the office should be clear. These offices should be established by a general executory decree if they are going to be established as long-term offices, or they should be established by a singular administrative decree if they are being established solely for one person to fulfill and then to be reevaluated.

What kinds of issues/structures should be considered? In thinking about concrete structures, I take my lead from Hahnenberg, thinking about "formation," "authorization," and "workplace."[53] One point to remember when dealing with canonical structures: the law will outline the ideal; flexibility is incorporated into that. Flexibility is needed to address reality. Thus, for example, legislation might require that lay ecclesial ministers obtain a certain level of education. Yet, the law can recognize that at times experience in life can substitute for education. This is clear in the norms, for example, requiring that officers of the tribunal have certain levels of education, and yet permitting someone without that level of education to occupy the office when necessary, and with permission from the proper authority. Following are some general ideas for offices held by lay ecclesial ministers.

Qualities. What qualities should lay ecclesial ministers possess? *Co-Workers* speaks of being in a canonically regular marriage, prayer, knowledge of and adherence to church doctrine, regular celebration of the sacraments, leadership ability, chaste living, etc. (31). What qualities are required for different ministries/offices?

Formation.[54] Euart comments, "Formation for lay ecclesial ministers involved in parish leadership is a critical focus for the future."[55] She highlights formation for lay ministers in leadership: "the skills training, education, and competency required for certain leadership positions cannot be overlooked," and also "education and training for seminarians as well as for deacons . . . and the skills needed for collaborative models of parish leadership."[56] Questions arise from these comments regarding the following:

> educational requirements for different ministries (should there be standard requirements throughout the episcopal conference? or should that be something at the level of the universal law, like requirements for ecclesiastical degrees?[57])
> putting in place some educational programs for different ministries, as well as a list of required courses for different ministries
> what other formation is required or recommended?[58]
> what are the expectations for ongoing formation? (*Co-Workers*, 50–52)

Authorization. John Huels writes, "An authorization is the legal empowerment, granted by means of an administrative act of the competent authority, which enables a person to perform lawfully an act of ministry or administration other than an act of the power of governance. An authorization is any non-jurisdictional faculty."[59]

What are the ministries (offices)[60] for which the bishop's authorization is needed?

Which ministries should be constituted as offices?[61]

What should the authorization state in writing?

How long should it be valid for?[62]

How should the community learn of the authorization? Should it be done at the same time as a liturgical ceremony to inaugurate the beginning of the lay ecclesial minister's ministry?

How should the lay minister's authorization function within the parish or diocesan context? Henk Witte gives an example from the Dutch Episcopal Conference: "The Dutch bishops wanted to see the formation of 'pastoral teams' for parishes to ensure 'that the specific value and position of the different pastoral assignments be taken seriously' and to facilitate mutual support."[63]

Workplace. Issues to be addressed in the workplace are the following:

the necessity of "job descriptions" for offices that include rights and responsibilities

duration of the offices

establishing some kind of system like "incardination" for lay ecclesial ministers,[64] so that lay ecclesial ministers have stability in service, both in their offices/roles as well as in the diocese[65]

building a system so that lay ecclesial ministers can transfer from diocese to diocese[66]

putting into place pay scales for different ministries

what happens if things go wrong (office of conflict resolution)[67]

Should formation in collaborative ministry with other ministers be legislated?[68] Pastors, assistant priests, deacons, religious, and lay ecclesial ministers often work together. What structures are in place or should be in place to ensure that the ministry is effectively accomplished?

Anne Asselin highlights another area for legislation when speaking about canon 517 §2:

> What is not quite as clear in the Code of Canon Law and what somewhat blurs the situation envisaged in this canon is the exercise of the power of governance by a lay minister . . . What is important is determining to what point a lay ecclesial minister may take decision in the parish for which he or she is responsible. It is unthinkable that the lay minister who finds himself or herself alone to administer a parish should always have to turn to the priest-moderator for every decision that needs to be taken in the day-to-day administration of a parish.[69]

Structures for Regions

It might be more feasible to work on some of the above in ecclesiastical provinces, where the needs and practices of a specific region are more homogeneous than the needs and practices of the whole country. As an example, in 1999 the bishops of Ontario published Lay Pastoral Associates in Parish Settings: Perspectives, Considerations and Suggestions.[70] They address some practical matters for their region, for instance, the pastoral mandate by which the diocesan bishop names a person as a "lay pastoral associate"; the purpose of the mandate is to give stability and protection to both the diocese and the lay pastoral associate. In addition, there should be a contract, signed by the diocese, the parish, and the pastoral worker. One concern is when pastors change. If there are laypersons working on parish teams, then care must be taken in the appointment of clergy to ensure that all understand the mandate to work together.

Finally, there are the questions of how and whether lay pastoral associates can be transferred, and how lay pastoral associates can have a voice in diocesan ministry, perhaps through a diocesan council for parish ministry.

Structures for Dioceses[71]

The kinds of structures that the diocesan bishop should put into place are the following:

a diocesan office for the laity and lay ministry[72]
a diocesan office for conflict resolution/due process[73]
general executory decrees establishing the different offices, as well as singular administrative decrees providing for the office and contracts or agreements between the diocese or parish and the lay ecclesial minister[74]

Conclusion

To answer the question, what difference does authorization make? It makes a difference if it is known in the community that a lay ecclesial minister has been sent (authorized) by the diocesan bishop to serve in a specific community. It is time to encourage such legislation, especially in individual dioceses.

Notes

1. E. Hahnenberg, "The Vocation to Lay Ecclesial Ministry," *Origins* 37 (2007): 181.

2. USCCB, *Co-Workers in the Vineyard of the Lord: A Resource for Guiding the Development of Lay Ecclesial Ministry* (Washington, DC: USCCB Publishing, 2005), 54.

3. S. Euart, "Lay Ecclesial Ministry and Parish Leadership Options: Canonical Reflections in Light of *Co-Workers in the Vineyard*," in *Lay Ecclesial Ministry: Pathways Toward the Future*, ed. Zeni Fox (Lanham, MD: Rowman & Littlefield, 2010), 114.

4. Ibid.

5. *Co-Workers* notes, "The support of the pastor has been found crucial to the success of lay ecclesial ministry within parish communities" (55).

6. See, for example, H. Witte, "The Local Bishop and Lay Pastoral Workers: A Newly Created Function in the Church and Its Impact on Episcopal Collegiality," *The Jurist* 69 (2009): 85, where he describes the experience of the Netherlands and notes, "Some local bishops welcomed and supported the lay pastoral workers; others did not . . . even within a diocese, a continuity of policy was not guaranteed. A new bishop could easily change the hitherto open policy of his predecessor."

7. L. Orsy, *Receiving the Council: Theological and Canonical Insights and Debates* (Collegeville, MN: Liturgical Press, 2009), 78.

8. P. Lakeland, "The Lay Ecclesial Minister: Is S/he a Theological Monster?," *Concilium* 1 (2010): 61.

9. J. A. Coriden, "Pastoral Ministry in the Parish: A Theological Consensus and Practical Issues," in *Service for Union with God and with One Another: Essays in Honor of Sister Rose McDermott, SSJ*, Institutiones Iuris Ecclesiae I, ed. R. J. Kaslyn (Washington, DC: Catholic University, 2010), 103.

10. Ibid., 106.

11. R. J. Castillo Lara, "Il posto del diritto canonico in una visione conciliare della Chiesa," in *Iustus iudex*, ed. K. Ludicke, H. Mussinghoff, and H. Schwendenwein (Ludgerus-Verlag, 1991), 13.

12. A. Borras, "Quelle regulation canonique pour les ministères de laics? Du code au droit particulier," *Studia canonica* 40 (2006): 349.

13. S. K. Wood, ed., *Ordering the Baptismal Priesthood: Theologies of Lay and Ordained Ministry* (Collegeville, MN: Liturgical Press, 2003).

14. E. Rinere, "Canon Law and Emerging Understandings of Ministry," in *Ordering the Baptismal Priesthood*, 79–80.

15. R. Pagé, "Full-Time Pastoral Ministers and Diocesan Governance," in *Canon Law Between Interpretation and Imagination*, Monsignor W. Onclin Chair, 2001, p. 30.

16. A. Asselin, "Vingt ans après la promulgation du Code de Droit Canonique: Qu'en est-il du service des laics dans l'Église?," *Studia canonica* 38 (2004): 103.

17. T. Green, "Contemporary Challenges to Episcopal Governance: Reflections on the 2004 Directory on the Ministry of Bishops and Other Pertinent Texts," *The Jurist* 68 (2008): 431.

18. Euart, "Lay Ecclesial Ministry and Parish Leadership Options," 114.

19. Coriden, "Pastoral Ministry in the Parish," 123.

20. I take into consideration those who stress that we should not rush in these matters, for instance, Hahnenberg in "Vocation to Lay Ecclesial Ministry" cautions: "Let's not rush to force lay ecclesial ministry into some imagined normative shape of ministry. Let's give ourselves as a church enough time to reflect on the ways this new reality is inviting us to rethink the very categories we use" (179).

21. Ibid.

22. J. Coriden, "Necessary Canonical Reform: Urgent Issues for Action," in *Canon Law Between Interpretation and Imagination*, 22. At pp. 22–23 he suggests changes to some canons that would open certain offices in the church to laity.

23. Coriden, "Pastoral Ministry in the Parish," 123.

24. J. Provost, "Temporary Replacements or New Forms of Ministry: Lay Persons with Pastoral Care of Parishes," in *In diversitate unitas*, Monsignor W. Onclin Chair, 1997, p. 65.

25. A. Asselin, "Lay Ecclesial Ministers in the Present Parish Structure and Some Suggestions for the Future," *Forum* 17 (2006): 145.

26. T. Green, "Contemporary Challenges to Episcopal Governance: Reflections on the 2004 Directory on the Ministry of Bishops and Other Pertinent Texts," *The Jurist* 68 (2008): 420–21.

27. Ibid., 426.

28. E. Hahnenberg, "Bishop: Source or Center of Ministerial Life?," *Origins* 37 (2007): 107, recalls that "presbyters depend on the bishop not for their ministerial power but for the exercise of their power." He applies that to all ministers: "Might we not . . . imagine the bishop as not only the center of a *presbyterium* but also the center of a *ministerium*— . . . a ministerial community that includes, among others, lay ecclesial ministers."

A. Hagstrom, "Lay Ecclesial Ministry and Questions of Authorization," *Origins* 37 (2007): 109, considers Hahnenberg's question of whether the bishop is the source or the center of ministry in his diocese and notes that *Co-Workers* (and indeed the Code of Canon Law) "presents a vision of the bishop as source and font of ministry."

Coriden, "Pastoral Ministry in the Parish," 106, takes up this language: "The diocesan bishop is the center and coordinator of ministry within the diocese, but he is not the source or font of its ministries."

Susan Wood, "Baptism: Common Call to Service," *CLSA Proceedings* 72 (2009): 10, explains, "lay ministry does not arise out of a bishop's ministry, as stemming from his Sacrament of Order, but out of baptism in cooperation and collaboration with the bishop."

29. *Co-Workers*, 5. At pp. 10–11: "Previous documents from our Conference have called such women and men 'lay ecclesial ministers' and their service 'lay ecclesial ministry.' We continue that usage here with the following understandings. The term 'lay ecclesial minister' is generic. It is meant to encompass and describe several possible roles . . . 'Lay ecclesial minister' is not itself a specific position title. We do not use the term in order to establish a new rank or order among the laity. Rather, we use the terminology . . . to identify a developing and growing reality."

30. Ibid., 12, citing Congregation for Clergy et al., Instruction, *Ecclesiae de Mysterio*, On Certain Questions Regarding the Collaboration of the Non-Ordained Faithful in the Sacred Ministry of the Priest, August 15, 1997, in English translation in *Origins* 27 (1997–98): 397, 399–409, practical provisions, articles 1, 2.

31. Ministry is necessarily a public function in the church, exercised in the name of the church. Living out one's baptism by spreading the gospel is not "ministry" in this sense.

32. Coriden, "Pastoral Ministry in the Parish," 100.

33. Some of this list was taken from R. McDermott, *"Co-Workers in the Vineyard of the Lord*: A Canonical Analysis," *The Jurist* 67 (2007): 441–43.

34. Euart, "Lay Ecclesial Ministry and Parish Leadership Options," 102, speaks of laypeople serving "in Catholic schools and colleges, health care facilities, social service agencies, diocesan chanceries, and other types of ministry."

35. J. D. Davidson, T. P. Walters, B. Cisco, K. Meyer, E. Zech, *Lay Ministers and Their Spiritual Practices* (Huntington, IN: Our Sunday Visitor, 2003), 22, citing the subcommittee of the USCCB, Lay Ecclesial Ministry: The State of the Questions, 1999.

36. J. Huels, "Towards Refining the Notion of 'Office' in Canon Law," *The Jurist* 70 (2010): 396–433.

37. Code of Canon Law, Latin-English Edition, New English Translation (Washington, DC: Canon Law Society of America, 1999).

38. Huels, "Towards Refining the Notion of 'Office' in Canon Law," 397.

39. A. Asselin, "Les agents de pastorale dans la structure actuelle des paroisses et quelques propositions pour l'avenir," *Studia canonica* 39 (2005): 115.

40. Huels, "Towards Refining the Notion of 'Office' in Canon Law," 409. Different authors approach the mix of ministries differently: Susan Wood, "Conclusion:

Convergence Points toward a Theology of Ordered Ministries," at the end of the first Collegeville Ministry Seminar, spoke of the ordained, the installed, and the commissioned. See Wood, *Ordering the Baptismal Priesthood*, 256–57. See also Coriden, "Pastoral Ministry in the Parish," 106, who distinguishes: "1) ordained: (bishop, presbyter, deacon) . . . ; 2) installed: (e.g. pastoral associate, director of religious education) . . . ; 3) commissioned: (e.g. lector, cantor, minister of Holy Communion)."

41. Huels, "Towards Refining the Notion of 'Office' in Canon Law," 425–26.

42. J. Beal, "Lay People and Church Governance: Oxymoron or Opportunity," in *Together in God's Service: Toward a Theology of Ecclesial Lay Ministry*, Papers from a Colloquium (Washington, DC: NCCB, 1998), 108.

43. A. Borras, "Quelle regulation canonique pour les ministères de laics? Du code au droit particulier," *Studia canonica* 40 (2006): 356. See pp. 358–59 for a list of possible areas in which to develop offices for lay ecclesial ministers.

44. Ibid., 364.

45. Huels, "Towards Refining the Notion of 'Office' in Canon Law," 413. At p. 427 Huels explains the consequences of creating offices when they should not be created, warning that if an appointment looks like the conferral of an office, the person will have the rights and duties inherent in an office as outlined in canons 48–58, as well as 193, and 1734–39.

46. Ibid., 414. Other means of establishing offices are statutes and custom (cf. 414).

47. For Huels's argument why a singular administrative decree must be used when the decree confers the office on a particular person, see p. 415: "the office created by a singular decree ceases once the officeholder vacates the office."

48. Ibid., 428, n. 90: "For extraordinary ministers of communion, the faculties are those of cc. 910, §2; 911, §2; and 943. The delegation of faculties is also appropriate for the extraordinary ministers of baptism (cc. 861, 2), the lay assistant at marriages (c. 1112), lay ministers of the word and sacramentals (cc. 230, §3; 766; 1168), and those who lead Sunday celebrations in the absence of a priest or conduct funeral services (*Ecclesiae de mysterio*, arts. 7, §1; 12)."

49. Ibid., 429. At p. 432 he concludes that it is up to the diocesan bishop to determine which offices he deems important for his diocese.

50. Pagé, "Full-Time Pastoral Ministers and Diocesan Governance," 30.

51. Coriden, "Necessary Canonical Reform," 22–23, suggests changes to some canons that would open certain offices in the church to laity.

52. R. McCord, "The U.S. Bishops and Lay Ecclesial Ministry," *Origins* 37 (2007): 103.

53. Hahnenberg, "Vocation to Lay Ecclesial Ministry," 181.

54. *Co-Workers*, 36–49, speaks of different aspects of formation: human, spiritual, intellectual, and pastoral.

55. Euart, "Lay Ecclesial Ministry and Parish Leadership Options," 116.

56. Ibid.

57. The Code outlines educational requirements, for example, for the offices of bishop (c. 378 §1.5), seminary professor (c. 253 §1), vicar general (c. 478 §1), judicial vicar (c. 1420 §4), judge (c. 1421 §2), defender of the bond (c. 1435).

58. McDermott, *"Co-Workers in the Vineyard of the Lord*: A Canonical Analysis," 452, speaks of the intense formation programs undergone by "candidates for vocations to the clerical and consecrated life" and states, "One can reasonably see that the present formation of the lay faithful . . . pales somewhat in comparison to these intense formation programs."

59. J. Huels, *Empowerment for Ministry: A Complete Manual on Diocesan Faculties for Priests, Deacons, and Lay Ministers* (Mahwah, NJ: Paulist, 2003), 32. At p. 10, n. 15, Huels reminds us that the authorization is "for a ministerial act or an act of administration done in the name of the Church."

Coriden, "Pastoral Ministry in the Parish," 117, objects: "there is no adequate reason for the final restrictive clause, 'other than an act of the power of governance.' . . . it has been well established that lay persons can be granted and do exercise the power of governance."

60. An important point would be agreement on the name of different ministries or offices. One example of different titles is found in Coriden, "Pastoral Ministry in the Parish," 119–20, who uses the example of canon 517 §2. He explains that the most common title is "pastoral administrator." On p. 119, he notes the CARA special report from 2005, which did a study of the actual practice in the United States where "this particular ministry has been given thirty-six different titles." Finally, Coriden evaluates the different titles used, and proposes "pastoral administrator" as his preferred title. The same could be done for different ministries, so that a common understanding of ministries and their titles arises. At p. 120, Coriden concludes, "If something does not have a name, its very being is suspect."

Euart, "Lay Ecclesial Ministry and Parish Leadership Options," 113, gives a list of possible titles for this "figure . . . pastoral or parish life coordinator, parochial minister, pastoral administrator, pastoral leader, parish director, or resident pastoral minister." She cites a 2009 CARA Report (footnote 36) stating that "parish life coordinator" is the most commonly used. At pp. 115–16, Euart addresses the complexities of "titles for canon 517 §2 roles," noting, "Titles matter; they describe or illustrate the role and functions performed by the person holding the office." She highlights the concern of the 1997 interdicasterial instruction *Ecclesiae de Mysterio* on not confusing titles and outlines attempts by the USCCB to come to some consensus on titles. She concludes, "Today, the suitability of terminology remains an unresolved issue . . . it seems important for the future that an effort be made to identify, if not a common title, two or three titles that might be selected as appropriate designations for this new role" (116).

Huels, *Empowerment for Ministry*, 176, speaks of the pastoral administrator and notes, "the diocesan bishop is competent to decide what to call this office within the diocese."

61. Provost, "Temporary Replacements or New Forms of Ministry," 61, gives an example: "a diocesan law could create the office of a lay person who participates in pastoral care, determine the obligations and rights that go with the office, and resolve various other issues in terms of how the lay person relates to the parish structures, the priest moderator, and the diocese." Provost continues, "Why is this a question worth addressing? There are certain legal effects which follow if the position is an ecclesiastical office. The position itself has to be established by a competent authority . . . Once established, it has the stability inherent in the notion of an ecclesiastical office; it should have a certain duration, and not be started and stopped at whim. The office is entitled to a description of its rights and obligations" (61).

62. Coriden, "Pastoral Ministry in the Parish," 121, argues for a stable appointment for a specific period of time for the example of "pastoral administrators" (c. 517 §2). He writes, "A suitable stability of office is a high value, both for the individual minister and for the community being served."

63. H. Witte, The Local Bishop and Lay Pastoral Workers: A Newly Created Function in the Church and Its Impact on Episcopal Collegiality, 106, where he is citing a 1990 document by some members of the Dutch Episcopal Conference.

64. *Co-Workers* speaks of the possibility that "lay ecclesial ministers might transfer from one diocese to another in the region with the approval of the sending and receiving bishops" (57).

65. M. Wijlens, "Ecclesial Lay Ministry, Clergy and Complementarity," *CLSA Proceedings* 64 (2002): 28, gives an example from some German dioceses: "Upon having completed a successful education as 'pastoral workers,' the diocesan bishop receives them within the context of a celebration of the Eucharist, into the 'service of the diocese.' In this ceremony, they promise obedience to the bishop and his successors and obtain a [civilly valid] contract for an indefinite time with the diocese. They also receive a mandate for their first concrete assignment." At p. 28, n. 2, she speaks of an example of the "pertinent sections from the liturgical celebration in the diocese of Münster" in which "the diocesan bishop and the lay person enter into a mutual commitment: the bishop promises to provide for a fitting position in the diocese, the lay person promises obedience to the diocesan bishop and his successors. Moreover, the spouses promise to assist their partners." See pp. 40–47 for the texts from the dioceses of Münster (Germany) and of Basel (Switzerland).

66. McDermott, *"Co-Workers in the Vineyard of the Lord*: A Canonical Analysis," 458, citing Hahnenberg, states, "One issue raised by the National Association of Lay Ministry is that of portability of benefits designed for lay ecclesial ministers moving from one diocese to another." *Co-Workers*, 63, no. 4, addresses the issue of "portability of benefits."

67. *Co-Workers*, 64, no. 6, speaks of "grievance procedures."

68. A. Asselin, "Consultation in the Parish: A Needless Burden, a Necessary Evil, or a Worthwhile Opportunity?," in *In the Service of Truth and Justice:*

Festschrift in Honour of Prof. Augustine Mendonça, ed. V. G. D'Souza (Bangalore, India, 2008), writes, "Lay leadership formation is one thing, but what about the formation of pastors as leaders of these newly structured parishes?" (135).

69. Asselin, "Lay Ecclesial Ministers in the Present Parish Structure," 142.

70. Assembly of Catholic Bishops of Ontario, Lay Pastoral Associates in Parish Settings: Perspectives, Considerations and Suggestions, September 1999. The document can be found at http://acbo.on.ca/englishweb/publications/pastoral.htm (accessed June 17, 2010).

71. Beal, "Lay People and Church Governance," 108, speaks of a "preference of many dioceses in the United States for issuing 'policies' and 'guidelines' instead of promulgating 'particular laws.'" At pp. 108–9, Beal encourages dioceses to promulgate laws regarding ecclesiastical offices held by lay ecclesial ministers for the stability of the office. In addition, establishing such offices makes the relationship between the diocesan bishop and the office holder clear to the community.

72. McDermott, "*Co-Workers in the Vineyard of the Lord*: A Canonical Analysis," 456, suggests this: "Given the USCCB's concern for the role of the laity in the Church over the past two and a half decades, it would seem appropriate to have an office for the laity and lay ministry in each diocese. This office would serve at the diocesan level in a similar manner to that of the Pontifical Council for the Laity at the universal level. Likewise, it would complement the offices for clergy and members of consecrated life."

73. J. Coriden, *The Rights of Catholics in the Church* (Mahwah, NJ: Paulist, 2007), 130–31, speaks of "alternative dispute resolution," which would include conciliation, mediation, and arbitration. He notes that "many dioceses have offices of due process . . . and some of them are active and successful. However, many other dioceses have them 'on paper' only."

74. McDermott, "*Co-Workers in the Vineyard of the Lord*: A Canonical Analysis," 457, notes that such contracts or agreements "protect the rights of both the diocese or parish and the lay person, particularly in providing for termination and guarding against any unjust removal from office or ministry." These contracts or agreements would also provide norms for remuneration, health benefits, pensions, etc.

Chapter 8

Developing Lay Ecclesial Ministry[*]

Francis Cardinal George, OMI

Aristotle said that a small mistake in the beginning has enormous consequences at the end. In considering this increasingly important topic of lay ecclesial ministry, major errors could easily arise from the way we often address any topic in the United States. Ours is a pragmatic culture. Results in action and activity define the meaning of ideas and even create a person's identity. Often we ask, "What do you do?" when we really mean, "Who are you?" To come to a correct sense of lay ecclesial ministry, it is a mistake to start with what somebody does or doesn't do. Ministry obviously is an activity, a function, but it doesn't adequately define the person who does it. Nor should one begin with models, especially those not based in Holy Scripture, nor with human roles or with power or authority. I would like to suggest that it is more true to say that ministry is not a profession, rather than to assume that it is. There are professional elements that identify a ministry, of course, but a profession is organized in order to control and pass on a certain body of knowledge and certain skills. Professionals serve others, but on the professionals' terms; and the professional person is accountable primarily to the profession itself, which usually controls its own accrediting processes. Ministry, by contrast, begins not with control but with going out to the poor on their terms and on God's, not on ours. It means being accountable in ways that are rather complex but that become evident as the minister works to maintain his or her life with integrity.

The great bugaboo that sometimes shapes discussion of ministry in general in the church today is the fear of clericalism. Clericalism is not automatically created by titles or clothing or history. Clericalism is a sinful attitude that removes a person from being accountable. An ordained priest might be very informal ("Just call me Bob") and still be totally clerical because he's not accountable. Neither his bishop nor his parish council can influence his activity. He's accountable only to himself and his own ideas. That's clericalism, and it's found in many places in the church and other social organizations. Unaccountability is often particularly in evidence when people declare themselves prophets.

What I'm going to say now shouldn't be surprising. Bishops, after all, are not supposed to be original. We hand on what we have received. We make sure that the basic elements of our response in trusting faith to the truths of God's self-revelation are remembered, repeated, and relived in every generation. In speaking about lay ecclesial ministry, therefore, I will argue that we should begin with relationships.

Relationships tell us who we are. We're all born somebody's daughter, somebody's son. Only later do we establish a certain personal sense of self by reason of choices we make or actions we undertake. Our life is spent growing into the relationships that are given to us before we are self-conscious, before we know who we are. Relations are basic to identity and to self-understanding. One is part of a social network before one does something, before one acts. We are incorporated into the human race, to begin with, and into a particular human family. Basic relations are both ineradicable and eternal. They last beyond the grave.

Most of us were incorporated into the family of God by parents or grandparents who brought us to the church to be baptized. When we think of church, we should think, first of all, of the network of relationships that Vatican II called "communion." In 1985, when the special synod called to examine the reception of Vatican II defined the ecclesiology of "communion" as the basic theology of church in the Second Vatican Council's documents, some expressed surprise until they went back to the Latin texts of the council and discovered how frequently *communio* appeared, even though it was translated into English using several different terms: community, society, fraternity, along with communion.

The ecclesiology of a council called to be an exercise in ecclesial self-consciousness solved an impasse that had been with us since the Counter-Reformation. When the Reformers defined the church as a spiritual reality, as invisible as is grace itself, and when, in reaction, the Counter-Reformers, particularly St. Robert Bellarmine, insisted that the church is a visible society, like the Kingdom of France or the Kingdom of Naples, in order to safeguard the visible structures willed by Christ as part of the church's constitution, a division was built into the understanding of church that reinforced conceptually the experience of separation between Protestants and Catholics.

Counter-Reformation ecclesiology didn't, of course, deny the primacy of grace and the faith and other infused virtues that are the invisible realities given by Christ to his church, but its stress on the visible gifts created tensions not only with Protestants but also with society. The problem of the church in the world of nation-states became the problem of relating two perfect societies, perfect not in the moral sense but in the sense that both church and state were complete, possessing everything necessary for each to fulfill its purpose. In a sense, both church and state became self-contained and the problem of their interrelationship exhausted the discussion of the relationship between the church and the world.

Resituating the relation between a united church and a divided world was the reason for calling the Second Vatican Council. The natural trajectory of Protestantism is to make the church publicly a department of state and privately a spiritual support group. Luther took refuge with the German princes, who protected him from the authority of pope and emperor. He insisted then that the only public law was civil law, and the only private law was individual conscience, unmediated by the church. Luther burned the books of canon law along with St. Thomas's *Summa Theologiae*. There is no public reason; there is only faith and the Scripture that elicited it. There is no public discipline except that imposed by the will of the civil rulers. In a society whose ethos is secularized Protestantism, like that of the United States, the Catholic Church's claim to retain her own canon law and to defend her faith philosophically using natural law theory makes her appear to most Americans as "a state within the state." Because the state is supreme, at least in all matters visible, the Catholic Church's self-definition is resented.

The Reformers reduced the sacraments of the church to two. Because the church has no visible governance structures willed by Christ, Protestants do not claim to have a sacrament of holy orders. They have believers called from among the baptized and commissioned to be ministers of God's Word, servants who function as preachers to help people understand Holy Scripture; but no one is ordained to govern the church visibly. Christ is head of his church, of course, and governs his people, but Christ has ascended into heaven and is invisible; and there is no way that his headship can be visibly present to his church here and now. The Reformation was about church governance as much as it was about salvation by faith. In an invisible church, there is no public mediation of

God's will for his people; the Holy Spirit inspires the human authors of Scripture and inspires as well those who read it. Literacy became almost a precondition for church membership. The Reformation could hardly have happened before the invention of the printing press. For Catholics, of course, the church is "mother," an interior voice who mediates one's relationship to God, a community within whose bosom relationships are given and explained. The ecclesial family existed before its inspired memoirs were written.

The Vatican II description of the church as communion finessed both the tension between the invisible and visible church and the conflict between church and state, which has been transformed into a dialogue between faith and culture. In prayer and worship, the church listens to Christ and receives his gifts; in dialogue with cultures, the church listens to the world and comes to an understanding of how Christ's gifts are to be shared in a particular place and time in order to be a leaven transforming society and its institutions, including the state. The church is a network of relationships based upon sharing the gifts of Christ. If one receives a gift, a relationship is established. If your grandmother knits socks for you for Christmas and you do not accept them, you not only refuse the gift but you also weaken or break the relationship with your grandmother. A gift is a commodity with a person attached. From the exchange of gifts, real relationships are created. Communion is not a metaphor for church; it names a network of real relationships based on accepting and offering in turn the gifts that Christ has given his people. There are many different relationships, because there are many different gifts. The council emphasized three of the visible gifts: the proclamation of the Gospel in its integrity, the seven sacraments of the apostolic churches, and apostolic governance, passed on from generation to generation by the Twelve and their successors in the episcopal college. These are the visible gifts that relate to the triple *munera* of Christ himself: teacher or truth, priest or life-giver, and shepherd or way. Everything in the church speaks of Christ. To state, as does the council, that Christ's church "subsists" in the visible Catholic Church is to affirm that all the gifts Christ wants his people to enjoy are given and received in Catholic communion.

More basic, of course, are the invisible gifts of grace: faith, hope, charity, the infused virtues, and charisms to build up the body of Christ. The church makes invisible gifts visible, because she is a sacramental church. Ministries in the church are based on the gifts given sacramentally, and the sacraments, in turn, are instituted for the sake of mission. The various ministries, like the various sacraments on which they are based, insert the members of the church variously into the church's mission. While the gifts and the ministries are multiple, the mission is always simple. The purpose of the church, the "why" of the church, is to introduce the world to its Savior in every age until he returns in glory to judge the living and the dead. The church introduces the world to its Savior by making available his gifts to all peoples: the visible gifts and, through them, the invisible gifts so that, in constantly increasing the numbers that share Christ's gifts, the church will continue to expand until the end of time. Sharing spiritual gifts, whether visible or invisible, is called evangelizing. Sharing material gifts is called stewardship.

In every case, the gifts are shared by means of various ministries, some of which are structurally or constitutionally essential for the church and many of which come and go according to the demands of the mission in particular times or circumstances. The essential gifts establish offices in the church; other gifts that are given not just for the sanctification of an individual believer but truly for the sake of the church herself are charisms. The document on the church from the Second Vatican Council, *Lumen Gentium*, distinguished between offices and charisms, whether individual or institutionally established. This distinction enables the church to discern which ministries are essential and which are necessary but not of the essence of the church.

How are sacraments understood in a relational ecclesiology? The sacraments are actions of the risen Lord. They create new relationships within ecclesial communion by connecting people to Christ in his various mysteries. The sacraments establish a new creation. They are more than the naming of a gift already present. When a little child is baptized, she is brought into the church building as a creature of God, one who has received the gift of existence from her Creator and the gift of existence as a human being from her biological mother and father. A rational creature, made in God's image and likeness, she is worthy of every dignity because of her relationships. Even though it is spiritually sterile because of the consequences of original sin, the relation of creation in creatures is real. When she is baptized, however, a new relationship comes into the child's existence. The child is carried out of the church building with a new relationship to the Father. No longer just a creature of God, a baptized person is a son or a daughter of God. They may dare to call God "Father" because they are now identified with Christ, God's only begotten Son. The consideration of God as creator is basic but philosophical and not dependent upon historical revelation. The recognition of God as Father is possible only because we have received, in baptism, the gift of the Son's own life. That relationship is permanent, just as the relationship to one's mother and father is permanent, no matter how one's life is lived. One can never be unbaptized, just as one can never be unborn.

Confirmation seals baptism and enables a son or daughter of the Father to face the world publicly as a disciple of Jesus Christ, able to take personal responsibility for the church's mission. When we are baptized, chrism is placed on our heads, sanctifying our bodies and therefore our entire selves. When we are confirmed, chrism marks our foreheads with the sign of the cross. We relate to the world as one called to evangelize, to give witness to Jesus Christ.

Beyond the relationship of sonship, the relation of Jesus to the Father, made visible in baptism and sealed in confirmation, the relationship of Christ's headship of his church is also made sacramentally visible. The sacrament of marriage makes visible the relationship between Christ and his church, his spouse, but marriage is not eternal; it ends with death. The relationship between Christ and his church is made visible permanently in the sacrament of holy orders. When they are ordained, the hands of a priest are anointed for sacred service and the head of a bishop is anointed for the sake of governance. Ordained bishops and priests receive, then, a new relationship not to the Father but to the church. Orders do not bring an intensification of the baptismal relationship; they establish a new relation that defines the life of an ordained priest, bringing him into Christ's own authority to govern the church by calling him to sacrifice his life for Christ's people. Every ordination of a priest is a sign that Christ continues to govern his people. Every ordained priest is called to love the church as Christ loved her and offered himself up for her.

Because holy orders is the sacrament of ecclesial governance, every bishop and priest has a title. There is no laying on of hands outside of an ecclesial communion governed by a local bishop. Vatican II recovered the sense of diocese as local or particular church and not just a jurisdictional circumscription. A diocese (or eparchy) is a church headed by a pastor who is a bishop. The episcopacy is the fullest form of priesthood because it gives authority to govern a people in a particular place in communion with the universal church, with and under the Bishop of Rome, the head of the episcopal college. A bishop is a pastor in the fullest sense, not just a priest with added jurisdictional authority. Parishes are not local churches; they are eucharistic communities that form and reform as necessary, headed by priests who are in visible communion with a local bishop. The ordained priest, like the bishop and in communion with him, has power over the eucharistic body of the Lord because he has authority over the ecclesial body of Christ. A priest is not ordained for a parish. His title is that of his diocese or religious order, although he may or may not exercise the ministry of pastor in a parish. Every baptized Catholic, therefore, has three pastors: the priest who is pastor of his or her parish, the bishop who is pastor of the local church and whose name is mentioned in the celebration of every Mass, and the pope, pastor of the universal church, whose name is also mentioned in the celebration of the Eucharist throughout Catholic communion. When the three pastors teach and act in communion, the church is visibly united and possesses internal peace.

There is, therefore, no ordained priesthood without explicit relationship to a church. Some apparently think that one can be ordained without a title, without people, without a church, as if ordination were a personal charism, a purely personal prerogative that one can claim just because of personal desire or personal competence in serving. Holy orders is an ordering, a relationship made visible, not an external certification for ministry. Heads have members, just as members have heads. In Catholicism, both are visible. Catholic communion is visibly established through the sacraments of baptism and holy orders. Vatican II completed or reformed Aquinas's theology of ordained priesthood, which defined the priest by relation to the Eucharist. By refocusing the priest's identity on pastoral charity and the relationship of headship, the council reminded the church that the Eucharist is possible only because of ordained priests who have authority from Christ to bring his people into unity around the altar. Pastoring is primarily a work of love, not of jurisdiction or law, although regulation of even a loving community is necessary if it is to be a visible communion. The church is a new creation, not a society borrowing its visible organization from worldly models.

The church looks at society, looks at people, and doesn't see individuals and their rights or even individuals and their gifts. Our particular society protects individual rights, often to the detriment of the common good, because it is based upon seventeenth-century social contract political theory, which is useful as far as it goes. If it goes too far, then the political reality exhausts the social reality, and that is a formula for totalitarianism. The church, for her part, looks at people and sees persons and their relationships. In Catholic social teaching, the family is the basic unit of society, not individuals.

How does lay ecclesial ministry fit into this theological vision? As lay, it would seem to speak of the world. As ecclesial, it speaks of the church. As ministry, it seems to speak of function rather than relationship. Essentially, lay ecclesial ministry is a particular form of participation in pastoring, in caring for people by keeping them connected to, related to, Jesus Christ.

Sacramentally, lay ecclesial ministry is based on baptism and confirmation; but because it brings the minister into the pastoral relationship proper to the ordained priest, something besides the conferral of holy orders has to be intrinsic to lay ecclesial ministry precisely as ecclesial. This is the calling from the local bishop that brings a new relationship into ecclesial communion. Sacramentally, baptism brings one into Christ's relationship to God the Father, and holy orders brings one into Christ's relationship to his church. There is, however, a relationship made visible among baptized believers in the way they care for one another in Christ. Christ's love is active in teaching children how to pray, in passing on the faith through example and witness, in visiting the sick and the homebound, in supporting the works of the church. These activities create a relationship of church to church, of member to member. Keeping the members of Christ's body related to one another as his disciples can be done informally and in passing or in an explicit manner and more permanent manner by calling and commissioning from the bishop, establishing with him a new public relationship. Lay ecclesial ministers are codisciples of Christ with other laypeople, but are so publicly in the name of the church because they have been called to take on responsibility for strengthening the bonds of communion under the direction of an ordained pastor. Lay ecclesial ministry is not done intermittently as a service to others, even in Christ's name, but institutionally, in an established manner for the sake of the church's mission. Lay ministry, in its many forms, becomes lay ecclesial ministry when the bishop calls the person and then commissions him or her to a particular parish or to some other institutionally based task. Because of that call and commission, the minister participates in the function of pastoring, but analogously so and from a baptismal sacramental base.

Within this sense of ecclesial communion, its ministries and its mission, the Archdiocese of Chicago has distinguished five components in the process of formation and in the public establishment of a lay ecclesial minister. There is, first of all, an interior call or grace. A period of discernment helps determine whether or not an attraction to lay ministry, as opposed to Christian service in the world, is truly an interior call from God. This discernment usually takes place in the parish with the help of the pastor and, perhaps, a personal spiritual director.

To test this initial discernment, a candidate enters into formation programs. These are both academic and personal. The archdiocese has instructed the universities and other institutions that teach future lay ministers that there are eight areas of theology that have to be covered in any program used by future lay ecclesial ministers. The school gives its own master's degree, in theology or pastoral studies or in divinity. The seminary faculty enters into the final stages of this academic formation to be sure that the theological vision of the lay ecclesial ministers is consistent with the theology courses of the seminarians, since they will be working together in the parishes and other institutions of the archdiocese.

Along with the academic formation and the acquiring of pastoral skills, the candidate receives personal formation supervised by the lay ecclesial ministry office of the archdiocese. The purpose of this personal formation is to help the candidate grow in the spiritual life and to help the bishop and the archdiocese learn that the person is trustworthy and can be entrusted with responsibility for other believers. This program is called Together in God's Service. Most of the laypeople in the program are active in their parishes and so are well known not only to their parish pastors but also to the auxiliary bishops or myself. We do not call someone who isn't known personally to those responsible for pastoring in the archdiocese.

When the academic preparation and the skills acquisition and the personal formation are all completed, the candidate is certified by the diocese. Certification is testimony to the readiness of the candidate to be called by the bishop into lay ecclesial ministry in the archdiocese. This call is then given in a public ceremony, because the lay ecclesial minister has public responsibilities in the church. The lay ecclesial minister is not just a hired worker in a parish, even though most are employees in parishes. There is an archdiocesan commitment to them, to be of assistance in helping them find a ministerial position. There is mutual accountability, not of the same kind as obtains for an incardinated priest but nonetheless meaningful. With the call from the bishop comes a commissioning, a sending of the lay ecclesial minister to a particular parish or institution in the archdiocese. This commissioning specifies where the called minister is to go to be part of the archdiocesan mission. Its terms are negotiated by the parish pastor and the lay ecclesial minister and approved by the archdiocesan office for lay ministry.

Two forms of lay ministry are recognized as ecclesial in the Archdiocese of Chicago: pastoral associates and directors of religious education or catechetical leaders. We have talked about youth ministers and music ministers and several other forms of ministry being recognized as "ecclesial" in the sense outlined above, but either because some of the positions don't seem to have much permanency or because the responsibilities are more for a function than to people or because the need for a master's degree is too daunting, the archdiocese at this time has instituted lay ecclesial ministry only for pastoral associates and catechetical teachers of the faith.

The life and ministry of lay ecclesial ministers strengthens the church's mission by complementing the life and ministry of ordained priests. The people are loved and cared for with expertise and personal responsibility. The church becomes more evidently the place where the face of Jesus Christ can be seen more clearly and the grace of God becomes more readily available. With the help of lay ecclesial ministers, the gifts of Christ are more easily shared.

Notes

* This chapter is an adaptation of a keynote address at the 2011 Collegeville National Symposium on Lay Ecclesial Ministry, available online at http://www1 .csbsju.edu/sot/symposium/CardinalGeorgeKeynote.htm.

Part IV

Rituals of Authorization and Their Pastoral and Theological Significance for Lay Ecclesial Ministry

Chapter 9

Rituals Matter
What Diocesan Rites Can Tell Us about the Emerging Theology of Lay Ecclesial Ministry

Graziano Marcheschi

What questions, issues, concerns, and theologies regarding the service of laity in the church are implicit in the design and implementation of a rite of "calling" or "authorization"? Does understanding ministry as "function" vs. "relationship" affect the language and symbols of a rite? Do rites of calling clarify or blur the distinction between the ordained and the authorized?[1]

At an archdiocesan meeting, I referenced remarks made by some participants in Chicago's first "calling rite," lamenting that for several the event apparently held little significance.[2] Immediately, a pastoral associate who had participated in Chicago's third and most recent calling ritual reacted with disbelief. Her experience and that of many colleagues in her vicariate contrasted sharply with what I had reported.[3]

With enthusiastic energy, zeal even, she spoke of how the group with whom she experienced the rite has developed a vocabulary that includes the words "candled" and "candling," references to the sacramental each received at the rite from the hands of Francis Cardinal George.[4] "We use the term 'candled' as a way of identifying our call to lay ecclesial ministry," she said. "As we have grown in our understanding of our ministerial role, it has become for us the symbol of our vocation."

She spoke of how the "called" lay ecclesial ministers in her vicariate proudly refer to themselves as having been "candled," and distinguish between those who have and those who have not been through "candling." "We speak of the perspective we share as 'the candled,' and how it differs from those who are *not* candled," she said. This group of twenty-plus ministers has put their candles in places of honor in their ministerial settings. For her and her friends, the rite and candle were hugely significant. She had assumed her experience was typical, and was surprised that participants from the first rite hadn't found *calling* to be the profound event she experienced. "It's very much a part of our identity," she explained; "the calling, the candle speak to us of the relationship we've embraced within the archdiocese."

She later wrote to elaborate: "The candle represents both the fire of our baptism and, having received it from our Ordinary, our ecclesial relationship to the Archdiocese. When we talk to other parish ministers, who may be questioning the significance of participating in the 'candling' ceremony, we hold up the candle as the light that illuminates our path," she said. "We hold on to our candles, as the one true reminder of our call and of our ecclesial role. And we recognize that the formation processes that the candling rite completes are what shape our ministerial identity."[5]

This anecdote serves to illustrate a basic premise of this essay: rituals speak. And, therefore, rituals matter. In a church that professes *Lex orandi, lex credendi*, one must pay attention to the creation and evolution of rituals. Because they speak of Christ and his body, the church, rituals must speak truthfully. They must communicate faithfully what the church understands about Christ's saving activity and help those who participate to better apprehend the flow of grace within the life-moment brought to a particular rite.

As the thousands of women and men serving in parishes throughout the country built a legacy of commitment and service; as the roles of pastoral associate, director of religious education, youth minister, and many others achieved differentiation, local recognition, and legitimacy; as those serving longed for and requested recognition from their bishops, lay ecclesial ministry became the object of sustained scrutiny on the part of the US hierarchy. And rightly so because those serving deserved the clarity and support that recognition from church authority brings, and because those in authority have a responsibility to exercise governance in a way that fosters and guides the use of the gifts brought by lay ecclesial ministers, "not to control the Spirit, but to test all things and hold fast to what is good" (AA 3, 24; 1 Thess 5:12, 19, 21; c. 394).

When US dioceses began recognizing lay ecclesial ministers through public rites, a new moment dawned in the life of the church in America. Every public, ecclesial act makes a statement, either about what Christ is doing or about what his body, the church, is doing. In the sacraments we recognize the risen Christ saving and sanctifying his people. But what do we recognize in a public rite of calling or commissioning? What is the action and who is the "actor(s)"? Though illustrative, the anecdote above is not presented to make a case for adding "candling" to the liturgical lexicon, nor to endorse sacramentals or even "calling" rites, but to illustrate the power of liturgical action and to ask what can be learned from examining the contours of a particular rite.

Are They Necessary?

Before examining specific rites, however, a prior question demands attention: do we need them? The answer depends on one's definition of ministry and on one's understanding of "authorization,"[6] and prior to that, "vocation."[7] The ideological camps stand far apart. Regarding notions of vocation, Edward Hahnenberg of John Carroll University helpfully names the sides as "too-personalized" and "too-institutionalized," saying that, on the one hand, "vocation is too often reduced to an inner voice, whispered by God directly to an individual in the depths of her or his soul," while, on the other hand, "the task of *authenticating* a ministerial vocation . . . [is] placed almost exclusively in the hands of the ordained."[8] Hahnenberg doesn't question the personal dimension of vocations nor the hierarchy's role in authenticating them, but he rightly worries about their "isolation and their separation,"[9] and about pitting personal and institutional responses against each other, that is, "the individual's sincere conviction that 'I have a call' juxtaposed against 'the bishop's unwavering insistence that "Nobody has been called until I call them." ' "[10] A rite of calling will necessarily pick a point along this continuum, either focusing more on the individual's response to the Spirit's impulse, or asserting that the bishop's call is essential for service to constitute public, authorized ministry.[11]

Baptism or Orders?

At the root of the debate lies one's understanding of baptism and holy orders. Lacking a balanced understanding of either sacrament easily leads to one of two egregious errors: laicism or clericalism.[12]

To focus the discussion, let's first recap the evolution of lay ecclesial ministry in the post–Vatican II church. It has been asserted by some that the council *required* Catholics to understand that Christianity is for ministers only.[13] No longer bound by a worldview that saw laypersons as the passive recipients of the mission of the clergy, laity discovered their own mission and vocation. Holy orders no longer held center stage. In its place, baptism assumed the central role. While there was but one mission entrusted to the church, there were a multitude of ministries, gifts, and calls given to God's people. The call to holiness was universal, not reserved to clergy and religious.

Vocabulary soon shifted. Rather than the "lay apostolate," people began talking about "lay *ministry*." Lay ministry became whatever lay-people did: what they did in their workplace was "marketplace" ministry; what they did within the church was "ecclesial" ministry. Soon ministry became the most ubiquitous term in the post–Vatican II lexicon. Ministry could be just about anything a person did to live and spread the Gospel.

But from these good intentions, confusion spread because when everything is ministry, nothing is ministry. Francis Cardinal George has addressed this issue with his typical, clear-minded candor:

> I think that, at times, the universal call to holiness got misinterpreted . . . as a universal call to ecclesial ministry. Perhaps the clericalism sometimes found in the pre-Vatican II Church continues to operate among those who think one cannot be holy except through doing ministry. There were a few years when everything was called "ministry," from preaching the homily to cutting the grass. The essential distinction between the generous service which is the natural outgrowth of a holy life and the various ministries and offices of the Church is part of the teaching of Vatican II. (The Universal Call to Holiness, 3)[14]

This "*essential* distinction" has been an issue of no small significance for those involved in formation of laity for service in the church. If the call to ministry flows solely or primarily from baptism, then talk of episcopal "calling" or "authorization" sounds hollow, making the push for hierarchical approbation redolent of the error of clericalism.

When holy orders was the hub of the ministerial wheel and the mission of Christ was seen as entrusted solely to the hierarchy, it made sense to ask, "If holy orders is everything, what is baptism for?" Cardinal Avery Dulles asserted that the error of clericalism forgets the baptismal theology of Vatican II and so "overemphasizes the value of ordination . . . that the active power conferred by baptism, confirmation, and matrimony are unduly minimized."[15] The push for ritualizing and authorization could appear to manifest the clericalism experienced by a colleague in upper diocesan administration who was asked by her vicar general, "You do know it's priests who run the church, don't you?" or of the clericalism, reported by Richard Gaillardetz, manifested by a pastor who told his pastoral associate, "At the end of the day, my ministry comes from God, what you do is a job."[16]

As important as it is to stand vigilant against a demeaning clericalism, we must also acknowledge its opposite pole: laicism.[17] If, instead of ordination, everything flows from baptism, then the question becomes, What is holy orders for? Is priesthood just an "intensification" of the call received at baptism? Some divinity school students, myself included, have encountered the notion that "priesthood" exists on a continuum, that the ordained just have a higher "dose" of the same priesthood shared by all the faithful. Of this error, Dulles says, "it so emphasizes baptism as to imagine that it confers all rights and powers in the church, so that ordination would not be understood as giving any new sacramental and hierarchical powers."[18] This error, just as virulent as any clericalism because it fails to respect the movement of the Spirit in assigning different gifts and different ministries, characterized a woman who refused to attend Chicago's first rite of calling, saying, "I don't need any bishop laying hands on me. I got all the authorization I need from the Holy Spirit."[19]

Ministry or Discipleship?

A calling rite is not an ordination[20] but neither is it a redunking in the pool of baptism. There's no question the Second Vatican Council helped the church rediscover baptism as the "foundational sacrament of ministry" and provided a "clearer recognition that ministry is not just for the ordained."[21] But while baptism makes it *possible* for a Christian to be a minister, it does not *make* one a minister of the church. No baptismal theology can ever make holy orders obsolete nor give lay ministers automatic authorization to serve within the church. Baptism makes us disciples, but saying it makes us all ministers ignores reality. When religious orders sprang up, they were recognized not as a lesser degree of orders but as a new charism, a new form of Spirit-given life and service that required recognition, support, and authorization to grow and flourish.[22] Lay ecclesial ministry is on the same trajectory.

If LEM represents more than the universal call to holiness and if it encompasses a fuller form of service that is neither common to all the faithful nor necessary for responding to one's baptismal call, then we must consider questions of authorization for lay ecclesial ministry and ponder the design of rites of authorization. Such rites will need to view baptism as the necessary antecedent rather than the efficient or proximate cause of lay ecclesial ministry.[23] And if baptism is not the answer to the questions, What makes the service of the laity "ministry," and what makes lay ministry "ecclesial?" we must conclude, without questioning the necessity of baptism, that the proper answer is "the bishop." For some, this will not be a particularly attractive notion. But, in light of Roman Catholic tradition, ecclesiology, and canon law, it seems to be the only notion that makes sense.

Interiority

Besides the Scylla and Charybdis of laicism and clericalism, another danger lurks in the murky waters surrounding the lay ecclesial ministry debate, and it can influence the design of public rites of authorization. This distinctively American leaning is an overemphasis on interiority. Americans tend to glorify the personal and subjective, giving it normative authority. But how one "feels" neither determines whether one is *called* to ministry ("I have a vocation because I feel good inside . . .") nor whether what one does *constitutes* ministry ("If you feel in your heart that making sandwiches at the local restaurant is a way of helping people nourish their bodies, then what you're doing is ministry . . ."). While lay ecclesial ministry "*emerges* from a personal call," it is about much more than the way I "feel" about what I'm doing.[24]

Through this lens, it becomes easier to distinguish ministry done in the name of the church from baptismal discipleship. In "discipleship," interiority *is* paramount. Discipleship is about holiness, which is another way of saying it is all about how one sees life and what one sees *in* life. A disciple recognizes the "Godness" of life and of all people. One who has given his or her life to God sees and does things differently. "Motivation" distinguishes the "disciple" sandwich-maker from the "non-disciple" sandwich-maker.

Vatican II teaches that one's inner attitude can transform the challenges and trials of daily life into something salvific. What might be the source of anger or cynicism for one becomes the source of holiness for another (LG 41). Thus, the lawyer who sees work on behalf of her clients as a way of incarnating justice, or even the grocery clerk who sees bagging groceries as helping customers feed and nurture their families, is living out discipleship, while the lawyer who is simply "making a buck," or the checkout clerk who hates his job and the people he's serving, is doing nothing of the kind.

But what is true of "discipleship" is often misapplied to lay ecclesial ministry. Of course, we expect anyone who answers the call to ministry to desire to serve God and others and thus grow in holiness; but that "internal" desire is not the only or even the primary criterion that distinguishes certain work as "ecclesial ministry." Though a case like the following would be tragic, consider a priest who no longer cares for his people and simply goes through the motions, no longer motivated by love or genuine piety. If that priest celebrates Mass and the sacraments, hears confessions, buries the dead, and visits the sick, like it or not, he is doing genuine ministry. "Genuine" here must be understood as "true" or "real," not as "ideal" or "exemplary." While the priest's interiority affects the state of his soul, it does not change what he does from being ministry to being something else. Why? Because "it's not all about him."

Interiority is primary and necessary in hearing the "call" to ministry, but what *constitutes* LEM comes from outside the minister, and that is authorization. The 1999 USCCB document Lay Ecclesial Ministry: The State of the Questions explicitly addresses this point:

> The word "ecclesial" denotes not only that the ministry of these lay persons has a place within the *communio* of the Church, but also that *it is to be submitted to the judgment and supervision of the hierarchy. It is not simply an activity undertaken on personal initiative.* (16, emphasis added)

By saying that "identity as a lay ecclesial minister is partly a question of personal awareness and partly a matter of recognition by official Church authority" (ibid., 7–8), State of the Questions moves us out of the realm of interiority and disposition and into the realm of "law."[25] Catholic notions of vocation are about more than individual experience or desire. All baptized Christians are called to share in Christ's saving work as priest, prophet, and king. But when they do so through public activity that is authorized by the church, we call it "ecclesial ministry."

If these assumptions are correct, a liturgical rite of authorization will need to give a clear nod to the personal but much greater emphasis to the *action of the church* manifest in the rite. If rites simply celebrate subjective attitudes rather than the activity of Christ or his church, they become irrelevant. Calling rites are not ordinations, but they must be more than an individual's declaration of willingness to serve or a bishop's acceptance of that service. While both should occur within authorization rites, the action of the church in *calling* one to ministry remains primary.

At the same time, however, rites of calling must never be used to gut the notion of lay ecclesial ministry, reducing it to lay "assisting" or lay "helping," turning authorization into an ecclesial pat-on-the-back of those who help the clergy do *their* ministry. Church authorities who design such rites must first answer the question, can laity be called "ministers"? Canon law primarily reserves that title to the ordained.[26] And some bishops would prefer to see the usage remain limited. They worry that referring to laity as ministers begins to blur the legitimate line between lay and ordained. Some object that use of the term creates a new class within the church, turning laity into a lower rank of clergy. Even some *lay* critics fear this usage smacks of elitism and clericalism, that is, "You can't do God's work unless you are clergy?!?"

Function or Relationship?

Worry about such blurring can be eliminated by understanding ministry as "relationship" rather than "function." And this applies first to our understanding of priesthood. When priesthood is understood primarily as function, as it too often is, the ministry of laity will inevitably threaten some clergy. If LEMs perform some of the *functions* of priesthood, and perform them well, the *interaction* of LEMs and priests can easily devolve into issues of who gets to do what. If priestly ministry is just about the functions of presiding, preaching, and pastoral care, someone will eventually ask, Does not the one who is most *skilled* at those functions possess the greater authority, indeed, the greater imperative to perform them?

Ontology is the other common way of understanding priesthood. I will not undertake a discussion of the theology of ontological change, but a recovery of this sometimes derided aspect of church teaching would benefit both clergy and laity. Bishop William Lori of Bridgeport, Connecticut, argues against a purely functional approach that erases the distinction between the ministerial priesthood and the common priesthood of the faithful.[27] While he acknowledges the abuses that can result from overemphasis on ontological change, he calls on his priests to recognize that in ordination they take on Christ, the one whose ministry was characterized by selfless service to others and who freely gave his life for the sake of all.

Rejecting ontology in favor of function and insisting the priest *is* what he *does* sometimes becomes an argument for widening access to priesthood beyond its current male-celibate confines. The assertion that preaching, presiding, and teaching are not *just* functions but *essentials* of priesthood is arguably true. But sometimes that claim walks alongside the assumption that if you don't have the gift, you don't get the ministry. Ministry should be entrusted only to those who possess the gifts, and if there aren't enough male celibates who qualify, then perhaps the net needs to be cast wider.

In a dialogue between American university professors and German priests and lay ministers who had crossed the Atlantic for an immersion experience of the church in the United States, one of the Germans asked an American theologian, "Aren't you reducing priesthood to function?" The American unapologetically responded, "Yes," adding he had been such a "doer" all his life and that it came naturally to make that assumption. Another American added, "We *are* what we *do* consistently."

Given the currency of such attitudes, it is imperative that seminarians and lay ministers acquire a sound understanding of priesthood. Overemphasis on function can lead to a service-oriented, sociological approach to ministry. Proliferation of "ministries" does not always make for holier women and men; better "served" does not necessarily mean better "disciples." The church's first responsibility is to introduce us to Christ, not to create social events for every age group and programs for every need. People can be very engaged in parish and still not know Christ. We even can teach Scripture without ever really teaching Christ.

The church needs priests who are spiritual fathers. Ideally, the "best and the brightest" should fill seminaries and staff parishes. But what the church needs most are men who excel in holiness, who model a life of prayer, who understand the struggles and joys of the spiritual life, who have wrestled with demons and angels, who find God in all of life, who know the saints and number them among their friends, who are committed to empowering the poor and marginalized, who pray regularly, who can speak openly and unashamedly of their own faith and their relationship with Christ, who make no apologies for their priesthood, who humbly embrace the call to be icons of Christ in a world that largely ignores him, who are true servants, and who recognize that in Christ strength is made perfect in weakness. And the same can and must be said of lay ecclesial ministers.

At age four or five, my daughter Amanda asked me, "Do you know *why* I love you, Daddy?" Her explanation surprised me: "I love you," she said, "because I know you love me *more* than I love you." That day she taught me what it means to be a father. From my *relationship* with my children I derive my agenda: to be the one who loves them more than they love me. I would propose that their relationship with parishioners gives priests and lay ecclesial ministers their agenda: to become living icons of God's love, imitating Christ by loving people into wholeness and holiness.

In this notion of relationship theologies of function and ontology meet. As Cardinal George emphasizes throughout the interview cited here, relationship defines the identity of the lay ecclesial minister as well as of the priest. And the relationships are multiple, for one enters into relationship not only with those served but also with the *bishop*.

This discussion of function and relationship gets at the core of what is said and done in a rite of calling to lay ecclesial ministry. Such rites should manifest the conviction that relationship constitutes lay ecclesial ministry, not functions. Study and experimentation will yield language and symbols that can make that truth liturgically explicit.

Can We Call Them Ministers?

As previously noted, bishops' reservations about authorizing LEMs often stem from fears about the erosion of priestly identity.[28] The late Cardinal Joseph Bernardin addressed this concern in his 1985 pastoral letter on ministry:

> For many years, priests were *the* ministers of the community. Now, the emergence of various ministries may find a priest asking questions about his ministerial identity. "If people who aren't ordained can do many of the things I do, what is the meaning of my priesthood?" "How am I different," "What difference does ordination make?" . . . these questions bespeak a deep-rooted tension centering on priestly identity.[29]

Cardinal Joseph Ratzinger, now Pope Benedict XVI, lamented that "a loss of the meaning of the sacrament of Holy Orders" and "the growth of a kind of parallel ministry by so-called 'pastoral assistants' "[30] are resulting in a darkening cloud of confusion looming over and obscuring the special identity of priests. His concern was chiefly directed at European nations where he saw abuses that bear little or no resemblance to lay ministerial praxis in the United States. But while US experience is an ocean away from what caused worry elsewhere, what others do and how Rome reacts eventually impacts the wider church.[31]

When the US hierarchy met to discuss the State of the Questions document, bishops broke into small discussion groups. While most instinctively referred to the laypeople working in their dioceses as "ministers," one younger bishop asked, "Can we *call* them ministers?" He offered lay ecclesial "worker" and lay ecclesial "personnel" as alternatives.[32]

But that horse, as they say, has long since left the barn. It would be nearly impossible to reverse the usage that has become so common and widespread. Cardinal Avery Dulles[33] traced the consistent, though sometimes guarded, use of the term in papal, conciliar, and episcopal documents over the past forty-five years, concluding that the reality of laypeople exercising genuine ministry in the church has been consistently acknowledged and affirmed.[34] Even the 1997 interdicasterial instruction *Ecclesiae de Mysterio* did not forbid a careful use of the term "minister."[35] Though Vatican II never speaks of "lay ecclesial ministry," it clearly intended for laypeople to be involved in the internal life of the church, as well as in the world.[36] It was Cardinal Dulles's assertion that "laity" and "ministry" can be linked legitimately that ended the US bishops' debate over the *Co-Workers* document and secured its passage. Consequently, any rite that authorizes laypeople's participation in church service must unreservedly and unashamedly name it ministry.

Concern over erosion of priestly identity requires bishops to decide whether LEM is a lasting charism and a genuine work of the Spirit or a stopgap measure helping us deal with the current reduction in ordained ministers.[37] A bishop's answer to this question influences his approach to rituals of authorization and his understanding of the meaning of being authorized. Chicago's Cardinal George has made it clear that those he calls to lay ecclesial ministry have a direct relationship with him as archbishop. Though employed by local pastors, "they are," in his words, "not just the pastor's hired help."[38]

Bishops won't approve rites of authorization if they believe laypeople can't be called ministers; they won't authorize if they think lay ecclesial ministry is just about responding to a *personal* call from the Holy Spirit; they won't ritualize if the role of the church is not seen as essential in empowering those who serve. Rites of authorization must tell ministers that their service is exercised not only on their own initiative but also as a publicly recognized and authorized action within the local church. Lacking that, laity can't be expected to seek or value participation in such rites. A ritual that merely says we "acknowledge" what you are already doing lacks real meaning.

When planning the Archdiocese of Chicago's first calling rite, Cardinal George asked that all current ministers "discern" whether they had a "vocation" to ministry and then request "calling" to that ministry in the archdiocese, so a plan was designed. But the cardinal questioned the theology inherent in the design that asked people to discern "the vocation they received *years ago from the Holy Spirit.*" The cardinal explained that "no one has a vocation until the Church says they have a vocation, because vocation comes *through* the church." In response to "What do we say about these people and all the years they've been working?" he responded that the calling rite would "make *explicit* the vocation that had been *implicit* for these many years." However, the cardinal concluded it was inappropriate to require people who had been serving for decades to discern if they had a vocation, so the discernment process for veterans was scrapped.[39]

Seeking proper balance between too-personalized and too-institutionalized an approach, we turn now to the calling rite implemented within the Archdiocese of Chicago and a variation on the rite implemented elsewhere. I present the Chicago model because of my familiarity with it (full disclosure: I had a major hand in designing it). Though still "in development" and far from perfect, I believe it promotes the ecclesial commitments espoused in this chapter. I will count on the generosity of the reader to trust that comparison and contrast are used to endorse a theology of LEM and ways of making it liturgically explicit, not to compare dioceses or their leadership.[40]

My comparisons and contrasts will focus on language choices that focus either on the individual's *response* to his or her Spirit-given summons or on the necessity of the *bishop's call* for service to be *ecclesial* ministry. Given my own preferences and biases, I will argue for one approach over another, a given formulation over its alternative, the inclusion of certain terminology over its omission, etc. But in no way do I intend to denigrate those who embrace other approaches or theologies. Were I making the case for "green energy," I might favor wind power and extol its merits knowing full well that other "green-minded" individuals might argue as strenuously for solar or geothermal energy. I cite Chicago's rite and allude to an actual "adaptation" made elsewhere in the hope that highlighting the similarities and differences will illumine the foregoing discussions regarding vocation, interiority, function vs. relationship, and discipleship vs. ministry, etc.

Chicago's rite, celebrated three times by Cardinal George,[41] took the form of a Liturgy of the Word that included a renewal of baptismal promises, thus setting the rite within the baptismal context that is universally recognized as the indispensible root of all ministries in the church. Each time, the rite was celebrated on a Sunday at a local parish, proclaiming scriptural texts chosen especially for the occasion.

Completion of Chicago's required formation program (Together in God's Service [TIGS]) does not immediately qualify one for "calling." Prior to calling comes certification, which requires current employment and at least two years of pastoral experience.[42] While some possess the requisite experience even before they complete the formation program, many still must complete part or all of the two years of service before qualifying. Only individuals who already serve in full-time parish positions qualify for calling in Chicago. The first two celebrations of Chicago's rite were comprised entirely of parish ministers who were "grandparented" by virtue of their long service to the archdiocese. None had participated in the required formation program. Not till the third celebration of the rite did graduates of TIGS participate in the liturgy.

While Chicago's rite was intentionally titled a "calling rite" that confers "authorization," the rite adapted from it was christened a "commissioning rite" that avoided the language of "authorization." The designers of the adapted rite commented that

> *commissioning* was chosen over *calling*, because that language is more relational and carries echoes of Christ's Great Commission. We wanted to suggest that participants would go forth together to carry out Christ's mission in the world. "Authorization" seemed too juridical, while commissioning was rich and relational.[43]

Of course, commissioning, too, is a form of authorization, for to "be sent" there must be a "sender." The reticence of this diocese to speak of *authorizing* ministers might reflect reservations of two kinds: one, on the part of lay liturgy planners who preferred plural language redolent of community; the other, on the part of the bishop who perhaps was hesitant to employ language that said "too much" about the lay participants in the liturgy. The word "calling," I believe, carries stronger vocational implications than "commissioning." Though he wanted the language of the rite "to have a baptismal connection to the rest of the Eucharistic liturgy within which it was celebrated," the ordinary also wanted "to avoid any confusion with the rite of ordination."

In Chicago's rite, the archbishop asks the candidates, "Dear friends . . . Are you resolved to unite yourself more closely *to God and His Church* by your commitment to lay ecclesial ministry?" The adapted rite drops the words, "and His Church." This omission places the participant's assent within a less ecclesiological context, making it a personal covenant between the individual and God, rather than a public covenant between the individual and Christ's body, the church. Committing oneself to "His Church" acknowledges the importance of the concrete and particular. It speaks of incarnation, of Christ present in the particular ecclesial body within which one serves.

Chicago's rite asks its candidates, "Are you resolved to *love the church as Christ's body* and, through your ministry, to help those you serve to act justly, love tenderly and walk humbly with God?" The reformulated text asks, "Do you resolve to be faithful to the church . . . ," omitting mention of loving the church as Christ's body. Chicago's language assumes that it is desirable, in a public rite for individuals embracing church ministry, to acknowledge the church not just as institution but as Christ's very body that we are obliged to love in order to serve.

Chicago's rite also asks, "Are you resolved to *minister in cooperation with the pastors of the Church*, leading Christ's people in love and fidelity?" The adapted text does not include "in cooperation with the pastors of the Church" but uses the word "collaboratively," yielding, "Do you resolve to humbly serve Christ's people collaboratively . . . " This innovation, once again, produces a less *ecclesial* emphasis. Seen alone, the wording is innocuous, but contrasted with the model from which it differs, it makes a statement.

The Chicago text continues its ecclesial emphasis by asking, "Are you resolved to minister according to the mind of the Church, anchored in the faith which comes to us from the Apostles?" The reformulated text leaves out that question altogether because, according to the planners, the earlier promise to "be faithful to the church" makes it redundant. That Chicago asks its candidates for this explicit affirmation not only underscores its ecclesial focus but also suggests a conscious desire to incorporate its LEMs into the community of diocesan ministers.

In the adapted rite, the bishop *begins* by asking candidates to "express [their] intent and commitment to serve"; he *ends* saying he "formally *acknowledge[s]* and *accept[s]* [that] commitment." This language stresses the *initiative* of the *individual* making the commitment, something the bishop acknowledges and accepts. Chicago's "calling rite," I think, puts the focus on the church's action rather than on the individual's. The individual expresses his or her desire to serve by participating in the ritual; but in the rite, it's the church taking the initiative. Of course, the stirring of the Spirit within the individual has already occurred, but the church is proactively serving as the Spirit's mouthpiece.

I asked the designers of the adapted ritual if their rite acknowledges a *commitment to serve* or a *vocation*. They replied,

> The weight is on the commitment and intent *coming from the individual*. Calling is not explicit here. The Bishop asks for the intent of the individual; his [the Bishop's] piece is to commission. But the Bishop's intent to commission is meaningless unless it is *received* and something happens with it.

The vocation issue was the engine that drove Chicago's process, whereas vocational language was not a major factor in the design of the adapted rite. According to its designers, the central ideas manifest in their liturgy are

1. that lay ecclesial ministers are called by virtue of baptism;
2. that the commissioned are a professionally trained group within the church who make a public commitment recognized by the bishop of the diocese; and
3. that the commissioning liturgy parallels the other liturgies that bring individuals into ministry.

In contrast, Chicago's rite was designed to manifest

1. the need for *authority* in addition to baptism; and
2. the "calling" of candidates, rather than their "recognition" by the diocesan bishop.

However, *both* rites intended to parallel the liturgies that bring others into ministry.

As mentioned above, in the adapted rite the bishop addresses the candidates, saying,

> You have been led to respond to your baptismal call through lay ecclesial ministry. . . . Therefore, on behalf of the Church, I formally acknowledge and accept your commitment to serve and I commission you as Lay Ecclesial Ministers for the Diocese.

Here we find a striking omission in Chicago's rite. The dialogue with the bishop in which candidates promise fidelity to the church and her teaching concludes without the archbishop speaking specific words of acceptance or authorization. Such might be implied, but the words don't say it. This lack of specific language undercuts the integrity of the rite, something Chicago will need to address.

When we consider possible reasons for celebrating liturgies of calling/commissioning/sending, we quickly discover there are many. Each expresses a *need* that may reside within the individual or in the community. Recognizing that need is multivalent is critical because the alternative is operating out of assumptions that may be false or misleading. For example, an individual might dismiss the question of participating in a diocesan ritual, saying, "I don't need it. I already feel called and empowered for my ministry." But does that attitude overlook the community's need to recognize its ministers and the responsibility of the bishop to call them? Conversely, a bishop who assumes the diocese does not need an authorization ritual because he already has an employer/employee relationship with his lay ministers may be overlooking the need of individual ministers for recognition and affirmation and the needs of the community for sacramental signs of the contribution of laity to the ministerial work of the church. To better understand the need for rituals of authorization, let us briefly examine the possible motives, both personal and ecclesial, for celebrating them.

Personal Affirmation

A legitimate, pastoral motive is personal affirmation. Schools of ministry sometimes engage in "sending" rituals at the conclusion of their degree programs. Primarily, these are intended to give public recognition and affirmation, but they don't answer the student's question, In whose name will I serve? Affirmation is important, but it was not the primary motive of either of the rites examined. Affirmation can be given in other ways than a formal, diocesan rite.

Role Affirmation

A less personal and more sociologically oriented goal might be affirming the *role* of lay ecclesial minister. In this scenario, it is not the individual assuming the ministry who takes center stage; it is the ministry itself. That the church, while still evolving a theology of lay ecclesial ministry and still tripping, at times, over how to speak of lay ecclesial ministers, would publicly welcome the service of the laity and name it genuine ministry is truly prophetic.

The diocese using the adapted rite asserted that participation in the diocesan institute that prepares their laypeople for church service is only *one way* to be formed for ministry. The graduates [of our institute] stand as professional ministers but we are not trying to say there aren't other professionally trained ministers in the diocese. Others are no less professionally trained; they just haven't been through this rite [of commissioning].

Participation in the institute enables one to refer to oneself as a *commissioned* lay ecclesial minister, but others *may* call themselves lay ecclesial ministers, just not *commissioned* LEMs.

In Chicago, only pastoral associates and directors of religious education can be "called," and only those who have been called are designated lay ecclesial ministers. Asked about those currently exercising the responsibilities of PA and DRE, but without having participated in the calling rite, Cardinal George remarked,

> They are not lay ecclesial ministers in the official sense. . . . They are people who are doing the work of pastoral administrator or Director of Religious Education, but without really being in the category of Lay Ecclesial Minister.

In the cardinal's view, those who decline calling are performing a function, doing a job, not exercising ministry. Chicago draws a sharper line between those who are "called" and those who are not.[44] The important difference between them lies in the new relationship embraced by those who are called.[45] It should be noted, however, that while Cardinal George argues convincingly that the essence of ministry is relationship, Chicago's current rite never uses the word.

Doctrine

Another goal of a diocesan rite might be safeguarding the integrity of church teaching by publicly eliciting a candidate's promise of fidelity to church doctrine and discipline. This motive was clearly at work in the design of both rites I examined.

Ontology

No one would assert that an ontological change occurs in one who is commissioned or called. Baptism and holy orders confer a permanent character that changes a person at his or her core. A calling rite does no such thing. However, implicit in Chicago's approach to authorization is a conviction that calling is an invitation to a new *relationship* with the church community, not merely to a new *function* in the church. Unlike marriage, there is no permanent bond established, but the new relationship defines the individual's role and sets his or her agenda. Priesthood doesn't deputize someone to perform a particular function; it initiates a man into a new relationship. Calling to LEM is also about more than initiating someone into a role that is defined by its responsibilities. In the final blessing of the adapted rite the bishop prays, "Let your Spirit uphold them always *as they take up their new responsibilities* among the people of this Diocese." Chicago, as Cardinal George's numerous interview comments suggest, would likely substitute "relationship" in that blessing formula.

Episcopal Role

Chicago's rite emphasizes the role of the bishop in establishing a new relationship between minister and community. In the diocese utilizing the alternate ritual the connection to the bishop is less overt. Despite language that asserts the prerogative of the bishop to commission, representatives of the diocese noted approvingly that at a meeting of 150 diocesan ministers who were asked if they believed they had been *authorized* for their ministry, all raised their hands in affirmation, though only *fifteen* had actually participated in the diocesan commissioning rite. Some felt authorized by virtue of being hired by their local pastor; some because of having finished the diocesan program for religious educators; others felt "authorized" by the Holy Spirit.

The Chicago ritual explicitly intends to say of LEM that while baptism makes it possible, *authorization* makes it happen. The other diocese considers its diocesan program *important* for those who *participated* in it. But there are others, they said, "who have not experienced the call to serve as *commissioned* lay ecclesial ministers, and we don't think that diminishes what they do." Cardinal George would call the work of those who are not designated ministers of the diocese "a job" instead of "ministry," arguing that a more restricted use of "ministry" avoids a subjectivity that views anything and everything as ministry.

Conclusion

As the church continues to wrestle with the questions presented by the service of lay ecclesial ministers, the need for rites of authorization will grow more apparent. In designing those rites, liturgists will need to work from an informed theology of lay ecclesial ministry. While that theology is still evolving, it seems unlikely the basic questions will change: Does one focus on baptism, asserting authorization flows from that sacrament and needs only to be acknowledged by ecclesial authority, or does one assert that while baptism is indispensible, so is hierarchical approval? Does emphasis on church authority result in too clerical a model for lay ministerial authorization? Can we insist that no individual serve in the name of the church until the church has *formally* entered into relationship with him or her?

Emerging rites of authorization will change the ministerial landscape. Grounded in an understanding of *communio* as the source and ordering of ministerial relationships, rites of calling can make explicit what the experience of the past forty-five years has already proven: new charisms and ministries still arise within the church in response to the needs of society.[46] The exercise of new charisms is a participation in the creativity God lavished upon his people, an honoring of the giftedness that characterizes Christ's body.

As St. Paul told the Corinthians, so the Second Vatican Council has affirmed: "there are different gifts, but the same Spirit . . . different ministries but the same Lord."[47] We are a "communion," living "unity in distinction." Baptism initiates us into deep communion or *relationship* with God and others that creates the pattern for our *ministerial* relationships.

This notion of communion grounds our understanding of lay ecclesial ministry and must guide our design of rites of authorization. In Catholic belief, the bishop *is* the center of unity and it is his responsibility to foster the gifts and ministries of the local church. A theology of communion recognizes that we are most fully church when all those being empowered by the Spirit are given an opportunity to serve.

The development of lay ecclesial ministry in the aftermath of the Second Vatican Council is a source of great hope for the church. The experience of so many women and men for the span of a generation offers persuasive evidence that the Holy Spirit has rained a new charism upon the body of Christ that must be acknowledged in joy, fostered without fear, and authorized in diocesan rituals that beautifully manifest the rich ministerial mosaic with which God has blessed the church.

Archdiocese of Chicago

Ministers of Our God, You Shall Be Called

Isaiah 61:6

Call to Lay Ecclesial Ministry
for Pastoral Associates & Directors of Religious Education
of the Archdiocese of Chicago[48]

Welcome: (by *Auxiliary Bishop*)

Today, for the third time in this great archdiocese, we celebrate the rite of Calling to Lay Ecclesial Ministry of Pastoral Associates and Directors of Religious Education. This moment of joy reflects the growing conviction within the church that lay ecclesial ministry is a new and lasting charism that greatly enriches the church's life.

The publication by the United States Conference of Catholic Bishops of a document entitled *Co-Workers in the Vineyard of the Lord* affirms our own lived experience and underscores the significant contribution made by those who, over a period of many years, have made church ministry their life's work.

Chicago is proud to be among the first dioceses in the country to recognize its lay ecclesial ministers through a public rite of calling. Those of you who join our candidates today—pastors, ministerial colleagues, parishioners, and family members—have contributed to the good work that these women and men have done for the church. It is right and fitting that you should celebrate with us today. With joy and gratitude, let us rise to begin our celebration.

Entrance Song: "The Summons"   John Bell
(Procession: Servers; Office Directors; Lectors; Deacon; Cardinal)

Greeting: (*Cardinal*)

> In the name of Christ we gather today to call to ecclesial ministry
> those whom we welcome with great gratitude
> because of their faithful service to this archdiocese

On this day, during the great season of Easter,
as we await the coming of Pentecost, the Church's birthday,
we are mindful that Christ calls some to ministry through His body, the
    church.

Today, we wish formally to call to ecclesial ministry
these sisters and brothers whose lives have, for many years,
been marked by loving service to Christ and his holy people.
We also call, today, the first graduates of the *Together in God's Service*
    program
who have prepared, through academic study and spiritual formation,
to respond to Christ's call to serve this local church as parish ministers.

Sprinkling Rite: (*Water bowl is brought to Cardinal for blessing*)

Cardinal: Dear friends,
            This water will be used to remind us of our baptism.
            We ask God to bless it,
            and to keep us faithful to the Spirit he has given us.

Brief silence

Lord God almighty,
Hear the prayers of your people:
We celebrate our creation and redemption.
Hear our prayers and bless + this water which gives fruitfulness to the fields,
and refreshment and cleansing to all. You chose water to show your goodness
when you led your people to freedom through the Red Sea
and satisfied their thirst in the desert with water from the rock.
Water was the symbol used by the prophets
to foretell your new covenant with the human family.
You made the water of baptism holy by Christ's baptism in the Jordan:
by it you give us a new birth and renew us in holiness.
May this water remind us of our baptism
and let us share the joy of all who have been baptized at Easter.
We ask this through Christ our Lord.
(*Cardinal processes through assembly*)

Sprinkling Rite Song: "Song Over the Water" Marty Haugen

(*When the Cardinal returns to his place and the song is finished, he prays the
opening prayer*)

Opening Prayer:

Cardinal: God our Father,
              you have caused the grace of baptism
              to bear much fruit in your servants.
              In your mercy, look upon them
              as they seek to confirm their offering of themselves to you.

              As the years pass by,
              help them to enter more deeply into the mystery of the Church
              and to dedicate themselves more generously to the good of all.

              We ask this through our Lord Jesus Christ, your Son,
              who lives and reigns with you and the Holy Spirit,
              one God, forever and ever.

First Reading: Isaiah 61:1-3, 6

Responsorial Psalm: Psalm 40   "Here I Am, Lord, I Come to do Your Will"

Gospel Acclamation: Celtic Alleluia

Gospel: Matthew 4:18–5:1-12   *Read by Deacon*

Homily: *Cardinal*

Renewal of Baptismal Promises: (*Cardinal ASKS ALL TO RISE*)

+Renunciation of Sin

Cardinal: Do you reject sin so as to live in the freedom of God's children?
                    Participants: I do.
Cardinal: Do you reject the glamour of evil, and refuse to be mastered by sin?
                    Participants: I do.
Cardinal: Do you reject Satan, father of sin and prince of darkness?
                    Participants: I do.

+Profession of Faith

Cardinal: Do you believe in God, the Father almighty, creator of heaven
                  and earth?
                    Participants: I do.
Cardinal: Do you believe in Jesus Christ, his only Son, our Lord, who was
                  born of the Virgin Mary, was crucified, died, and was buried, rose
                  from the dead, and is now seated at the right hand of the Father?
                    Participants: I do.

Cardinal: Do you believe in the Holy Spirit, the holy Catholic Church, the communion of saints, the forgiveness of sins, the resurrection of the body, and the life everlasting?

Participants: I do.

(Entire assembly responds with SUNG refrain)

Acclamation: "We do Believe"   David Haas

We do believe! This is our faith; this is the faith of the Church.
We are proud to profess it in Christ Jesus.

Calling Forth: (*Cardinal addresses those to be called to lay ecclesial ministry. He motions them to rise.*)

Cardinal: Dear friends, in baptism you have already died to sin and have been set aside for God's service. Are you resolved to unite yourself more closely to God and His Church by your commitment to lay ecclesial ministry?

Participants: I am

Cardinal: Are you resolved to strive steadfastly to live the gospel in your life as well as in your ministry by persevering in prayer, working tirelessly for charity and justice, and seeking wholeness in the support of a community of faith?

Participants: I am

Cardinal: Are you resolved to love the church as Christ's body and, through your ministry, to help those you serve to act justly, love tenderly and walk humbly with God?

Participants: I am

Cardinal: Are you resolved to minister in cooperation with the pastors of the Church, leading Christ's people in love and fidelity?

Participants: I am

Cardinal: Are you resolved to minister according to the mind of the Church, anchored in the faith which comes to us from the Apostles?

Participants: I am

Cardinal: May God who has begun the good work in you bring it to fulfillment before the day of Christ Jesus.

All: Amen.

(Cardinal moves to CENTER in front of ALTAR to DISTRIBUTE CANDLES. Agency Directors read names of Director of Religious Education and Pastoral Associate candidates. Individuals come forward for brief interaction with Cardinal and to receive a candle from him.)

Acknowledgement by Assembly:

(Cardinal invites assembly to acknowledge the participants with applause, after which they return to their seats in assembly.)

Cardinal:
   With our applause, let us show our gratitude
   for the gift these women and men have been
   and continue to be to this local church.

Intercessions:

Cardinal:
   My brothers and sisters,
   with joy at Christ's rising from the dead,
   let us turn to God our Father in prayer.
   He heard and answered the prayers
   of the Son he loved so much:
   let us trust that he will hear our petitions.

(Read by one P.A. and one DRE)

1. That pastors and all who minister may lead in faith and serve in love the flock entrusted to their care by Christ, the Good Shepherd, we pray to the Lord.
2. That the whole world may rejoice in the blessing of true peace, the peace Christ himself gives us, we pray to the Lord.
3. That our suffering brothers and sisters may have their sorrow turned into lasting joy, we pray to the Lord.
4. That the church of Chicago may have the faith and strength to bear witness to Christ's resurrection, we pray to the Lord.
5. That Christ may continue to call faithful women and men to serve his church as priests and deacons, in religious life and lay ecclesial ministry, we pray to the Lord.
6. That our gifts might be varied and many and our oneness in Christ assured, we pray to the Lord.

Cardinal:
Father,
You know our hearts and our every need.
Hear the prayers of your people.
Give us what you have inspired us
to ask for in faith.
In your mercy you sent us your son, Jesus Christ,
in whose words we now pray:

Lord's Prayer

Solemn Blessing:

Cardinal:
May God who is the source of all good intentions
enlighten your minds and strengthen your hearts
that you may live out your vocation
with faithfulness and generosity.
R. Amen
May he make each of you a witness
and a sign of his love for all people.
R. Amen
May the Lord enable you to travel in the joy of Christ
as you follow along his way,
and may your commitment never waver.
R. Amen
May almighty God, the Father, and the Son,
+and the Holy Spirit,
bless all of you who have taken part in this celebration.
R. Amen

Closing Song: "We Are Called"

Notes

1. For this essay, on May 6, 2010, I interviewed Francis Cardinal George of Chicago, who was the first ordinary to celebrate a Rite of Calling to Lay Ecclesial Ministry. Rather than append the interview or bring it repeatedly into the body of the essay, I have chosen to insert his comments as notes at those places in the chapter where they are most relevant.

2. At least at the time it occurred; though, significantly, one spoke eloquently of how the rite and the candle given him by Cardinal George grew in importance for him and his family as the years passed.

3. It should be noted that the participants in Chicago's first calling rite were individuals who were "grandparented," i.e., invited to participate by virtue of their years of ministerial experience and exempted from participation in the Together in God's Service program (TIGS), the archdiocesan formation program required for anyone who hopes to be called to ministry within the Archdiocese of Chicago. The speaker cited here and the colleagues whom she referenced completed their academic work under the aegis of the TIGS program and participated in its comprehensive formation process.

4. The seven-inch pillar candle bears the archdiocesan crest and is inscribed with words from Isaiah: "Ministers of our God you shall be called" (Isa 61:6b). See pages 175–76.

5. GM: *Ecclesiologically, what difference does the rite make?*

FCG: It means people who are in that class of lay ecclesial minister are publicly recognized in their vocation to the church; it's not a private choice, not part of a job description, it means the church recognizes and calls people to a vocation that is unique.

GM: *Some Theology Schools conduct rites of "sending" or "commissioning" of their students. How do those events differ from the diocesan event?*

FCG: I don't know what they are. I haven't looked at them. But a School doesn't send anyone or commission anyone; it's the bishop who does that in the Catholic Church. [The University events] could just be a recognizing that what they're doing has a religious component; that's fine. But no one can call someone to a vocation in the local church except the bishop or someone whom he delegates. Sending means we send you from our community, from our school, out into the church. That's ok. [Schools] can't commission because that means you have a particular assignment and the schools don't give that assignment, the bishop does.

6. GM: *What does "Authorization" mean? Is it a vocational word or a juridical word? Are you happy with that word or might another work better?*

FCG: We've been back and forth on it, but we've accepted it as the best word we have. Hopefully it's both [vocational and juridical]. But, I prefer the word "public" to law. Authorization is *public*.

7. GM: *What do you see as the VOCATIONAL dimension of LEM? In what ways is it like and in what ways different from vocation to orders?*

FCG: It's the baptismal vocation, with a certain qualification vis-à-vis the church. It's not a new sacrament, but I think it is a vocation.

GM: *You've often used the term "A vocation within a vocation." Please elaborate.*

FCG: Well it's a call to ministry and therefore a mission that situates you vis-à-vis the church in a new way. But it's based on the baptismal call to holiness and membership in Christ's body. I think it is a vocation; it's not just a function, it's a new relationship. It's a calling, but it is based on baptism and confirmation which are the fundamental call to holiness for everybody . . . and to service, and beyond service, to ministry.

8. Edward Hahnenberg, "The Holy Spirit's Call: The Vocation to Lay Ecclesial Ministry," address delivered at the National Symposium on Lay Ecclesial Ministry, 2007, Collegeville, MN, p. 6. Unpublished manuscript available at http://www1.csbsju.edu/sot/symposium/2007docs.htm.

9. Ibid.

10. Ibid.

GM: *Some argue that saying: "you're not called till I call you" ignores the graces conferred by baptism and overemphasizes the role of the diocesan bishop. What is your response to that critique?*

FCG: The graces conferred by baptism are sanctifying grace; baptism doesn't say much about ministry at all. The role of the diocesan bishop we believe is part of the apostolic constitution of the Church.

11. GM: *Why did you feel a public rite of calling was important for the Archdiocese of Chicago?*

FCG: It's the difference between ministry and mission. Ministry is a function and it can be prepared professionally and certified. But Mission is relationship. It speaks of a calling by Christ to relate to the church in a different way, and the bishop is the one who calls people to this kind of new relationship in the church. So it was very important that it be incorporated into the lives of Lay Ecclesial Ministers in Chicago.

GM: *You've said calling LEM's is akin to what you do when you "call" the young men at Mundelein Seminary to priesthood. What are the similarities and differences between the two "callings"?*

FCG: The bishop calls people to a new relationship with the church. In the case of Seminarians, that relationship will be definitely established through a new sacrament, Holy Orders. In the case of lay ministers, it's established in relation to Baptism and Confirmation, already received. But calling is similar. A bishop of a diocese publicly calls people to a new relationship in the church, a vocation.

12. Avery Cardinal Dulles, "Can Laity Properly Be Called 'Ministers'?," *Origins* 35, no. 44 (2006): 726–30.

13. For example, writing in the mid 1990s, Paul Wadell, CP, asserted that "no baptized Christian can be a faithful disciple without being a committed minister" and cited an address given by Bishop Howard Hubbard of Albany, New York, who said, "Baptismal life is inherently and inescapably ministerial. It is not as if a gospel ministry is a baptismal option. All of us by virtue of our baptisms are called *to ministry in the Church*" (italics added). Paul Wadell, CP, "Strengthening One Another in Christ: The Role of Spiritual Friendship in Ministry," *The Passionist* 31 (June 1997): 59.

14. GM: *You have written of the need to reserve the term LEM to certain activity within the church, so as to avoid misuses like "the ministry of cutting the grass . . ." Can you offer a succinct definition of LEM?*

FCG: It was defined in Co-Workers. Maybe that was too long. [I would say,] "Someone whose relationship to the church is set publicly by a call from the bishop in order to do ministry as commissioned by the bishop or another pastor."

15. Ibid.

16. Unpublished address delivered at the National Association for Lay Ministry National Conference, Minneapolis, MN, 2007.

17. GM: *In common practice, is the Church effectively negotiating the line between the extremes of "laicism" and "clericalism" or have the boundaries been blurred in ways that are counterproductive?*

FCG: It's fish and fowl. Baptism is necessary for salvation—it sets our direction to a life of sanctifying grace. Orders is not necessary for salvation. Most people who are saved are not ordained. So it's rather a relationship, not to God directly, but to the body of Christ . . . to Christ and his Church. Baptism makes one a creature, a son or daughter of God. It always puts one in relationship . . . puts one in relationship to God; ordination puts one in relationship to the church. It's fish and fowl.

Everyone has to be baptized, including people who are in orders. Baptism is the entry to the sacrament of orders . . . to a life of grace. It's the fundamental sacrament; it's necessary for salvation.

Orders is something else; it's a new relationship, not to God but the church—and it's sacramental so it's an action of Christ . . . but not necessary for salvation; it's for the sake of the people . . . baptism is for the sake of the one baptized. Marriage and Orders are social sacraments. You're married for the sake of your wife and family and you're ordained for the sake of the church. Both of them are ways of sanctifying yourself . . . Start with relationships, not functions. Ask: "Who's being related?" Focus on the mission, not just ministry.

18. Dulles, "Can Laity Properly Be Called 'Ministers'?," 730.

19. GM: *After citing this quote to Cardinal George, I asked the following question: Theology that asserts the centrality of the role of the Bishop is often badly misunderstood. You have stated that in Catholic ecclesiology "we gather round the bishop." Please discuss why the bishop is central in discerning and recognizing vocations?*

FCG: You gather round the bishop, because the bishop points to Christ. It's not about him personally. If you want a church where there is private interpretation of scripture, and private interpretation of mission, there are such ecclesial bodies, they're just not catholic. Ours is an apostolic church. And therefore the mission depends upon one being called by the bishop. People should not be ministering in the church if they don't understand Catholic ecclesiology.

20. GM: *Obviously, call to LEM and ordination are different in kind. One is a sacrament, the other a public rite. The theology of priesthood speaks of an ontological change in the ordained. What occurs in an LEM calling rite? Is this an optional, symbolic event that simply "recognizes" what someone is doing in the church, or is it a "necessary" event? If the latter, please discuss why.*

FCG: Ordination is a change in the relationship with the church that is permanent. It's an action of the risen Christ. It's a sacrament. A calling rite is a change in relationship that is public, but not necessarily permanent, and it's an action of the church, not an action of Christ. The action of Christ took place at Baptism. Sacraments are the action of Christ. The calling rite is a rite of the Church and therefore not permanent, necessarily. Marriage is an action of Christ, so it's permanent. We can't change that. We can't un-baptize people, we can't un-marry people, or un-ordain people. You *can* "un-call" somebody. It's public, however, and therefore it's necessary for being publicly a lay minister.

21. Roger Cardinal Mahoney and the priests of the Archdiocese of Los Angeles, As I Have Done for You, A Pastoral Letter on Ministry (April 2000), 11.

22. GM: *Religious orders rose up as a new charism in the life of the church. Do you see the flowering of LEM in the late twentieth century as in any way analogous to that earlier experience?*

FCG: Yes, I guess so . . . movements of renewal . . . in some ways, yes . . . It is analogous. It's a form of discipleship, but it's not radical discipleship and that is what religious life is. Most renewals are centered around a form of radical discipleship. There are some things that seem analogous. I think it's a movement of the Spirit for the sake of strengthening the church. Beyond that, however, the means are very different. Religious life is simply a witness to a radical gospel commitment. You don't have to minister at all to be a religious.

23. GM: *Some say baptism is the source of lay ecclesial ministry, so "ministry" can be done by all the baptized. Some prefer to emphasize the role of the ordinary as the source. Where do you situate the "locus" of a layperson's ministry in the church . . . Baptism? The Ordinary's call? Both?*

FCG: Well, it's both. Obviously, you can't be called if you're not baptized. Baptism enables you to serve, but it doesn't bring you into the realm of ministry directly. The baptized and confirmed have to live their lives as public disciples of Jesus in the world, but it doesn't mean that they have a ministry in the church. Everybody is called to serve the church in some fashion, but all service isn't ministry. Some people would reduce or restrict the term ministry just to the ordained, so if you want to use it for laypeople then the proper term is lay *ecclesial* ministers.

But, analogously, if you want to call a service some kind of ministry which is ad hoc, reading . . . something like that, that's all right. As long as you understand that that is really just a way of *doing* something, it's not a new way of relating. That's always the key . . . Does this establish a relationship or is it just a service? If it's just a service, you're not ministering in the first place. And if it does establish a relationship that is new, then you've got something that could be called a lay ecclesial ministry . . . or the ministry of the priest . . . the deacon . . . or the bishop. It's really both: if you don't have baptism—that's the door—nothing else follows; but there's nothing in baptism that talks about lay ecclesial ministry as such. And so if you're going to officially recognize it and establish that relationship, the bishop has to give the call.

24. GM: *Can you comment on the proper balance between a "too-personalized" and a "too-institutionalized" approach to vocation?*

FCG: The preparation [period] is the discernment of vocation and that's true for any vocation. The sense that somebody has of a "personal call" is not normative for the church. Somebody can feel called to whatever, and they can be sincere, but can be wrong. Subjectivity is nothing more than subjectivity; it's not publicly normative. Discernment is precisely to see whether or not the subject or disposition corresponds to the objectivity and the criteria that the church herself creates, otherwise you've got anarchy—a collection of individuals who have no relationship to anybody else because each one defines his or her rights to do whatever they want. That's not the Catholic Church. [The church] is the body, it's a set of interrelationships and the bishop is ordained to headship. So, sincere conviction is just a sincere conviction. So that's where discernment comes in. It's not a proper balance, it's a discernment. Does this subject or inclination really correspond to what the church expects of people who have this position?

25. GM: *I have asserted that in saying that "identity as a lay ecclesial minister is partly a question of personal awareness and partly a matter of recognition by official church authority," State of the Questions moves us out of the realm of interiority and into the realm of "law." Can you please comment?*

FCG: I agree with that. I would change the word "law" to "Public Order." There are a number of orders in the church, classes of people, and it's public, it's not just private. The church is not a private club. This attitude of "What I want to do I should be able to do," makes the church a private club and not the body of Christ. So, in a sense, it's not that it's *partly* a question [of personal awareness], it is *fully* a question of personal calling or inclination or talk of grace, and also *fully* a matter of recognition by official church authority. It's fully both.

26. For example, canon 903 states, "Lay people who possess the required qualities can be admitted permanently to the ministries of lector and acolyte. [436] When the necessity of the Church warrants it and when ministers are lacking, lay persons, even if they are not lectors or acolytes, can also supply for certain of their offices, namely, to exercise the ministry of the word, to preside over liturgical prayers, to confer Baptism, and to distribute Holy Communion in accord with the prescriptions of law. [CCC 437 and Ministeria Quaedam]."

27. Bishop William Lori, "Fitting Functional and Ontological Views of Priesthood Together," *Origins* 35, no. 44 (2006): 731.

28. GM: *Do you fear that authorization of laypeople erodes priestly identity?*

FCG: There can be aberrations of all things. Either this is a leading from the Holy Spirit or it isn't. If it isn't, then we should stop it. If it is, then we should meet the challenges. It should not erode priestly identity; see to it that it doesn't.

GM: *Do you think that authorization "clericalizes" the laity?*

FCG: Authorization doesn't clericalize the laity, it's not a new form of clericalism; it's not part of the sacrament of holy orders. It is, however, a recognition that these people are called to relate to the church and the mission in a new way, and to do ministry. . . . It becomes clear when you talk about mission and about relationship . . . that's where it becomes clear. [GM: That is, *there is no problem with using the term for laypeople, because it is a matter of relationships unique to each role, not a matter of functions and who gets to do them.*]

29. Bernardin, In Service of One Another (Chicago: Chicago Catholic Publishing, 1985), 6.

30. Ibid.

31. GM: *What about a "Protestantization" of the concept of ministry as Cardinal Ratzinger suggested in 1998?*

FCG: If indeed ministry is just a function, that's the Protestant point of view, it comes and goes. In that case, yes, to some extent, because [lay ecclesial ministry] isn't permanent—and it doesn't have to be. It's fair enough to say that it is analogous to Protestant ministry. Protestants don't have the sacrament of holy orders. What they have are baptized people who are called by the church to do a different kind of service—preach or whatever, temporarily, until they decide they don't want to do it anymore. So it's a functional thing. But it does change the relationship to the church.

We are open now for relationships that we weren't open to before. It is pretty much analogous to Protestant ministry. It's what the church would have if we didn't have the sacrament of holy orders, but, of course, we do. The analogy to the Catholic Church in the Protestant churches is found in baptism. Lay ministry . . . in the sense [that it is] based upon the priesthood of the baptized only, is very much like [Protestant ministry]. These people are not [ordained], and don't claim to have received the sacrament of holy orders. A Protestant minister is not the same thing as a Catholic priest. He is, as baptized, very like a lay minister in the Catholic Church.

32. GM: *What do you think of the reluctance among some to apply the term "ministry" to laypeople?*

FCG: Some would like to restrict the term to the ordained . . . and that's a rather strong opinion in certain circles of the church, but I think the church herself leaves it open, at least in the Code, and so we can do that. But you know, that's another part of the discussion that will go on. I think it becomes acute when people recognize that someone is trying to [call laypeople "ministers"] in order to relativize the ministry of priests.

33. Dulles, "Can Laity Properly Be Called 'Ministers'?," 726–30.

34. As was done by John Paul II in 1994: "For some time now it has been customary to use the word 'ministries' not only for the *officia* and *munera* exercised by pastors in virtue of the sacrament of orders, *but also for those exercised by the lay faithful in virtue of the baptismal priesthood*" (John Paul II, Participation of the Laity in the Priestly Ministry, address given in Rome, April 22, 1994, n. 4, emphasis added).

35. Congregation for the Clergy and Seven other Roman dicasteries, *Ecclesiae de Mysterio*, trans. Some Questions Regarding Collaboration of Nonordained Faithful in Priests' Sacred Ministry, *Origins* 27 (Nov. 27, 1997): 397–409, esp. 402–3.

36. The Decree on the Apostolate of Lay People asserts that laypersons should "exercise their apostolate therefore in the world as well as in the church, in the

temporal order as well as in the spiritual" (AA 5, and again in 9). AA 10 goes further in specifying the varied ways laity share in Christ's triple *munera* within the church: "Their activity within the church communities is so necessary that without it the apostolate of the pastors will frequently be unable to obtain its full effect. Following in the footsteps of the men and women who assisted Paul in the proclamation of the Gospel (see Acts 18:18-26; Rom 16:3), lay persons of a genuinely apostolic spirit supply the needs of their brothers and sisters and are a source of consolation to the pastors no less than to the rest of the faithful (see 1 Cor 16:17-18)."

37. GM: *You've said that even if Chicago's Mundelein Seminary were full of young men seeking priesthood, you would still want laywomen and men ministering in the Archdiocese. Why?*

FCG: I think our people are well served by lay ministers . . . many of them are women. Our ability to see things, to reach out is broader, wider, and also deeper, I think, because these people are now involved full-time in ministry. I think that's something that is a great step forward. I think our people are better ministered to because we have lay ecclesial ministers. They don't replace priests. There are things that make a priest unique; but nonetheless, in terms of serving the people, I think the complex of ministry is richer.

38. GM: *Please discuss the difference it makes that LEMs are not "merely the pastor's hired help."*

FCG: Hopefully it will make a difference in the parish where they recognize that the LEM is part of the called ministers in the church, it's not just a job, it's a calling, and it's a relationship. They will recognize that in the generous donation of self that the minister brings to the area of his or her own expertise. I think that has to work itself out in each ministerial situation. I recognize my relationship with them by meeting with them once a year, by being open to their problems and discussions, and doing my best, with the help, often, of the offices in the pastoral center, who are eager to help them. Let's say someone has to make a transfer. Well, it's not just up to them to go around and hunt for a job. We have to try see to it, since they're recognized and called LEMs, that they're able to continue their ministry—if they choose to. So there's a certain sense of obligation to them; it doesn't work itself out in great detail all the time, but it's there.

39. GM: *Does the Church have a responsibility to recognize the various "calls" the Holy Spirit may be sending out among God's people? How can the church better steward the responsibility and power to recognize and authorize?*

FCG: While a calling is not a right, and it is a grace freely given by the Spirit, I would say a calling is by the bishop, it's not by the Spirit. Hopefully, the Spirit has already called; that's where we talk about subjective inclination and objective dissemination. The calling is by the bishop. If the discernment is good, the bishop knows that he is making public what the Holy Spirit has done in the heart of that person, signifying therefore a new relationship to the church. That's new.

The Spirit always works through the bishop, if it's *public* . . . If the various calls the Holy Spirit is sending out among God's people have a public repercussion, then the church has to look at it and discern.

[In a Rite of Calling] hopefully the Bishop is doing something because the Holy Spirit has given an internal impulse first. If there's no personal inclination, you don't call somebody. That's why I call people to orders; I say, Do you want to be a priest? If they don't want to be a priest, I'm not going to call them.

GM: *Should the church be on the lookout, recognizing that the Spirit works in hidden ways?*

FCG: We always do. Every time people act with really wonderful generosity, it needs recognition and we have to have a sign. The Holy Spirit is a Spirit of love who is moving among us, but you don't have to have a ceremony about that, necessarily. It depends on what kind of charism you have. If it has a permanent impact on the body of Christ and it is not just given for personal sanctification, then we should look at it. That's why it's important you used the example of religious orders, those orders have to be approved by the church.

40. It should be noted that access to liturgical rites is not yet a reality in many, if not most, dioceses. Some object that the endorsement of such rituals might cause those who lack access to feel relegated to second-class status. To say one "needs" to be called by the bishop could, indeed, cause one who has not been called to wonder, "Am I truly an LEM? Do I have a vocation?" This very valid concern, however, is not a reason to step away from rituals of calling but is motivation to advocate with greater urgency for their implementation. A similar argument has often been made in regard to requiring graduate-level preparation of lay ecclesial ministers. That some lack access to graduate education should not be a reason to lower standards but should provide motivation to strive all the harder to make it universally available.

Furthermore, ritualizing is what we Catholics do. We celebrate the significant milestones of life and we do it with signs and symbols that remind us of our identity and of Christ's pervasive presence in our lives. Should the embrace of God's gift of lay ecclesial ministry be treated any differently?

41. Currently, Chicago's rite is a biennial event.

42. In Chicago, calling and commissioning are separate moments that occur after certification. The framework that leads to recognition as a lay ecclesial minister involves a five-step process:

1. *Call from God*—experienced as a vocational call by the individual and tested by prayer, reflection, spiritual direction, and discernment with pastors.
2. *Training and preparation*—that is, academics and spiritual formation. Academics is professional preparation at one of Chicago's Catholic academic institutions, with core courses toward a master's degree identified by the archdiocese. Spiritual formation includes the significant impact of the academic courses, as well as more intentional formation activities like spiritual direction, discernment, retreats, and formation days.

3. *Certification*—professional credentialing granted by the appropriate arch-diocesan office after reviewing transcripts, interviews, ministerial experi-ence, etc.

4. *Call by the bishop*—public "call" of the individual to lay ecclesial ministry by the archbishop ritualized in a public ceremony. "Call" is a one-time event for the individual that is not repeated.

5. *Commissioning to a specific ministry role in a local parish*—LEMs are commis-sioned by the archbishop to a parish in much the same way that priests and deacons are sent. Accomplished by means of a letter, commissioning establishes a relationship between the lay ecclesial minister and the arch-bishop, naming the individual a minister of the archdiocese. Commission-ing is repeated each time an LEM takes on a new ministerial assignment.

43. Interview conducted on May 19, 2010. The comparison of these liturgies is intended to uncover the differing assumptions and theologies embodied in each rite, not to critique the work of another diocese. Therefore, I have chosen not to name the diocese or personnel who created the adapted rite.

44. GM: *Is a pastor's relationship with those on his staff who have been called any different from his relationship with those not called?*

FCG: I think he has an obligation to see the difference in commitment of people who are called and also the difference of the church's relationship to them. It doesn't mean a *personal* relationship . . . you may like someone not called more than someone called, but the pastor should be able to count more on those who are called. Their commitment is public; therefore he should be able to count on them in a way that might not be the case with someone who doesn't want to be called. Those called should be more dependable, trustworthy, put the church first, and live a God-fearing life. In that sense there's a commonality between the ordained pastor and these ministers. If a pastor chooses to welcome an LEM, it's like welcoming an associate pastor. They are like the associate pastor, but they don't govern.

45. *Two final comments from Cardinal George regarding relationship:*

GM: *Can you comment on those who have come to value the experience of calling only after an initial period of ambivalence?*

FCG: They grew in the relationship.

GM: *If a person decides to leave ministry after having been called, should that some-how be acknowledged?*

FCG: What are you going to do? Take back their candle? Blow it out . . . ? [laughs]. The person should write a letter to the bishop, and the bishop should write back saying thank you and God bless you. The relationship has changed.

46. Bernardin, In Service of One Another, 23.

47. See 1 Cor 12:4-7.

48. Because this moment in the life of the archdiocese presented an opportunity to create a lasting rite for local use and, perhaps, a model for other dioceses and because the vocation of lay ecclesial ministers was going to be ritualized pub-

licly, it seemed important and necessary to create a rite that spoke the church's language and flowed from her rich tradition. For these reasons, though adapted to this unique setting, some of the language and prayers utilized in the rite are taken from the English translations of *The Roman Missal* © 1973 and *Rites of Religious Profession* © 1974, International Commission on English in the Liturgy Corporation. All rights reserved.

Chapter 10

Leadership, Ritual, and Lay Ecclesial Ministry

Zeni Fox

Why did the US bishops develop the document *Co-Workers in the Vineyard of the Lord*? Tracing its evolution, from the early conversations in the Committee on Pastoral Practices, to the commissioning of the national study of the "new parish ministers" that was undertaken by Msgr. Murnion, to the designation of a subcommittee to study the matter, it becomes clear that confronted with a new expression of ministry, they desired to provide leadership in responding to it. The effort to understand this reality theologically and to provide guidance in its development charted the course of their work. As they themselves suggest in the conclusion of *Co-Workers*, this process needs to continue. Therefore, this chapter will explore two related aspects of their document: the affirmation that lay ecclesial ministry is a leadership role, and that public prayer and ritual can be a significant part of an authorization process for the lay ecclesial minister and for the community. In the first part, leadership theory will be used, both to explore ways in which lay ecclesial ministers are indeed leaders and to suggest why public prayer and ritual have a value in designating them as leaders. The second part presents some personal experiences that gave rise to the question this chapter addresses, and that link the two aspects of the question, leadership and ritual. In the third part, interviews with a select group of lay ecclesial ministers will be summarized, noting their experience of public prayer and ritual as part of an authorization process. The intention is to provide one answer to the question, why include ritual as part of the authorization process of lay ecclesial ministers as leaders in their communities?

Part One: Leadership and Lay Ecclesial Ministers

Introduction

Co-Workers outlines four characteristics of the ecclesial service per-formed by lay ecclesial ministers; one of these is leadership in a particular area of ministry. (Of course, there are other leaders, including ordained leaders, e.g., pastors, and lay leaders, e.g., members of the parish coun-cil, but the focus of this chapter is on lay ecclesial ministers.) Roles such as that of pastoral associate, parish catechetical leader, youth ministry leader, school principal, and director of liturgy or pastoral music are cited as examples. (*Co-Workers* includes those who are not paid for the exercise of such roles, an important consideration in rural and inner-city settings, and in various cultural groups.) The emphasis on leadership, and therefore on roles such as these, was not meant to diminish the im-portance of the service of the many laypeople who take on many other roles in ministry, such as lectors and catechists, but rather to provide one way of describing the smaller group that is the focus of their document. The other three characteristics the bishops name—authorization of the hierarchy to serve publicly in the local church; close mutual collaboration with the pastoral ministry of bishops, priests, and deacons; and appropri-ate preparation and formation[1]—are in many ways closely connected to the leadership responsibility. The leadership role *calls for* authorization, collaboration, and significant preparation.

Sometimes the popular understanding of leadership is overly fo-cused on a command and control model, a hierarchical valuing that sees leadership as the work of only the person "at the top" of the organiza-tion, whether that be a corporation or a church. However, a study of leadership theory suggests that it is much more dispersed in any system, and more complex than simply the exercise of authority or wielding of coercive power. Although there are many disciplines that can help to elucidate the meaning of leadership, including a study of examples from Scripture, a framework drawn from organizational theory will be used here to reflect on leadership and lay ecclesial ministers. One reason for utilizing this domain of research is that most of the work on leadership today is in the for-profit arena (with business school professors doing much of the research and writing).[2] Here perspectives from various theorists of leadership will be utilized, and applied to ministry in the church, and more specifically to lay ecclesial ministers.

Diverse Perspectives on Leadership

Various definitions of leadership assist in understanding particularities of the functioning of lay ecclesial ministers as leaders. Gibson, Ivancevich, and Donnelly state, "When one individual attempts to affect the behavior of others in a group without using the coercive form of power, we describe the effort as *leadership*."[3] The authors emphasize that influence rather than coercive power is central, note that the context of all leadership is relational, and see the accomplishment of goals as the focus. This definition does not use cross-cultural language but does encompass the diverse forms of leadership that emerge in specific cultural communities. In the context of church ministry, this definition is congenial. It invites us to reflect on the example of servanthood that Jesus presents to his followers, and on the church as a communion, "a mystery of Trinitarian communion in missionary tension" (*Pastores Dabo Vobis* 12, as quoted in *Co-Workers*, 19). It also reminds us that leadership is directed toward a goal, continuing the mission of Jesus: "joining in God's work of bringing [the] Kingdom [of God] to realization" (*Co-Workers*, 18). In other words, leadership is not primarily about the leader, not his or her status nor aggrandizement, but rather about the humble service of communal life and the mission of the church.

Research on parish ministers echoes these themes. For example, regarding religious educators, "(they), found, through interviews and discussions, that successful programs are characterized by shared responsibility on the part of a significant number of people in the parish and by leadership whose vision translates into program planning." Among the specific factors noted was "a strong sense of community and camaraderie among catechists."[4] Research shows that lay ecclesial ministers invite parishioners to be involved in many different ministerial roles. In addition, they work with various decision-making groups, including committees, planning teams, and advisory boards; 75 percent have personally formed such groups.[5] Certainly, when working with volunteers coercion is not an option; rather, influence exercised through relationality and setting of goals is central.

Gibson, Ivancevich, and Donnelly comment on a dynamic in hierarchical organizations: "the appointed manager may direct, instruct, or command; but unless followers have some choice to follow or not follow, there's no leadership . . . Through an ability to influence, the leader creates and uses the power and authority received from the followers."[6] In a parish, lay ministers are involved voluntarily. They serve as liturgical ministers, catechists, coaches, workers for charity and justice, etc., out of a sense of baptismal commitment and/or of perceived need in their community. Lay ecclesial ministers serve in a leadership position relative to these many lay ministers active in the parish, providing direction and coordination for the efforts of all. Their ability to lead is a function of their use of the power and authority received from the followers. This is true both in the more "organizationally focused" patterns that exist in dominant culture communities and in the more "charismatically focused" (this is meant organizationally, not theologically) patterns often found in other cultural communities.

A digression will illustrate this point. A manager in an industrial plant exercises influence with the workers—until they decide to go on strike. When they do, they withdraw the power and authority they had previously granted to the manager. Similarly, in society power and authority are granted to a leader, even a dictator, until such time as the populace withdraws their assent to such leadership. The "flower power" revolution against Marcos in the Philippines was such an event; the people simply did not grant authority and power to the president, despite the tanks aligned against them. In the church, the almost universal use of birth control by Catholics has been cited as an example of the withdrawal of the previous granting of authority to the hierarchy in this area of life. In parishes, such a process is more likely to occur by parishioners' withdrawal from parish activities (including financial support), or from the parish itself. Vibrant parishes with many ministries are a testament to the leadership ability operative in that setting—the granting of power and authority by the parishioners to the leaders, to influence their vision and actions, their participation in the mission of the church.

Leaders as stewards and teachers. Peter Senge states that the traditional definition of leadership, which is focused on "special people who set the direction, make the key decisions, and energize the troops," is deeply rooted in an individualistic and nonsystemic worldview. He faults this understanding because he sees it as "based on assumptions of people's powerlessness, their lack of personal vision and inability to master the forces of change, deficits which can be remedied only by a few great leaders." Instead, Senge envisions leadership as a function of a learning organization, in which "leaders are designers, stewards, and teachers," working in concert with their colleagues. The task of the leader becomes one of *"inspiring* (literally, 'to breathe into') the vision of a learning organization."[7] The Constitution on the Sacred Liturgy of the Second Vatican Council emphasizes the need for full, conscious, and active participation in liturgical celebrations—making this point fifteen times in this short document. Liturgy is the font and summit of our life as a community, and therefore this vision is aptly applied to the life of the community in general. All are called to be active participants in the mission and ministry of the church. Senge's definition invites such a consideration of the role of the entire community. In the church, all are strengthened in their role as disciples by the sacraments of initiation, and empowered by the ongoing presence of the Spirit. All are part of an organization ever learning new ways of joining in God's work of bringing the kingdom, especially by reading the signs of the times in each new age and place. The role of the leader as steward of the gifts, the charisms, of all in the community, and as teacher of ways of discerning what God calls us to today, is consonant with this view of church. Here church is understood as organization, but even more as community.[8]

Reflecting on this definition, one could say that the vision of the church proposed in Vatican II that emphasizes the charisms of many is at once a cause for the emergence of lay ecclesial ministry, and an informing perspective in the way that lay ecclesial ministers function in their roles. They are indeed designers, stewards, and teachers. The plethora of new approaches that have emerged in pastoral ministry (for example, the numerous ways of involving parents in the faith formation of their children and the multiple new social justice initiatives undertaken by teens and parish communities) are an indication of their role as designers of the new. At the same time, both the husbanding of resources and the handing on of the tradition illustrates the stewardship role.

In every domain of pastoral ministry, teaching is a central focus. This teaching is not focused in a narrow way only on the task to be performed but rather in a way that enriches the understanding of and appreciation for our Catholic tradition. For example, lectors are provided opportunities—workshops, printed and audio resources, reflection groups—to grow in knowledge and appreciation of the Scriptures they proclaim, and choirs and cantors are invited to explore the theological import of the hymns they sing. The leadership of lay ecclesial ministers has expanded the capacities of ecclesial communities as learning organizations, embodying the vision of a conscious and active faithful, given us by Vatican II.

Leaders and adaptive work. Another theorist, Ronald Heifetz, focuses in particular on the reality that at times human organizations are confronted with a problem for which no adequate response has yet been developed; in fact, at times the problem itself is not yet fully understood. Addressing such problems requires adaptive rather than technical work. "Problems that cause persistent distress do so because the system of accepted dependencies being applied to them cannot do the job. We look to our authorities for answers they cannot provide."[9] The leader cannot do adaptive work alone; the usual dependency on leaders to solve such problems is counterproductive. In parishes today, many such problems are present: the disassociation of young adults from our faith communities, the sometimes acrid division between conservative and liberal members, the impact of an increasingly secularized society on the processes for handing on the faith to children, and the changing demographics of parish communities, to name just a few. The dual tasks of defining the problem, and seeking solutions, require leadership that engages others in the search for a direction. Perhaps in these situations at times lay leaders may be better able to invite parishioners past the clergy dependency that often characterizes Catholics, and into an active engagement in adaptive work. Heifetz's definition of leadership emphasizes not dominance but rather "conferred power to perform a service,"[10] especially the difficult service of keeping a focus on adaptive work that needs to be done. This emphasis on the performing of a service is consonant with the understanding of ministry as service to the community.[11]

Lay ecclesial ministers as leaders. Evidence of the success of lay ecclesial ministers in providing leadership is found in the studies of Philip Murnion and David DeLambo. Murnion states that measuring effectiveness is not an easy thing to do, in part because the church rarely spells out measures for this, and in part because church leaders do not embrace common standards for parish life. Therefore he chose to use the category of "contributions" as a measure, and concluded, "The most important statement to make is that the vast majority of all consulted [the ministers themselves, pastors, other ordained ministers, and active parishioners] agree that the lay and religious parish ministers make a significant contribution to parish life." He further stated, "Clearly, there is broad agreement that the greatest impact has been made in the parish's ability simply to reach more people, the enabling of parishioners to feel at home in the parish."[12] Murnion considers the fears of some that the new parish ministers (today we would say lay ecclesial ministers) substitute for the parishioners' own ministry to one another, creating a kind of "staffism." Rather, he notes that parishioners affirm that "the lay ministers helped people to get involved in religious education, youth ministry, liturgy, pastoral care for one another and in other kinds of concerns. . . . The new parish ministers, for the most part, seem both convinced about the need to involve parishioners and adept at doing so. Furthermore, the parish ministers and the parishioners largely agree about parishioners' readiness to volunteer."[13]

It is worth noting here that at times bishops have expressed various hesitations about the role of lay ecclesial ministers as leaders. One of these is the idea that a new state, or new caste, is being developed. For example, in a paper tracing the evolution of *Co-Workers*, Sr. Amy Hoey quoted one bishop who said, "All of the talk about 'substantial collaboration with the ordained,' 'authorization,' 'public ritual' seems to suggest a new state in the Church. Obviously, the document does not say this straight out. But the effect, to me, is the same."[14] On a similar note, in his recent book Bishop Clark mentions the concern of a bishop that lay ecclesial ministry "is causing a new caste or class system to be created in our dioceses." (Bishop Clark goes on to say that his own experience "has not at all indicated that a new ranking or class system is emerging among the people [he] knows who are engaged in ministry.")[15] Bishops' concerns about "elitism" are sometimes heard as well. The understanding of leadership developed by Senge places an emphasis on the leader as within the community, part of the community, not standing outside it, certainly not above it. It is from within the body that the leader is able to exercise influence. Whereas at one time in history, a strongly hierarchical model of leadership was the norm in society, today there is greater and greater emphasis on participation in creating and working toward goals, and on leaders who are working *with* their communities in doing this.

Bases of Influence

A further dimension of leadership theory that is useful for our analysis here is that of the interpersonal bases for power, or influence. Gibson, Ivancevich, and Donnelly name five: legitimate, reward, coercive, expert, and referent.[16] Hersey, Blanchard, and Johnson add two more: information and connection.[17] These authors argue that influence is key to an understanding of leadership (which Senge does not), and that this influence is derived from diverse sources. The sources of expert and information influence are rooted in knowledge; referent influence derives from personal charisma and/or from confidence, rapport, and trust built over a period of time; coercive influence depends on force and the exercise of sanctions; connection influence is the result of who one knows; reward influence flows from the ability simply to provide things that people would like to have. While it may be true that a lay ecclesial minister who is new to a parish has knowledge (perhaps a master's degree, perhaps years of experience in another setting), it takes time for competence to become clear to parishioners. In addition, the lay ecclesial minister is still in many ways an anomaly in the worldview of Catholics who expect priests and sisters to provide all leadership, which causes further resistance to these new ministers. Often such a new minister does not have a network of relationships in a new setting, the source of connection influence, and has not yet built relationships that would engender confidence, rapport, and trust. The new minister does not have—and hopefully would not want to have—mechanisms of force or sanctions available. On the other hand, in nondominant culture communities young people from within the parish are often nurtured into leadership roles by elders; therefore their connective power is strong. In these communities charismatic leadership is often highly valued, and the gift of leadership is its own "expert" base, often with little reference to academic or diocesan credentials.

While each of these sources of influence could be pondered at length, it is legitimate power that is of particular interest in this analysis. Legitimate power is described as "the perception that it is appropriate for the leader to make decisions because of title, role or position in the organization."[18] However, "subordinates play a major role in the exercise of legitimate power. If subordinates view the use of power as legitimate, they comply. However, the culture, customs, and value systems of an organization determine the limits of legitimate power."[19] Although the language of "subordinates" and "compliance" does not describe parish life, the principle that legitimacy *is granted*, which was mentioned above, is relevant to our concerns. Years ago, a colleague in a diocesan office with responsibility for DREs described the difficulty they had by saying, "The parishioners think she is just Mrs. So and So, and what right does she have to make decisions about religious education." This captures a dimension of the culture that did not grant legitimacy to the person who had been designated by the pastor as precisely the one to make the decisions about religious education. In a culture where the legitimacy of the priest (and also of the vowed religious) is quite taken for granted, the legitimacy of the lay ecclesial minister often must be earned over a period of time. The issue here is not primarily the difficulties this poses for lay ecclesial ministers but rather the limitations it places on their ability to lead effectively in the parish. The research of Ruth Wallace with pastoral administrators of parishes[20] suggests that one way to augment the perception of legitimacy is by the use of a ritual of authorization.

Part Two: Personal Experience

Often research questions arise from personal experiences, experiences that precede the concepts that later shed light on them. Leadership, authorization, ritual—the ideas explored in this chapter—were first encountered through experiences such as those presented here. The reader is invited to reflect on his or her experience relative to these questions, seeking the grounding in reality that gives conceptual analysis particular value.

The first anecdote highlights the problem of not being authorized in some public way. In 1969, when I began my ministry in a parish (not described with that language at the time), I was the first layperson on the staff (one of the first staffs in that diocese to include other than clergy) and the first director of religious education in the parish. Despite the fact that I had the full support of the pastor, and that I was very well credentialed for the position, I struggled for acceptance in executing my role. At a retreat conference, I met a Protestant minister who said, "I expect that you find it difficult to be accepted as a leader in your parish." I was surprised that he would say this, until he continued, "Ordination authorizes someone for leadership, and an ordained person has to mess up rather badly before trust is withdrawn. You have to work very hard to gain trust each time you work with new people." I recognized the truth of what he said, especially when I reflected on the difference in the way that vowed religious and newly ordained priests were able to begin in their roles in leadership. This insight shed light on my situation, and heightened my awareness of the importance of authorization—even though that was not the language I used at the time.

Increased awareness of the importance of authorization came some years later from a couple, Rita and Joe, who were involved in a youth ministry certification program. They had worked for a number of years with three other couples, providing volunteer leadership for their parish's ministry effort, but only they had enrolled in the program. After the first year, the pastor designated Rita and Joe as youth ministers, and listed their names in the bulletin. Leadership was still shared by the four couples; Rita and Joe were not paid; the only change was the listing in the bulletin. Rita and Joe were surprised that the parents were much more supportive of their efforts after they were officially designated for their role by the pastor. (They said that for the teenagers it did not matter, and with them all four couples were still equally received as leaders.) At the time I described this to myself as the extension of the pastor's mantle of authority to include Rita and Joe, with the simple action of publicly naming them as youth ministers and listing them as such in the bulletin. Once again, the importance of authorization caught my attention.

Over the years, I noted a certain evolution of rituals and blessings, "informal authorizations," which occurred through the spontaneous actions of varied communities and community leaders. One instance was at a university offering graduate degrees in ministry, where I taught for many summers. The students were from all over the world, many quite experienced in ministry. They included laypeople, vowed religious, and priests. Each year, the summer would end with the celebration of a Mass, in the university chapel. The students planned the liturgy—choosing liturgical ministers (presider, readers, musicians, etc.), planning the music, and developing a blessing ritual. These rituals varied from year to year, but always the gathered community blessed those who were graduating, with an emphasis precisely on their ministry in the church. For example, one year, the assembly was invited to extend their hands in blessing as the names of the graduates were called, and the leader proclaimed, "We send you to the Church of . . ."—and here a variety of places, Scotland, India, North Carolina, among numerous others, were named. Each time, the assembly responded, "Amen." The summer school community was a temporary one; it had no official role in designating persons for ministry. Many of the graduates were returning to the ministries in which they had been involved before coming to study; others were embarking on a new ministry, sometimes in a new place; some were still seeking a place of employed ministry. Nonetheless, it was clear that the prayer of the gathered community, the simple ritual, was very meaningful for brothers, laypeople, priests, and sisters. My judgment was that because Catholic sensibilities are so attuned to the sacramental dimension of all of life, and to the place of ritual in celebrating this sacramentality, *of course* such rituals would evolve naturally. Of course, this was not a formal authorization, but for some the action of the community strengthened them in their understanding of their role in the church, and for all the celebration had meaning.

This conviction was strengthened when a second institution at which I taught developed an annual Mass of blessing for graduates, at the initiative of the students. The graduates planned the Mass, and developed a ritual to be celebrated within it. Each year each group symbolized their commitment to ministry in a particular way. Once, each graduate received a lighted candle, with the invitation to then light the candles of all who were present, sign of going forth with the Light of Christ. Another time they were blessed with oil, symbol of their commitment to ministry. The ritual, the symbols, arose from their experience of church, their knowledge of our Scripture and tradition, their conviction that they are indeed involved in the work of the church, in ministry. Participants reported that the Mass of blessing was deeply meaningful for them, and for their guests: family, friends, pastors, colleagues. (Students often said that families did not understand what they were doing, why they were studying for a degree. That such a ritual was experienced by their families meant a great deal to the graduates.) Neither the institution nor the gathered community was authorizing them for ministry, but nonetheless, the experience of being blessed, of being prayed for, was very significant for the men and women involved, even those who were vowed religious, though for them to a lesser degree. One could say that the celebration of blessing strengthened the participants for their role in the church.

I myself was prayed for and blessed before I began a pilgrimage to the church of the poor in Peru, sponsored by the Christian Brothers. It was the simplest of rituals, at the end of a Mass in a small retreat house chapel, attended by the nine participants and our leader, and some neighborhood people who had come in for the Mass. And yet it moved me to tears. When I reflected on the experience, I realized that in all my years of service in the church, this was the first time that a community prayed for me, the first time that I was blessed in a formal way. I understood more fully the gratitude of the students who experienced the power of the sacramentality of such rituals.

Finally, a research-based analysis of the role of ritual is offered by Ruth Wallace in her study of pastoral administrators of parishes without a resident pastor (those ministering under canon 517.2). She indicates that she found that those who were officially, ritually installed in their role by the bishop were more readily accepted by the parishioners.[21] My interpretation of this is that the mantle of authority was visibly extended over them, allowing them to function more fully in their roles, from the beginning. The public, ritual authorization facilitated their exercise of leadership—in the language of leadership theory, it granted them legitimacy in their role.

Part Three: The Experience of Lay Ecclesial Ministers

In an effort to learn whether the use of a ritual of authorization does indeed help lay ecclesial ministers lead more readily because they have been clearly legitimized, I conducted interviews with men and women in several dioceses.[22] Because Catholic ecclesiology defines the local church in relationship to the bishop, I believe that his presidency at such rituals is important. Furthermore, I did not consider the rituals that mark the end of a program of formation, but only those designed as an aspect of the authorization process and conducted by the bishop. Therefore, only lay ecclesial ministers from dioceses with such a ritual were interviewed. Some interviews were done by phone, some as focus groups conducted in the diocese. Most of those interviewed had been authorized in part through a ritual initiated by the diocese. However, in an effort to more fully investigate this question, I also interviewed some lay ecclesial ministers who had not been authorized in such a way.[23] Those interviewed included people who serve in a wide diversity of roles, in both parish and diocesan positions, such as pastoral associate, director of religious education, director of music, and business administrator. Some have been in their roles for over twenty years, some were new to employed positions, the majority having about seven to ten years of experience. Most of the interviewees were from the dominant culture, with a smaller representation from the African-American and Hispanic cultures. For most, the celebration of the ritual followed, sometimes by many years, their being hired to be a member of a parish or diocesan staff. This was a limiting factor in the research on the effect of the ritual on their leadership, because it required remembering a sometimes distant experience.

The Ritual

I asked first about the nature of the authorization rituals. They were sometimes celebrated in local parishes, more often in the cathedral. The bishop was the one authorizing. The context was a Mass, with the authorization ritual placed within the larger celebration. Elements varied— participants entered in procession with the liturgical ministers; unlit candles were carried, and then lit by previous graduates of the program; pins were given; certificates were conferred; people were called forth.

Family and friends were invited, as well as pastors and parishioners. The personal response to the celebration varied. The presence of guests was mentioned by many. A common note was the importance of having family present. One woman said, "We all invited our families. This showed the importance of the occasion—though I am not sure that they yet understand." Another said, "I was floored that all my family came," and another, "I was glad that my family went to the Cathedral, because they made sacrifices as a result of my participation in the program." One man admitted that he did not remember much about the occasion, several years back, but said it was good for his family. For some, family members were their only guests. The importance of their pastor's presence is caught clearly in a comment on his absence: "My pastor did not come. I was disappointed, and felt let down. He did not recognize that this was important. However, I did not allow that to overshadow the whole event for me." The significance of the presence of colleagues was described by one man: "I had joy because several peers were called at the same time that I was." Some participants invited people from their parish to come. A pastoral associate said that she plays the piano at morning Mass, and had rather casually invited the older women who attend to come. "They came," she said, and they were so honored to have been asked, so moved by what they saw. "I was so humbled," she concluded.

Personal Response to the Ritual

Many of those interviewed spoke with considerable feeling of what the celebration meant to them, personally. Some enthusiastic, general responses included, "It was just gorgeous. I didn't know what I was coming to, but it was just wonderful, beautiful." "It was amazing, I felt uplifted, affirmed in ministry." One woman said, "I might have not gone; I was pressured to do so—but I am so glad, it meant so much." And another commented that a friend had said, "My insides are shaking, I can't stop crying." A woman who had been involved as a DRE for almost twenty years before participation in a ritual of authorization said, "It empowers you, and that felt good." On the other hand, a number of the men interviewed said that they did not remember that much about the ritual.

Several people mentioned a very specific response, of gratitude: "I felt affirmed being called, and had an experience of gratitude"; "I felt enormous gratitude that I was called, and felt humbled." Some remarked on the experience of God within the celebration. "I felt God's presence there. I had a calling all of my life, and now God was affirming it." And, "I felt as though God were saying, 'Good job, I am well pleased with you.'" Some indicated the importance of the event by their actions at a later time. A woman said, "I keep my letter saying that I was sent to St. Dorothy parish in a special place." And a man explained, "We light my candle at Sunday dinner—with my teenage kids there—and the one we use now is a replacement of the first one, which was used up."

Ritual and Authorization

One question posed to the interviewees was, "Did the fact that you were so authorized make any difference in your exercise of your role in the parish—relative to other leaders, relative to the people you serve in your ministry?" The fact that most participants in the study held leadership roles before the ritual of authorization, and that the rituals were generally celebrated some time ago, means that this data is at best suggestive—and of course, they could only report their personal perception of "any difference." As one participant said, "I was already doing the job, and the ritual seemed like an add-on." However, many helpful points were made by these men and women whose experience and theological background gave them a valuable perspective.

One comment summarizes a part of the answer to the question: "The ritual was wonderful, but what is really different?" Another said, "The ritual itself did not make that much difference." Two kinds of reasons are offered, some relative to the individual minister's self-understanding, some to the understanding of parishioners and priests. The first category included answers such as, "I already had a sense of calling from my Baptism, and from my pastor, and from my connection with the parish"; another stressed the importance of competence gained through academic study, and recognized by the pastor. The most telling comments were in reference to parishioners: "Ritual is not on the radar of most people; they don't know what it is"; "After the ceremony, when the priest tells the congregation, they don't know what it means"; "These terms mean nothing to the people in the parish." A few also commented on priests' perceptions: "I am not sure that the ritual means anything relative to the way the priest relates to us in our roles"; "The new priest is trying to understand"; and, "I am not sure that the priest knows what to do with us." (One conclusion was offered, relative to priests: "Priests should have a course on lay ecclesial ministry, on DRE's." This comment was greeted with a spontaneous chorus of yeses, in the focus group.)

Despite these many hesitations about the effect of a ritual, many participants spoke about ways that it is important *to them*, not only in a personal sense, but precisely in reference to their ministry. "For me, the ritual was an affirmation that I have a place; the homily said that we have a place as a lay minister." "Being blessed said to us that indeed we know what we are doing"—and another added, "And that gives me more confidence." "The ritual is an acknowledgement by the bishop that we are performing a ministry, that we are servant leaders." "It was very important to me to receive from the bishop the recognition that I am properly formed—not for the sake of my ego, but as an acknowledgement." "Being commissioned by the bishop gives legitimacy, even if only I know it," and another added, "Commissioned not to a *job*, but to ministry in the diocese." "In retrospect, I view being called as a source of challenge, strength, affirmation." "Ritual is important for *us* in taking the authority that we need to minister." A final comment summarizes much of what was said: "Being part of the ritual, we began to see ourselves as part of a larger group. People don't understand our role. Ritual is important to us. We are still struggling with where we fit. Ritual is good for us."

Participants showed an awareness of the complex issues relative to leadership, influence, and authority, discussed in part 1 of this chapter. One said that parishioners and priests alike ask, "By what authority are you doing this?" She then added, "It helps when they know that it requires a different education to be certified. When they know that I am, they are more willing to accept my authority. If they don't know, they say, 'Who are you to tell me.'" One woman noted a particular aspect of the question of authority and influence when she observed, "In the business world, women are accepted. But in the church, women are not well accepted in leadership—as the contrast with the acceptance of deacons by church leadership shows." A man observed, "Being commissioned by the bishop gives legitimacy, even if only I know it."

Ritual and the Parish

Because participants in this study were identified through diocesan offices, most of the rituals participated in were diocesan, conducted by the bishop. However, many comments about parish-based rituals were made, some by those who had also experienced such a ritual, and some by those who said that a parish setting would be more helpful. As one woman said, "The value of ritual is not in question here, but where it takes place could be discerned, and fine tuned. It would have highlighted the ministry more if it were in the parish." A man said that the rite of installation of a pastor and the ritual for lay ministers had a lot in common, but the first was local, "and that affirmed more than the rite of calling did." "The people would see us in a new way" if the ritual were in the parish, another added. Those who had experienced a parish ritual, in addition to the diocesan one, spoke with feeling about the experience. "The whole parish blessed me, and everyone was invited to affirm me. The children's choir surprised me by singing my favorite songs." "It was more personal in the parish, with those I would be serving. It took my breath away." "In my own parish, it was more emotional." In one case, a parish reception followed the Cathedral celebration, and a woman commented, "It was more personal; they were so happy for me, even if they did not know what they were happy for."

Authorization without Diocesan Ritual

Those interviewed who had not been authorized in part with a ritual included men and women, Hispanic and Anglo, lay and vowed religious, serving in varied roles in parishes and dioceses, for a short time and for many years. I asked them, "What is the effect of your preparation for ministry on your acceptance in your role?" In general, they reported that academic preparation (an expert base of influence) did not help acceptance. One woman said, "My preparation (an MDiv) did not endear me in any way." Another with a rich background of experience and a diocesan certificate said, "I had no prior connection with the parish. I met great resistance—'we should do it the way we did in the past'—but having the pastor behind me made an incredible difference." Another who had an MA spoke of conflict with a priest who said, "Ordained people (and men) do not work for non-ordained people (and women)." She added that if the pastor had more clearly authorized her, this would not have been so.

On the other hand, connection influence was significant. One woman with no diocesan or academic credential who now supervises a staff of ten in the parish said, "I am in the parish I grew up in. People called on me rather than the pastor for many things." A man said, "I came into the role with no pastoral experience, but I was well known by the pastor and the parishioners. A parish group helped to acclimate me to my role."

Some ministers commented on difficulties regarding authorization. One man said a parent had complained to the archbishop, saying, "Who does he think he is; he's a nobody." (The pastor had responded, "He is not a nobody. He's the DRE.") However, when asked whether an authorization by the bishop would have been helpful, the answers were negative: "I am not sure if people would know the difference"; "Way out where we are, we do not have that much relationship with the diocese"; "It does not matter, because the pastor is the on-site person."

Indirectly, the respondents indicated that it was the experience of doing the ministry that gave them authority in their role. A pastoral associate said that in an emergency she was called upon to lead a celebration of Sunday worship without a priest, and "that did more for the people to believe that I was and did what the pastor said I was."[24] Another said that "when placed on the regular hospital and wake schedule, my role was more recognized." A DRE said that "authorization was settled in the course of ministry, when I made requirements, and asked for commitments." One woman said simply, "The community authorized me."

Some other ways of being authorized were named. A sister said, "Being a vowed member of a religious community does have some privilege. I don't feel that I need to be authorized. My authorization comes from my religious community." A parish administrator who grew into the role from being a secretary said, "When the position became more formalized, and I had a new title which was listed in the bulletin, I was sort of validated with authority. I found more acceptance then."

Asked whether they were ever prayed for by the congregation, one woman replied, "No, but what a beautiful idea that is!" Another said that when she was leaving the parish, the people blessed her, and added (with tears in her eyes), "if only that had been reversed." A young Hispanic woman described her welcome, along with another intern, to a parish far from home. "They were waiting for us, praying for us, they held a ceremony of welcome." One man pointed out that the Canon of the Mass includes prayers for all ministers, and another that on catechetical Sunday that, although he is not commissioned, the community does pray for him. And one woman said that to be prayed for by the community "would foster validation more than anything else." Clearly, being prayed for by the community in which one serves was seen as something most valuable by these lay ecclesial ministers.

Conclusion

Leadership theory suggests that the influence of lay ecclesial ministers, their capacity to lead, would be strengthened if their legitimacy in their role were made clear to all involved, especially when they are new in their position. Anecdotal evidence suggests the importance *for the ministry* and *for the ministers* of processes of authorization, and for rituals of blessing as a dimension of authorization. For Catholics, with our rich sense of sacramentality, ritual has special resonance. A formal ritual of authorization celebrated by the bishop was posited as a particular way to grant such legitimacy; this hypothesis was tested through interviews of lay ecclesial ministers.

However, the interviews with lay ecclesial ministers who had been authorized officially at a diocesan ceremony do not support the thesis that their influence, their authority, was strengthened in this way, at least as they perceived it. Interviewees said that in part this is because the ritual took place after, sometimes long after, they began their ministry, and in part because parishioners (and some priests) do not see the ritual as granting legitimacy, and, in fact, may not even be aware of the ritual.

(An exploration of why, on the other hand, the ritual of ordination of deacons has clearly granted them legitimacy—even if not clarity about their role—could be instructive.)

Nonetheless, the rituals, the prayer of the community for them, the public affirmation of their role do have considerable meaning for the lay ecclesial ministers themselves. Parish-based rituals were especially meaningful for those who had participated in such. An added consideration is that it would be possible to develop parish rituals appropriate for diverse cultural groups. Furthermore, many who had not so participated said that the local ritual would be both more meaningful for them personally and more helpful in the eyes of the parishioners in granting legitimacy to them. Men and women who had not been authorized with a ritual indicated that being known in the parish before beginning in a new role was very helpful in being granted authority by the people. Even more important was the actual performance of ministry, over a period of time. While the interviewees who were not part of the ritual of authorization with the bishop did not see much value in such a ceremony, they viewed being prayed for by the community most positively.

This research does suggest that good order in the community, more effective leadership, and a deepened personal commitment and sense of meaning can be facilitated by public authorization of lay ecclesial ministers, with attendant ritual. However, the theological understanding of the place of lay ecclesial ministers in the life of the church, and of the meaning of any rituals that will be developed, needs maturing, both in the church as a whole and among parish clergy and people in the pew.

Notes

1. USCCB, *Co-Workers in the Vineyard of the Lord: A Resource for Guiding the Development of Lay Ecclesial Ministry* (Washington, DC: USCCB Publishing, 2005), 10–11, 9.

2. Lovett H. Weems Jr., *Church Leadership: Vision, Team, Culture and Integrity* (Nashville: Abingdon Press, 1993), 29.

3. James Gibson, John M. Ivancevich, and James H. Donnelly Jr., *Organization* (Boston: Irwin, 1994), 401. Emphasis in the original.

4. National Catholic Educational Association, *Toward Effective Parish Religious Education for Children and Young People* (Washington, DC: NCEA, Department of Religious Education, 1986), 5.

5. Zeni Fox, *New Ecclesial Ministry: Lay Professionals Serving the Church* (Franklin, WI: Sheed & Ward, 2002), 67.

6. Gibson et al., *Organization*, 402.

7. Peter M. Senge, *The Fifth Discipline: The Art & Practice of the Learning Organization* (New York: Doubleday/Currency, 1990), 340. Italics in the original.

8. A biblical reflection on this theme is offered by Kenneth K. Killinski and Jerry C. Wofford in *Organization and Leadership in the Local Church* (Grand Rapids, MI: Zondervan, 1973), especially chap. 11, 133–41,"The Church Organism and Community," which offers a Scripture-based analysis.

9. Ronald A. Heifetz, *Leadership Without Easy Answers* (Cambridge, MA: Belknap Press of Harvard University Press, 1994), 69–76.

10. Ibid., 57.

11. Robert Greenleaf was at the fore in presenting understandings of leadership as service. His *Servant Leadership: A Journey into the Nature of Legitimate Power and Greatness* (New York: Paulist, 1977) explores the servant as leader in varied settings, including business, education, and churches. There is an inspirational dimension to his work, which makes it a valuable resource for those who wish to explore deeper understandings of leadership.

12. Philip J. Murnion, *New Parish Ministers: Laity & Religious on Parish Staffs* (New York: National Pastoral Life Center, 1992), 81–82.

13. Ibid., 88.

14. Amy Hoey, "Concepts and Language of *Authorization* and *Vocation* in USCCB Documents on Lay Ecclesial Ministry," unpublished paper prepared for the Collegeville Seminar II, February 13, 2009, 9.

15. Bishop Matthew Clark, *Forward in Hope: Saying AMEN to Lay Ecclesial Ministry* (Notre Dame, IN: Ave Maria Press, 2009), 22.

16. Gibson et al., *Organization*, 370–71. They state that they use the terms influence and power interchangeably.

17. Paul Hersey, Kenneth H. Blanchard, Dewey E. Johnson, *Management of Organizational Behavior* (Upper Saddle River, NJ: Prentice Hall, 1996), 234–39.

18. Ibid., 237.

19. Gibson et al., *Organization*, 370.

20. Ruth Wallace, *They Call Her Pastor: A New Role for Catholic Women* (Albany, NY: SUNY Press, 1992). See further explanation of her research, below.

21. Ibid.

22. The sample size was small, thirty-two individuals from three dioceses. There is no study of dioceses in which the bishop presides at a ritual of authorization, including a blessing, which made identifying potential participants difficult. Based on polling of various ministry leaders, it would seem that there are not many dioceses that have such a ritual. Interviews conducted from July 2009 to March 2010.

23. I am grateful for the guidance offered to me by Dr. James Kelly, professor, Fordham University, a sociologist who gave me helpful advice as I began this project.

24. Catherine Vincie offers a probing analysis of the role of ritual, from both an anthropological and a theological perspective in "Lay Ecclesial Ministry and Ritual," in *Lay Ecclesial Ministry: Pathways Toward the Future*, ed. Zeni Fox (Lanham, MD: Rowman & Littlefield, 2010), 85–100. Relative to the perception of this interviewee, she says, "The ritual practice of acknowledging and exercising liturgical roles of lay ecclesial ministers would give added status and stability to this emerging reality" (90).

Conclusion

Points of Convergence
Vocation and Authorization for Lay Ecclesial Ministry

William J. Cahoy

In 2001 Saint John's University School of Theology·Seminary convened ten theologians in the Collegeville Ministry Seminar to consider the theology of lay and ordained ministry in light of the increasingly widespread practice of laypeople taking on ministerial roles in the Roman Catholic Church. The seminar published a collection of essays on this theme, *Ordering the Baptismal Priesthood: Theologies of Lay and Ordained Ministry*. The participants also identified seven "points of convergence" that they proposed as "principles to shape a theology of ordered ministries."

1. Theologies of ministry must begin with an experiential description of ministry today.
2. Baptism is an initiation into the life of Christ and the way of discipleship in the Church by which all participate in the mission of the Church. It is the ground for all discussion of ministry.
3. Mission is grounded in the divine missions of Word and Spirit, which flow from God's love for the world.

4. Ministry, grounded in baptism, is the building up of the Body of Christ for the mission of the Church. Ministry not only serves the internal needs of the Church but enables the Church to pursue its mission for the transformation of the world.

5. Within the diversity of the Spirit's gifts, the life, communion, and mission of the Church have been served by ordered ministries.

6. What is constant historically is the principle of sacramental order. What changes is how ministries evolve and are ordered.

7. These principles call us to an ongoing ecclesial discernment and a fresh articulation of an ordering of ministries (e.g., installation, commissioning) in the Church in order to recognize emerging ministries and changes in church practice.[1]

The participants in the Collegeville Ministry Seminar II endorse these principles that, together with conciliar documents and various episcopal statements, comprise a foundation on which to build a theology of vocation and authorization for lay ecclesial ministry.[2]

Inspired in particular by principles one and seven, the Collegeville Ministry Seminar II and the symposiums on lay ecclesial ministry of 2007 and 2011 have brought together practitioners from national ministry organizations, bishops, and theologians to engage in "ongoing ecclesial discernment" on the experience of ministry in the Roman Catholic Church in the United States. During this same period the US bishops have engaged in their own process of ecclesial discernment on the reality of laypeople in ministry in the United States and its meaning theologically and practically. The fruit of that discernment is *Co-Workers in the Vineyard of the Lord: A Resource for Guiding the Development of Lay Ecclesial Ministry*, approved by the US bishops in 2005. *Co-Workers* and the ongoing ecclesial reflection on the experience of laypeople in ministry have highlighted two topics for particular attention: vocation and authorization. These two topics are the focus of the second Collegeville Ministry Seminar and this volume.

The decades since the Second Vatican Council and its affirmation of the universal call to holiness have seen an explosion of ministerial opportunities for the baptized that do not require ordination or membership in a vowed religious community. We joyously celebrate this expansion of ministries, the opportunities it provides for the baptized to participate in the communion and mission of the church, and the increased capacity it gives the church to meet the needs of the community and the world. This is a manifestation of the bounteous gifts of the Holy Spirit bestowed on the people of God for the building up of the church and ultimately for our mission in the world as the sacrament of Christ.

Within this bounty of ministerial gifts and opportunities, we are focusing specifically on the *vocation* and *authorization* of lay ecclesial ministers. As a result of our research and conversations, we propose the following points of convergence as principles to shape a theology of vocation and authorization for lay ecclesial ministry. As described in chapter 2, these eight points were discussed and revised at the Collegeville National Symposium on Lay Ecclesial Ministry. The statements presented here in bold text were endorsed by well over two-thirds of the participants. In addition to being the positions of the authors, they represent a working consensus of this gathering of leaders from the forty-four ministry organizations and schools sponsoring the symposium.

1. **Lay ecclesial ministry is the work of the Holy Spirit.**

    The emergence of this particular form of ministry is one manifestation in our day of the abundance of gifts bestowed on the church by the Spirit for the good of the community and its mission in the world. In putting these gifts to work, lay ecclesial ministers are continuing the ministry of Jesus and participating in the evangelizing mission of the church.

    As in biblical times and in every age since, the Spirit calls forth the ministers and ministerial forms needed to serve the mission of Christ. In our own day, lay ecclesial ministry has emerged as laywomen and laymen have responded generously to a renewed awareness of the implications of their baptism and to the needs of the church and the world. The rise of lay ecclesial ministry is thus a sign of the continuing vitality and responsiveness of the church as it gives birth to new forms of ministry.

    Co-Workers affirms that "lay ecclesial ministry has emerged and taken shape in our country through the working of the Holy Spirit" (14). As a work of the Spirit, lay ecclesial ministry needs to be affirmed, celebrated, and incorporated more fully into the theology and ministerial structures of the church.

2. **Baptism is the foundational sacramental source that empowers the lay ecclesial minister to carry out the mission of Christ.**

    Christians who are called to serve as lay ecclesial ministers are sacramentally empowered for their ministry by baptism. Baptism initiates a person into the communion of the Trinity and the communion that is the church. Confirmation strengthens and Eucharist nourishes this communion, which continues the mission of Christ.

Lay ecclesial ministers receive the authority to exercise their ministry in a leadership role from the recognition that comes from competent church authority, following a period of vocational discernment and formation. However, the source of their ministry is first of all Christ, who, through the Spirit, draws all of the baptized into his saving mission.

3. **Lay ecclesial ministry is a genuine vocation to ministry discerned within the ecclesial community.**

   Lay ecclesial ministers are called forth by the Spirit of Christ. They have a genuine vocation to ministry. The vocation to lay ecclesial ministry is not a call to a particular state of life, nor is it necessarily a lifelong commitment. Yet lay ecclesial ministers *do* make a significant commitment to ministry, and they live out this commitment in concrete ways. For most lay ecclesial ministers, their response to God's call to ministry is a life-orienting decision, one that profoundly affects the way they relate to the church that is their home.

   Serving in a public role of ministerial leadership, lay ecclesial ministers have a vocation to ministry that is discerned through a process that is both personal and ecclesial—attentive to the gifts of the individual, the needs of the community, the mutual collaboration of various ministers, and the oversight of competent church authority.

4. **Lay ecclesial ministers enter into a distinctive set of relationships within the life of the church.**

   Their ministry is characterized by appropriate formation, the authorization of the hierarchy, leadership in a particular area of ministry, and mutual collaboration with the ordained and other ministers. These characteristics distinguish the ministry of lay ecclesial ministers from other ministries and from the broader participation of the lay faithful in the communion and mission of the church.

   Signed by the trinitarian seal and washed with the waters of new birth, lay ecclesial ministers witness to the communal relationship of divine life and seek to foster relationships of communion with other lay and ordained ministers and with all the people of God.

Co-Workers identified four distinguishing characteristics of lay ecclesial ministry: appropriate formation, authorization, leadership in an area of ministry, and mutual collaboration with the ordained (10). Taken together, these characteristics constitute a network of relationships—a "place" or position within the ecclesial community. For the lay ecclesial minister, these relationships shape a ministerial identity and guide ministerial activity. By grounding all ministry in the communion of the triune God and by reflecting on the relationship of lay ecclesial ministers to bishops, presbyters, deacons, and all of the faithful, *Co-Workers* underscores this fundamentally relational vision.

What distinguishes lay ecclesial ministers from other ministers and from the broader participation of the lay faithful in the mission of the church is not some special status or particular function. What marks their ministry as unique is their relationships within the life of the church. To use the language of the first Collegeville Ministry Seminar, lay ecclesial ministry is an example of an "ordered ministry" that involves a public, ecclesial repositioning in the community. This repositioning involves a new relationship with both the hierarchy and the other lay faithful.

5. Lay ecclesial ministers serve in the name of the church.

The call to lay ecclesial ministry is rooted in the baptismal call to holiness and mission that is incumbent on every believer. Lay ecclesial ministers receive a further call to serve formally and publicly on behalf of the church.

To say that lay ecclesial ministers minister "in the name of the church" is to affirm that they serve not on the basis of their own personal prerogative. Rather, by entering into a distinctive network of ecclesial relationships, lay ecclesial ministers serve on behalf of the whole ecclesial community, increasing the community's ability to carry out its mission in the world. This is signified and strengthened by the authorization of the community's ordained leaders. This public, ecclesial recognition is not to minimize the importance of individual gifts, personal discernment, or the intellectual, spiritual, and pastoral formation that are essential to Christian ministry. Instead, it is to affirm the way in which lay ecclesial ministers put these personal gifts in service on behalf of the body of Christ, since they are called to participate in more defined ways in the teaching, sanctifying, and governing work of Christ and the church.

6. **The bishop or his delegate authorizes the lay ecclesial minister for ministry in the name of the church.**

   Authorization is the act of entrusting one with a mission to perform a ministry in the name of the church. It confers the authority to minister in the name of the church; formalizes a relationship of communion with the bishop, the local pastor, and the community; defines the role the lay ecclesial minister will undertake in the community; and establishes accountability to church authority and the people served.

   All ministry comes from Christ through baptism. But those who minister formally and publicly "in the name of the church" take on a new relationship to the community, signified and strengthened by some form of authorization. Thus, while lay ecclesial ministers receive the power to minister from their baptism, the ability to exercise that power publicly in the name of the church depends on authorization. Given his responsibility for ministerial oversight within the local church that is the diocese, it is the bishop who authorizes the lay ecclesial minister, either personally or through a delegate or pastor.

7. **Public rituals provide an opportunity for the ecclesial community to receive, affirm, and celebrate the ministry of the lay ecclesial minister.**

   Rooted in the incarnation and a sacramental imagination, Catholic tradition and practice are rich in signs and symbols, typically embedded in and given meaning by rituals. In this community public rituals validate the vocation and authorization of the lay ecclesial minister to serve in the name of the church and help all members of the community celebrate the lay ecclesial minister's new role in the community and the community's increased capacity for ministry. The existence of such rituals should be welcomed and further developed by the ecclesial community.

8. **The presence of lay ecclesial ministry calls the church to provide systems of support and adjust parish, diocesan, and national structures and policies to more fully integrate this new reality in the ministerial life of the church in the United States.**

   The tradition of the church includes rich institutional structures and a system of law that support its communal life, its mission and ministry, and its ministers. It is time to create structures to support the growth and stability of lay ecclesial ministry in particular law (both at the diocesan and conference levels). These structures would help make lay ecclesial ministry a more stable experience in individual dioceses, and would help make lay ecclesial ministry better understood by both the lay and ordained faithful.

Notes

1. Susan K. Wood, SCL, ed., *Ordering the Baptismal Priesthood: Theologies of Lay and Ordained Ministry* (Collegeville, MN: Liturgical Press, 2003), 256–64.

2. We are using here and throughout our work the definition of lay ecclesial ministry from *Co-Workers in the Vineyard of the Lord*:

> Within [the many ministries of the baptized] is a smaller group on whom this document focuses: those men and women whose ecclesial service is characterized by
>
> - *Authorization* of the hierarchy to serve publicly in the local church
> - *Leadership* in a particular area of ministry
> - *Close mutual collaboration* with the pastoral ministry of bishops, priests, and deacons
> - *Preparation and formation* appropriate to the level of responsibilities that are assigned to them
> - Previous documents from our Conference have called such women and men "lay ecclesial ministers" and their service "lay ecclesial ministry." We continue that usage here. (10)

Appendix

The 2011 Collegeville National Symposium on Lay Ecclesial Ministry Cosponsors and Collaborating Organizations

Aquinas Institute of Theology
Archdiocese of Chicago Lay Ministry Formation Program
Association of Graduate Programs in Ministry
Bernardin Center for Theology and Ministry, Catholic Theological Union
Boston College
Canon Law Society of America
Center for Ministry Development
College of Saint Scholastica
Diocese of Saint Cloud
Federacion de Institutes Pastorales
Federation of Diocesan Liturgical Commissions
Franciscan University of Steubenville
Illuminare
Institute in Pastoral Ministries, Saint Mary's University of Minnesota
Instituto Fe y Vida
Jesuit School of Theology in Berkeley, Santa Clara University
Loyola Marymount University
Loyola University New Orleans
Ministry Training Source
Minnesota Catholic Education Association

National Association for Lay Ministry
National Association of Catholic Chaplains
National Association of Catholic Family Life Ministers
National Association of Catholic Youth Ministry Leaders
National Association of Diaconate Directors
National Association of Pastoral Musicians
National Catholic Council for Hispanic Ministry
National Catholic Educational Association
National Catholic Young Adult Ministry Association
National Conference for Catechetical Leadership
National Federation for Catholic Youth Ministry
National Federation of Priests' Councils
National Leadership Roundtable on Church Management
National Organization for Continuing Education of Roman Catholic Clergy
Northeast Hispanic Catholic Center
Saint Catherine University
Saint John's University School of Theology·Seminary
Tekakwitha Conference
University of Dayton
USCCB Commission on Certification and Accreditation
USCCB Committee on Cultural Diversity in the Church
USCCB Committee on Laity, Marriage, Family Life, and Youth
Villanova University
Washington Theological Union

Contributors

Charles Bobertz, PhD, is a professor of theology at Saint John's School of Theology·Seminary in Collegeville, Minnesota. He received his doctorate from Yale University in 1988 and was ordained to the permanent diaconate in 1997. He is the editor, along with Professor David Brakke, of *Reading in Christian Communities: Essays on Interpretation in the Early Church* (University of Notre Dame Press, 2002) and the author of a forthcoming book from Baker Academic Press, *A Liturgical Reading of the Gospel of Mark.* Dr. Bobertz has published widely in leading theological journals.

William J. Cahoy, PhD, is dean of Saint John's School of Theology·Seminary. He has been on the theology faculty at Saint John's since 1990, teaching both graduate and undergraduate classes. He has an MA in religion from Yale Divinity School and a PhD in systematic theology from Yale University. He serves on the boards of the Louisville Institute, the Society for Arts in Religious and Theological Studies, and the Collegeville Institute for Ecumenical and Cultural Research; and is a member of the Commission on Accrediting of the Association of Theological Schools. Dr. Cahoy has written on the work of Søren Kierkegaard, feminist theology, the identity of church-related colleges, the Catholic intellectual tradition, Benedictinism, and theological education.

Zeni Fox, PhD, is a professor of pastoral theology at Immaculate Conception Seminary School of Theology, Seton Hall University. She earned an MA in religious education and a PhD in theology from Fordham University. Dr. Fox is the author of *New Ecclesial Ministry: Lay Professionals Serving the Church* (Sheed and Ward, 2002). She edited *Lay Ecclesial Ministry: Pathways Toward the Future* (Rowman and Littlefield, 2010) and coedited *Called and Chosen: Toward a Spirituality for Lay Leaders* (Rowman and Littlefield, 2005). For over ten years, she served as an advisor to the bishops' Subcommittee on Lay Ministry as they developed *Co-Workers in the Vineyard of the Lord.* She lectures frequently throughout the country on this topic.

Francis Cardinal George, OMI, has been an American cardinal since 1998 and is currently archbishop of Chicago. He has previously served as bishop of Yakima and the archbishop of Portland. Cardinal George is a past president of the United States Conference of Catholic Bishops from 2007 to 2010. A member of the Oblates of Mary Immaculate, he had once served as provincial, or head, of the American province of his order; before that, he taught at several American seminaries. He was elected the moderator for North America at the 2008 General Assembly of the Synod of Bishops meeting.

Edward P. Hahnenberg, PhD, is the inaugural holder of the Jack and Mary Jane Breen Chair in Catholic Systematic Theology at John Carroll University in Cleveland, Ohio. He is the author of three books—*Ministries: A Relational Approach* (Crossroad, 2003), *A Concise Guide to the Documents of Vatican II* (St. Anthony Messenger Press, 2007), and *Awakening Vocation: A Theology of Christian Call* (Liturgical Press, 2010)—and numerous articles in academic and pastoral journals. Dr. Hahnenberg was a theological consultant to the US bishops' Subcommittee on Lay Ministry in its preparation of *Co-Workers in the Vineyard of the Lord.* In 2011 he received the Spirit of the Conference Award from the National Association for Lay Ministry in recognition of his contributions to the church's ministerial life.

Jeffrey Kaster, EdD, is the associate dean of administration for Saint John's School of Theology·Seminary. He is on the theology faculty at Saint John's University and the College of Saint Benedict and is the director of the Youth in Theology and Ministry program. He also served as chair of the 2007 and 2011 Collegeville National Symposia on Lay Ecclesial Ministry.

Graziano Marcheschi, MA, DMin, is director of Ministerial Resource Development for the Archdiocese of Chicago, where he recently concluded eighteen years as the archdiocesan director of lay ministry formation. He has been adjunct faculty at a number of institutions, including the Institute of Pastoral Studies, Loyola University Chicago. He contributed commentaries on the Pentateuch, Gospels and Acts for the Catholic Bible, Personal Study Edition (Oxford University Press) and has authored books on Scripture and preaching. He hosts a local cable television program, *The Church, the Cardinal and You*, and cohosts the archdiocesan morning radio program *Catholic Community of Faith*.

H. Richard McCord, EdD, is former executive director of the US Conference of Catholic Bishops' Committee on Laity, Marriage, Family Life, and Youth. In this capacity he was chief staff person for all lay ecclesial ministry projects, including the development of *Co-Workers in the Vineyard of the Lord*.

Hosffman Ospino, PhD, is assistant professor of theology and religious education at Boston College School of Theology and Ministry, where he is also the director of graduate programs in Hispanic ministry. His research and publications concentrate on the impact of culture in the church's educational and ministerial practices. He is the editor of *Hispanic Ministry in the Twenty-First Century: Present and Future* (Convivium Press, 2010). Dr. Ospino is currently an officer of the Academy of Catholic Hispanic Theologians of the United States (ACHTUS).

Lynda Robitaille, JCD, received her doctorate in canon law from the Gregorian University. She is a professor of canon law at Saint Paul University in Ottawa. She is active in giving presentations in canon law, and continues to publish. Dr. Robitaille belongs to professional associations of canon lawyers, including the Canon Law Society of America and the Canadian Canon Law Society. She has served on the executive boards of both societies in the past.

Susan K. Wood, SCL, PhD, a Sister of Charity of Leavenworth, Kansas, is professor and chair of the Department of Theology at Marquette University, where she also received her doctorate in systematic theology. She serves on multiple bilateral dialogue groups at both the national and international levels, including the Faith and Order of the World Council of Churches and the Joint Working Group. Dr. Wood is a board member of the Center for Catholic and Evangelical Theology. Her publications include *Spiritual Exegesis and the Church in the Theology of Henri de Lubac* (Eerdmans, 1998), *Sacramental Orders* (Wipf & Stock, 2010), and *One Baptism: Ecumenical Dimensions of the Doctrine of Baptism* (Liturgical Press, 2000), and *One Baptism: Ecumenical Dimensions of the Doctrine of Baptism* (Liturgical Press, 2009). She is the editor of *Ordering the Baptismal Priesthood* (Liturgical Press, 2003). Her present project is a study of the relationship between the permanent diaconate and lay ecclesial ministry.